HYPERLOCAL JOURNALISM

In the wake of the withdrawal of commercial journalism from local communities at the beginning of the 21st century, *Hyperlocal Journalism* critically explores the development of citizen-led community news operations.

The book draws together a wide range of original research by way of case studies, interviews, and industry and policy analysis to give a complete view of what is happening to communities as their local newspapers close or go into decline to be replaced by emerging forms of digital news provision. This study takes the United Kingdom as its focus, but its findings speak to common issues found in local media systems in other Western democracies. The authors investigate who is producing hyperlocal news and why, as well as production practices, models of community and participatory journalism and the economics of hyperlocal operations.

Looking holistically at hyperlocal news, *Hyperlocal Journalism* paints a vivid picture of citizens creating their own news services via social media and on free blogging platforms to hold power to account, to redress negative reputational geographies, and to tell everyday stories of community life. The book also raises key questions about the sustainability of such endeavours in the face of optimism from commentators and policy-makers.

David Harte is Associate Professor in Journalism and Media Studies at Birmingham City University, UK. Within the Birmingham School of Media he teaches on modules related to journalism studies, social media and alternative and community media. He supervises PhDs in the areas of journalism and community media. He has also published on the role of social media in media education and worked on creative economy initiatives within the West Midlands.

Rachel Howells is a journalist and media researcher. She has worked as a journalist for almost 20 years and was a founding director of the hyperlocal news co-operative Port Talbot Magnet and editor of its newspaper and website. Her research is focused on the decline of local newspaper journalism in Wales and the effects of this decline on both the production of news and local citizens. She sits on the National Union of Journalists' Welsh Executive Council and on the advisory board of the Independent Community News Network (ICNN).

Andy Williams is Senior Lecturer in the School of Journalism, Media and Cultural Studies at Cardiff University, UK. He has a number of research interests which intersect journalism studies and cultural studies, including the practice and political economy of local journalism, and the relationship between news and public relations. He is a founder member of Cardiff University's Centre for Community Journalism.

HYPERLOCAL JOURNALISM

The decline of local newspapers and the rise of online community news

David Harte, Rachel Howells and Andy Williams

LONDON AND NEW YORK

First published 2019
by Routledge
2 Park Square, Milton Park, Abingdon, Oxon OX14 4RN

and by Routledge
711 Third Avenue, New York, NY 10017

Routledge is an imprint of the Taylor & Francis Group, an informa business

© 2019 David Harte, Rachel Howells and Andy Williams

The right of David Harte, Rachel Howells and Andy Williams to be identified as authors of this work has been asserted by them in accordance with sections 77 and 78 of the Copyright, Designs and Patents Act 1988.

All rights reserved. No part of this book may be reprinted or reproduced or utilised in any form or by any electronic, mechanical, or other means, now known or hereafter invented, including photocopying and recording, or in any information storage or retrieval system, without permission in writing from the publishers.

Trademark notice: Product or corporate names may be trademarks or registered trademarks, and are used only for identification and explanation without intent to infringe.

British Library Cataloguing in Publication Data
A catalogue record for this book is available from the British Library

Library of Congress Cataloging in Publication Data
A catalog record has been requested for this book

ISBN: 978-1-138-67453-0 (hbk)
ISBN: 978-1-138-67454-7 (pbk)
ISBN: 978-1-315-56124-0 (ebk)

Typeset in Bembo
by Taylor & Francis Books

Printed and bound in Great Britain by
TJ International Ltd, Padstow, Cornwall

CONTENTS

List of illustrations	*vi*
Acknowledgements	*viii*
Preface	*ix*

Introduction		1
1	Hyperlocal news in context	15
2	The withdrawal of local and regional news journalism	43
3	Inside a news black hole – case study of a town with no newspaper	65
4	From lost pets to local corruption: What gets covered in hyperlocal news	89
5	Practising hyperlocal journalism – authenticity and reciprocity	114
6	Inside the hyperlocal newsroom	136
7	Sustaining hyperlocal journalism	172
Conclusion		190

Index	*205*

ILLUSTRATIONS

Figures

2.1	Average six-monthly circulation of the *Western Mail*	49
2.2	Turnover and profitability at Media Wales, 1999–2015	50
2.3	Staffing levels at Media Wales, 1999–2015	52
2.4	WalesOnline.co.uk average daily unique users, 2008–2016	54
2.5	Trinity Mirror Regionals/Trinity Mirror Publishing revenue breakdowns by platform, 2003–2016	54
3.1	How Port Talbot's public interest news is covered, 1970–2013	72
3.2	Percentage point difference in turnout average for local council elections compared with Wales average, 1973–2012	82
3.3	Percentage point difference in turnout average for general elections compared with UK average, 1970–2015	83
4.1	Hyperlocal's 'long tail' – distribution of stories across sites, 2012	98
4.2	Geographic spread of UK hyperlocals, 2012	100
4.3	What gets covered? Percentage of topics covered by hyperlocal blog posts, 2012 (n = 1,941)	101
4.4	Who gets to speak? Percentage of sources either directly quoted or indirectly cited in UK hyperlocal news (n = 1,873)	102
6.1	Compilation of photographs in the Taylors' home, representing where B31 Voices is produced	139
6.2	Completed 'blank' page in the *Tyburn Mail*	153
6.3	On the Wight newsroom	160
6.4	Live analytics screen for website visitors	161
6.5	Sally Perry's diary for 3 September 2015	164

List of illustrations **vii**

Tables

4.1 Functions of secondary source intervention in UK hyperlocal
blog posts (n = 421)   103
4.2 The focus of campaigns initiated and supported by UK
community news producers   106
4.3 The focus of investigations carried out by UK community news
producers   108
6.1 Facebook engagement according to subject matter, March 2014   141

ACKNOWLEDGEMENTS

The authors wish to thank the wide range of community activists, journalists, entrepreneurs, policymakers, consultants, investors and academics who either contributed to or helped shape the research within this book. Special thanks to Professor Ian Hargreaves, who led the research project out of which much of this research developed, and to Dr Jerome Turner, who carried out some of the research and co-authored several papers with us. We would like to thank the publishers for their patience with us.

PREFACE

This book brings together a wide range of research conducted in the UK that has focused on the emergence of hyperlocal journalism. The term 'hyperlocal' isn't ours, but its increasing use in the late 2000s and early 2010s within commentary about the decline of the mainstream local press resulted in a desire to find out more about it. Not just what it is, but also why it had become so widely referenced and therefore what expectations might be being placed upon practitioners. Thus, a research project was proposed and work took place to investigate hyperlocal publishing in the UK between 2012 and 2015 as part of a larger project investigating 'creative citizenship', supported by the Arts and Humanities Research Council (AHRC) under its Connected Communities scheme (grant number AH/J005290/1). David Harte and Andy Williams were co-investigators on this project. In parallel, Rachel Howells was carrying out her own research, funded by the Knowledge Economy Skills Scholarship and the Media Standards Trust, into what happens when mainstream local media retreat from a local town (described in chapter 3). Howells has not only worked as a journalist but has also run a hyperlocal website and newspaper for Port Talbot in South Wales. Similarly, Harte has run a news website for Bournville in Birmingham. This allows for a significant degree of insight into the nature of this form of journalism and the issues inherent in practising it. Additional funding for the case study of B31 Voices, discussed in chapter 6, came via the Research Councils UK as part of the Digital Economy Communities and Culture Network+ project. An element of the research (a survey of hyperlocal practitioners) took place in partnership with Steve Barnett as part of his AHRC Research Fellowship project, Media Power & Plurality.

This book is partially derived from the following articles published in academic journals and books, which have been adapted, extended and amended for this volume. It also draws on theses by Harte and Howells.

Harte, David (2013) "One every two minutes": Assessing the scale of hyperlocal publishing in the UK. *JOMEC Journal* [Online]. Available at: https://jomec.cardiffuniversitypress.org/articles/abstract/10.18573/j.2013.10240/

Harte, David (2016) "Tell it like it is": The role of community not-for-profit media in regeneration and reputational change. *Ethical Space: The International Journal of Communication Ethics*, Vol. 13, No. 2, pp. 35–47.

Harte, David (2017) *An Investigation into Hyperlocal Journalism in the UK and how it Creates Value for Citizens.* PhD Thesis, Cardiff University.

Harte, David, Dovey, Jon, Agusita, Emma & Zamenopoulos, Theodore (2016) From networks to complexity: Two case studies. In: Hargreaves, I. & Hartley, J. (eds) *The Creative Citizen Unbound: How Social Media Contribute to Civics, Democracy and Creative Communities.* Bristol: Policy Press, pp. 129–152.

Harte, David & Turner, Jerome (2015) Lessons from "The Vale" – the role of hyperlocal media in shaping reputational geographies. In: O'Brien, D. & Matthews, P. (eds) *After Urban Regeneration: Communities, Policy and Place.* Bristol: Policy Press, pp. 131–145.

Harte, David, Turner, Jerome & Williams, Andy (2016) Discourses of enterprise in hyperlocal community news in the UK. *Journalism Practice*, Vol. 10, No. 2, pp. 233–250.

Harte, David, Williams, Andy & Turner, Jerome (2017) Reciprocity and the hyperlocal journalist. *Journalism Practice*, Vol. 11, No. 2–3, pp. 160–176.

Howells, Rachel (2015) *Journey to the Centre of a News Black Hole: Examining the Democratic Deficit in a Town with No Newspaper.* PhD Thesis, Cardiff University.

Williams, Andy, Barnett, Steven, Harte, David & Townend, Judith (2014) *The State of Hyperlocal Community News in the UK: Findings from a Survey of Practitioners* [Online]. Available at: https://hyperlocalsurvey.files.wordpress.com/2014/07/hyperlocal-community-news-in-the-uk-2014.pdf

Williams, Andy & Harte, David (2016) Hyperlocal news. In: Witschge, T., Anderson, C. W., Domingo, D. & Hermida, A. (eds) *The Sage Handbook of Digital Journalism.* London: Sage, pp. 280–293.

Williams, Andy, Harte, David & Turner, Jerome (2015) Filling the news hole? UK community news and the crisis in local journalism. In: Nielson, R. K. (ed.) *Local Journalism: The Decline of Newspapers and the Rise of Digital Media.* London: I. B. Tauris, pp. 203–223.

Williams, Andy, Harte, David & Turner, Jerome (2015) The value of UK hyperlocal community news. *Digital Journalism*, Vol. 3, No. 5, pp. 680–703.

Williams, Andy & Howells, Rachel (2018) The withdrawal of local and regional news journalism - report from South Wales. In: Mathisen, B. R. & Morlandstø, L. (eds) *Lokale Medier: Samfunnsrolle, offentlighet og opinionsdanning.* Oslo: Cappelen Damm, pp. 151–176.

INTRODUCTION

Within hours of the Grenfell Tower fire of June 2017 it emerged that warnings about the potential for such a disaster had been posted to a blog run by the Grenfell Action Group. The most widely quoted post had been written the previous November and contained a stark warning: "It is our conviction that a serious fire in a tower block … is the most likely reason that those who wield power at the KCTMO [Kensington and Chelsea Tenant Management Organisation] will be found out and brought to justice!" (Grenfell Action Group 2016). There had in fact been ten posts over a period of four and a half years (listed here: https://grenfellactiongroup.wordpress.com/2017/06/14/grenfell-tower-fire/) that highlighted issues related to fire safety, ranging from complaints about obstructions of emergency access routes to identification of the paucity of fire safety advice provided by the tower's management organisation. William Perrin from the community media consultancy Talk About Local describes the blog as "an excellent example of a classic hyperlocal site" (2017). For Perrin, this assessment is as much the choice of platform (the free-to-use wordpress.com) and design (the default two-column layout) as it is the content of the site. He notes the sheer volume of content (over 150 posts) that had been produced on this singular topic by concerned citizens. Speaking to the BBC in November 2017, Edward Daffarn, the blog's author and resident of Grenfell, said that the blog was meant to be a record of "how a community on a housing estate in the fifth richest country in the world could be ignored, neglected, treated with indifference" (BBC 2017).

Perrin finishes his post about the Grenfell blog by hoping that "the media make full use of the material on this excellent site to hold local power to account" (2017). Although that has happened in the aftermath of the fire, the bigger story has been the failure of the local press to take notice of the Grenfell Action Group's concerns prior to the incident. Or rather, the incident revealed that there wasn't much of a local press left to be able to take notice. Grant Feller had been a local

2 Introduction

reporter in Kensington and Chelsea almost 30 years previously, even then report-ing on Grenfell residents' health and safety concerns. In a column he wrote after the fire, Feller notes that a vibrant newspaper group with ten reporters "had access to people, information and events that made genuinely important stories"; he says, "I wasn't just a reporter. I was a conduit, a campaigner-by-proxy, an accidental member of a fractious, neglected and welcoming community that I knew nothing about until I landed that cub reporter job" (Feller 2017). In 2017, just one reporter covered the Kensington and Chelsea patch, as well as other patches, leading Feller (2017) to conclude:

> I don't know whether a vibrant local newspaper staffed by idealistic young journalists would have prevented the catastrophe all of London has been indelibly scarred by. But it could have. The warning signs were there and the pleas of residents' groups are plentiful.

Others have echoed his conclusion. "What if the royal borough of Kensington and Chelsea had a vibrant local newspaper scene", asks *The Guardian*'s Peter Preston (2017). The lack of media response to the various posts on the blog was evidence for Preston that the hollowing out of the local press, in the form of consolidation or closure of local titles, means that potentially serious community concerns can go unreported. He notes that local newspapers still matter because "without journalists to raise a ruckus, scandals slide by unchecked". Working alone, individuals "can't yet exert the simple pressure on officials that newspaper headlines still can" (Preston 2017). His assertion seems surprising in an age when newspaper readership is in decline and citizens are likely to be as highly networked and as noisy as journalists can be. However, research by Firmstone and Coleman (2015) backs up Preston's claim, suggesting that the perceived legitimacy of the role of the citizen journalist is questionable. They examined Leeds' media ecology to map out the relationships between mainstream media, communications officers in the local council and hyper-local citizen journalists. They found that whilst there is now a greater breadth to the local communications ecology, there are limits to the legitimacy of citizen journalism in the eyes of local communications stakeholders: "conservative perceptions of the media preferences and skills of the public serve to maintain the value of mainstream news media above that of digital media" (Firmstone and Coleman 2015: 134).

Yet as outlined in this book, the role of the 'noisy' citizen creating the "classic hyperlocal site" (Perrin 2017) is becoming increasingly legitimised – not just by academics such as ourselves, but by policymakers and professional news-making organisations (including the BBC), who are also noticing that many hyperlocal websites are building large audiences for their content and engaging effectively with their communities. This book is thus about those citizens who are making noise in Leeds, West London and elsewhere in the hope that their efforts do indeed hold local power to account, with or without the need for what remains of the local press to act as brokers for them. This book also notes the diversity of practice in hyperlocal blogging, which is as often benign as it is incendiary. What value might there be in creating content about lost purses, faulty street lights or dog poo? In terms of community-building, as we shall see, perhaps quite a lot.

In this introduction we draw attention to the ways in which hyperlocal publishing has been defined and how it has become part of scholarly, policy and industry discussions about the sustainability of local journalism.

The citizen as journalist

The role of the ordinary citizen in the formation of journalism represents a significant challenge to those whose profession it is to produce the news for print, online or broadcast. The 'citizen journalist' has seemingly entered the profession without the need for formal training and has arrived as newsgatherer, publisher, curator and, indeed, entrepreneur. Sometimes the citizen as newsgatherer is an altogether accidental affair as they bear witness to a breaking news event and instinctively reach for their smartphones to share images and words with whoever wants to see them. Professional journalists, adept at searching for fresh content on social media platforms, can then be seen pleading with the citizen for rights either to republish these images in their publications or to handle distribution rights. Such examples are likely to occur at dramatic news moments, yet the citizen – equipped with devices capable of taking images, shooting video, publishing to the Internet – also makes contributions to newsgathering at a more everyday 'hyper-' or 'ultra-' local level. Social networking status updates with observations of traffic hold-ups, bad parking, broken street lights and suchlike have become digital assets that are reworked into an emerging form of news operation where the seemingly trivial and banal takes its place alongside more traditionally journalistic content such as reports on crime and local public services.

This near-ubiquitous capturing of the ordinary everyday comes at a time when traditional local media are in decline. The newspaper industry's continued trend towards closure and retrenchment of their local and regional press titles (Oliver 2008) has resulted in concerns about the impact this may have on the public sphere (Siles and Boczkowski 2012). With fewer reporters on the ground and an admittance that local newspapers can no longer be papers of record (Sharman 2015), what then might fill the resultant democratic deficit? Who is left to hold power to account? Inevitably, attention has turned partly to the citizen. While most mainstream newsrooms would now recognise the value of the citizen as a newsgathering resource in capturing newsworthy moments as they happen, the decline of the local press has also created an opportunity for enterprising, civic-minded, digitally savvy individuals seeking to start news services for personal gain and/or for wider civic benefit. These services have come to be labelled as 'hyperlocal' news services by practitioners themselves, by investors, by regulators, by lobbyists and by academics. In the UK, they have been variously framed as a potential saviour of local journalism (Talk About Local 2011), an emergent area of the Internet economy (Nesta and Kantar Media 2013; Radcliffe 2012) and a mechanism to strengthen community

4 Introduction

cohesion (Carnegie UK Trust 2014). To some extent, therefore, hyperlocal has arrived as a fully formed notion within the media landscape, with the dominant view being that its contribution to ensuring a plurality of news sources in localities is of real value to citizens.

Definition and purpose of hyperlocal news

In their paper on "Defining Hyperlocal Media", Emily Metzgar *et al.* argue that the word hyperlocal "appears regularly in discussions about the future of the news media and potential alternative models, but there is no agreed-upon definition" (2011: 773). In general, the discussions they refer to describe Hyperlocal Media Operations (HLMOs, their term) as a kind of hybrid form of local news-making that has elements where "alternative newspaper movements combined the inter-active and broadcast abilities accompanying Web 2.0" (Metzgar *et al.* 2011: 774). For Metzgar *et al.*, it is necessary to address the issue of definition so that they, and future researchers, can distinguish between "all websites with a local orientation from sites that may more genuinely deserve the moniker 'hyperlocal'" (2011: 774). By those that "deserve" this, they mean HLMOs that produce original content rather than aggregate the content of others and where there is "an expectation that the content be original and that engaging with the site results in increased connection to the community" (Metzgar *et al.* 2011: 774). In essence then, they offer a kind of qualifying criteria for HLMOs, and they set out some US-based examples that exemplify the criteria. This in turn shapes the definition they settle on: "Hyperlocal media operations are geographically-based, community-oriented, original-news-reporting organizations indigenous to the web and intended to fill perceived gaps in coverage of an issue or region and to promote civic engagement" (Metzgar *et al.* 2011: 774). Metzgar *et al.* make the claim that the potential of HLMOs is in reinvigorating the public sphere, seeing the Internet as a way to broaden access for all to news and information: "The interactive media these sites use have not created a perfect Habermasian environment, but they have moved conditions forward toward a more ideal setting than has been possible before" (2011: 783).

Writing in 2007, Jan Schaffer reports on survey-based research on 500 hyperlocal citizen media sites in the US, arguing that this kind of news outlet acted as "a form of 'bridge' media, linking traditional forms of journalism with classic civic participation" (2007: 7). By 2009, distinguished commentators had already accepted that such community news operations had a role to play in sustaining US democracy (Downie and Schudson 2009). Although the market for local news in the US was still in steep decline in the mid 2010s, and community news start-ups faced many challenges around future economic sustainability, there were signs that smaller local news publishers were weathering the storm better than some of their mainstream counterparts. The Pew Research Centre identified 438 digital organisations in 2014 that produced original news regularly, most of them local in orientation, and found that these smaller, often non-profit, news sites were the biggest component of a growing US digital news sector (Jurkowitz 2014). Contrasting somewhat with this more mature and established hyperlocal media market, hyperlocal community news media are also a part of distinct European national media systems. Fröhlich *et al.* (2012), along with Bruns (2010), have researched the large German community news network MyHeimat. In 2010, Fröhlich's team found a national network of 37,000 citizen journalists collaborating with a number of regional news operations as well as publishing directly to a series of hyperlocal audiences (see Fröhlich *et al.* 2012). In the Netherlands, van Kerkhoven and Bakker (2014) identified 350 hyperlocal news websites publishing in 199 municipalities. These sites offer diverse, and often very locally relevant, news, but in common with many community news outlets worldwide, they often struggle to maintain themselves financially.

In the UK context, Charles Beckett describes hyperlocal journalism's potential to address the issues of a declining local press, eulogising about a "blossoming of hyper-local online ventures" and claiming that "hyper-local journalism is not simply a hobby or a pleasant localist addition. It is a potential amelioration of the drastic problem of declining professional regional and local news media" (2010: 11). Likewise, academics from Goldsmiths University in London argued that hyperlocal journalism could be part of a proposed new public service news consortium which could "develop and support hyperlocal media through the sharing of resources and online link up to encourage alternative voices" (Fenton *et al.* 2010: 2). Given the lack of empirical research, there is little surprise that academics often describe hyperlocal in fairly broad terms that frame it in line with Metzgar *et al.*'s view that its primary contribution lies in rejuvenating the public sphere. It is a similar case in UK policy documents, with the Labour Government, in its 2009 report *Digital Britain*, citing the "medium-term potential of online hyperlocal news" to contribute to a pending gap in the provision "between the old and new" (Department for Culture, Media and Sport and Department for Business Innovation and Skills 2009: 150). In 2009, the UK communications regulator Ofcom, in their review of *Local and Regional Media in the UK*, noted hyperlocal as being nascent in contrast to a developing US scene, with much of the UK material "hard to find, either because it does not attract a lot of traffic, or because it fails to deploy the strategies required to get a high ranking in traditional search engines" (Ofcom 2009: 45). By and large, they describe hyperlocal as an emergent element of an existing 'ultra-' (a prefix they say is interchangeable with 'hyper-') local media landscape that includes newspapers, radio, even television.

In their 2012 overview of the emerging network of hyperlocal websites, Ofcom claims that these sites have "the potential to support and broaden the range of local media content available to citizens and consumers at a time when traditional local media providers continue to find themselves under financial pressure" (Ofcom 2012: 103). Ofcom devoted a chapter of their annual *Communications Market Report* (2012: 103–111) to hyperlocal publishing, a recognition of substance that in this instance does draw on a definition given in a report published the same year by Nesta, a UK charity that invests in creative businesses and publishes research. In

6 Introduction

that report, written by former Ofcom employee Damian Radcliffe, hyperlocal is defined as "Online news or content services pertaining to a town, village, single postcode or other small geographically defined community" (2012: 9). This widely cited definition of hyperlocal encompasses services beyond news (though Radcliffe only gives examples of news services), yet narrows the field to online services and those operating within small geographic areas. Rather than settle on a single definition, Flouch and Harris (2010a) recognise the variety of such services, setting out to identify a taxonomy of hyperlocal forms. They studied 160 of London's citizen-run online initiatives and identified eight distinctive types. It is important to note that Flouch and Harris attempted to measure the civic purpose of such websites using a scale that suggests listings-only sites have low civic purpose whilst discussion sites score more highly. Such weighting may be arbitrary, but the sites that are most successful can "make a distinctive contribution to local social capital, cohesion and civic involvement" (Flouch and Harris 2010b: 6).

In the UK, an attempt has been made to maintain a database of UK hyperlocal sites, originally at http://openlylocal.com/hyperlocal_sites but since superseded by a list kept at http://localweblist.net/. The services listed on this resource encompass many of the types identified by Flouch and Harris (2010a) and also include a high proportion of sites that are using platforms developed by mainstream media organisations. In 2015, a new attempt was made to refresh the database of hyperlocal sites (by Talk About Local with financial support from Carnegie UK Trust). In this iteration of the database, the published inclusion criteria reject operations run by major news corporations: "If you are a big corporate trying to register dozens of new template sites then please contact us first as that isn't quite in the spirit of things" (Local Web List 2015).

Hyperlocal – local and global

In Radcliffe's 2012 report he recognises that "Hyperlocal can mean a whole town or city" (2012: 9). In a later report (this time for Nesta and Cardiff University's Centre for Community Journalism), he makes the point that hyperlocal publishers "define their coverage locality in different ways" (Radcliffe 2015: 17), qualifying his point by drawing on a 2014 survey of UK hyperlocal publishers which shows that 27 of 157 publishers ran services with a city-level reach, whilst most (n = 92) described their intended coverage as "quite local" (Williams *et al.* 2014: 13). Christopher Ali argues that 'local' has become an empty signifier "as a result of monopoly capitalism" (2017: 49). He notes how the local is put to use by policy-makers and policy-shapers to serve the financial interests of large, often global, media corporations rather than the needs of communities. There has been a retreat from the public-service orientation of local media as a public good, with 'local' being utilised discursively by both sides of the debate about whether the free market or the state should sustain local news. He makes the point that although the policy debate is often about geography, it feels a little redundant in an era where digital technologies can bring local concerns to global audiences (Ali 2017).

Similarly, Kristy Hess (2012) has attempted to rethink local media in terms of its 'geo-social' position in the digital landscape. Hess sees the emergence of the term hyperlocal as being evidence of "a reinvigorated interest in geography as media industry and entrepreneurs experiment with new business models in the changing technological landscape" (2012: 53). Borrowing from the work of Manuel Castells, she argues that small local newspapers act as nodes, holding "a degree of symbolic power in constructing the idea of 'community' and the 'local'" (Hess 2012: 56). Bruns *et al.*, in their examination of the emerging role of bloggers and citizen journalists in the 2007 Australian federal elections, also note the intersection between local and the wider world in how hyperlocal journalism operates:

> the choice for hyperlocally-based citizen journalism sites may be one between focussing on the establishment and sustainment of strong local clusters, informed by hyperlocal discussion, and between aiming for the infusion of hyperlocally sourced reports and commentary into wider national debates.
>
> *(2008: 7)*

Geography matters, then, but only in the sense that small media operations such as hyperlocals act as conduits to the wider digitally networked world and potentially help reinforce a sense of place. Hyperlocals are, in some sense, "local and global at the same time" (Castells 2012: 222).

Practitioners themselves, however, are keen to point to the extent of their geographic reach as a defining factor. An informal alliance of UK hyperlocal publishers came together in 2012 under the banner of the Hyperlocal Alliance. The group had 73 members as of April 2013 and a wiki in which their definition was outlined:

> A Hyperlocal is any web site which: – provides news and information aimed at a well-defined and relatively small geographically [sic] area with a population of less than 150,000; is created, owned and operated by individuals living and/or working in that geography; encourages and facilitates debate within the community.
>
> *(Hyperlocal Alliance 2013)*

Unlike other definitions cited, this stresses the need for the hyperlocal site to be run by locally based individuals and rejects the inclusion of automated content generators, that would be allowable under Nesta's criteria. A blog post by hyperlocal publisher Philip John (2011) expresses a degree of frustration with the term and some of the assumptions underlying it. He argues that hyperlocal websites are "just the *representation of communities via the internet*, not some sort of replacement" (John 2011, his italics). They are "topic niche"; that is, focused on a very narrow topic but in a specific geographic place. "*Hyperlocal is a **topic niche** where the topic is a small geographic area*" (John 2011, his italics and emboldening). Finally, drawing on contemporary examples, he usefully recognises the diversity of hyperlocal practice:

8 Introduction

> Saddleworth News is obviously a news site. King's Cross Local Environment is more of an activism site. Harringay Online is a social network. North Sixteen is just a Twitter account. Fwix is an aggregator. Brownhills Bob's Brownhills Blog is a personal opinion blog. According to our topic niche way of describing it, all of these are hyperlocal.
>
> *(John 2011)*

More recently, efforts to support and cohesively represent the sector have seen the launch of the Independent Community News Network (ICNN), a representative body seeking to "promote the interests of community and hyperlocal publishers and to champion new sustainable forms of local digital and print journalism" (ICNN 2017). The body has been developed by the Centre for Community Journalism, which is in turn funded by Cardiff University, but is intended to be run by and for its hyperlocal members. ICNN is structured democratically and is open to hyperlocals of all shapes and sizes, though at the time of writing the advisory board is considering membership criteria to ensure members adhere to a set of "core beliefs"; namely, that "news should be independent, community-focused, and should provide a high standard of quality public interest news" (Meese 2017). Of note here, additionally, is the conscious departure from the term 'hyperlocal' towards more widely understood descriptors of news such as 'independent' and 'community'. These choices arose from UK-wide consultations with hyperlocal news producers and demonstrate, perhaps, that definitions of the term 'hyperlocal' remain elusive or divisive even among practitioners.

Making hyperlocal pay

However the sector chooses to frame itself, the development of the ICNN as a representative body represents a significant moment of maturity and is an attempt to focus the sector on issues of the sustainability of local journalism. Martin Moore, writing for the Media Standards Trust, makes the point clearly: "the business model that supported news in the 20th century no longer sustains it in the 21st. Hardest to fund has been local news reporting. This is not peculiar to the UK but symptomatic of many mature western democracies" (2014: 27). Yet, as we demonstrate at points throughout this book, discussions of commercialisation and sustainability bring to the surface a tension at the heart of the discourse around what kind of journalism, and what kind of journalist, communities are best served by. The hyperlocal journalist that often emerges from the commentary to date represents something of an idealised figure, something closer to a social entrepreneur than a journalist, required to be civic-minded but also tech- and business-savvy. The 'hyperlocalist', empowered by digital technology and social media, must hold a diverse skill set well beyond that of the traditional local 'hack':

> You also need to invest time in developing relationships, promoting your site, and in some cases working to turn your operation into a viable business. As

the platforms become easier to use and more commonplace, human skills are becoming as important as technical ones. Community management, sales ability and other skills in communication and content promotion are all becoming increasingly important if you want your voice to be heard.

(Radcliffe 2012: 16)

Embracing this diversity of skills, argues Radcliffe, "can be fundamental in making hyperlocal pay" (2012: 16). Indeed, making hyperlocal pay has become a key preoccupation of commentators, further positioning the hyperlocal publisher as a "fictive" entrepreneurial figure (Jones 2014). Jones argues that there exists an idealised fictive entrepreneur (drawing on Bourdieu and Passeron's 1996 discussion of the fictive student). Such a figure – gifted, responsive – is framed within policy discussion as a role model whose level "only the handful of gifted, fictive students are able to achieve" (Jones 2014: 240). Jones finds that the "combative, status driven and all-conquering entrepreneur is still prevalent in contemporary business culture" and one that is situated in "historically masculine-framed ideas of entrepreneurship" (2014: 241). This situating of such idealised fictive figures is common in writings on citizen- or community-led journalism initiatives, argues Luke Goode, noting how much work on citizen journalists frames them as "fitting descendants of the radical pioneers of modern journalism prior to its corruption by commerce and vested interests" (2009: 1290).

Much then rests on the shoulders of this fictive hyperlocalist, although their precarity is recognised too: "Outside major UK cities local public interest news will rely on volunteers sporadically and inconsistently performing the functions of a Fourth Estate. As a consequence, while some areas may be well served, others will not be served at all" (Moore 2015: 78). This debate about the value of alternative local journalism as fourth estate is not new. Whilst much of the policy discussion cites hyperlocal as if it were a new and novel form of doing journalism in defined, small geographic areas, there is in fact, as Tony Harcup describes (2006: 129–132), a recent precursor to this debate. The significant 'wave' of alternative local newspapers in the UK in the 1960s and 1970s also, like the current hyperlocal titles, garnered attention from regulators (Royal Commission on the Press 1977). As with hyperlocal, the alternative press that Harcup describes was extremely varied and largely distanced from the journalism profession. Most such newspapers were: "produced by people with no formal journalistic training or background" (Harcup 2006: 131). Harcup argues that the era he was examining was not a "golden age" (2006: 137), for to see it that way would be to claim that current movements have less value. It is still the case that "dissatisfaction with the mainstream media persists" (Harcup 2006: 138), and therefore new models of alternative media will persist in order to facilitate "active citizenship".

Rethinking a definition of hyperlocal

In general, academics, commentators and even practitioners themselves have created a debate in which they seem to be having separate discussions with the hope

10 Introduction

of a similar outcome; that is, hyperlocal as a new 'grounded' model for the provision of local news to the benefit of citizens and driven by civically minded entrepreneurs. Metzgar *et al.* note how: "grant-making organizations have hailed HLMOs as a potential saviour for the struggling news industry. Scholars have proclaimed HLMOs a 21st-century breeding ground for civic engagement" (2011: 773). In his analysis of a hyperlocal news blog in Leeds, Tony Harcup argues that we need to resist simplistic categorisation of alternative forms of news production:

> They do not form a uniform "sector" any more than mainstream media are all the same, and it is only by exploring specific examples in depth that we can hope to dig beneath the labels to see what we can discover about the possibilities and potential of such journalisms.
>
> *(2016: 654)*

Yet for the most part, 'hyperlocal' is used as a collective term for the many different forms of operations that have appeared in this space, and those who seek to declare themselves, or declare others, as hyperlocal practitioners, must consider themselves as part of a very specific movement. In this regard, the work presented here looks at those hyperlocal news operations who, to use Metzgar *et al.*'s (2011) term, see themselves as "deserving" the hyperlocal moniker. The overlapping definitions and purposes that we have outlined above are symptomatic of the way the movement is being used to address the various interests of those discussing it. Each party wants to see hyperlocal journalism as delivering value in one or more ways in a number of areas; that is, addressing the decline of social capital within communities; developing new models of journalism enterprise; and addressing the 'democratic deficit' in the face of the decline of the local press. Maybe as a result of these diverse needs as well as the diversity of practice by existing hyperlocals, we can see the difficulty of arriving at a singular, clear definition of hyperlocal. What there is consensus on is that there are gaps to be filled. Or, at least, perceived gaps: "HLMOs represent the latest attempt to fill the perceived gap in public affairs coverage and follow in a long history of media reform and citizen journalism efforts" (Metzgar *et al.* 2011: 782). In the UK, hyperlocal news publishing does seem to have a collective identity built around the perception that it is 'filling the gap' (as we reveal in later chapters).

Purpose of this book

In part, this book therefore offers detailed insights into how effectively hyperlocal news operations in the UK can contribute to the public sphere. The research presented here inevitably asks questions about the value of hyperlocal publishing in the context of its potential fourth estate role given the decline of the local press, a detailed case study of which is offered in the early part of this book. Yet to solely discuss this aspect would be to limit our gaze too narrowly. By focusing "on the social and cultural dimensions of hyperlocal news alongside its economic and political importance" (Hess and Waller 2016: 206) there is the opportunity to theorise the value of acts of media creation carried out by the full range of professional and non-professional social actors who produce and interact with hyperlocal information systems. Thus, we seek to address the question of the value for citizens of these operations as information nodes dealing with the often banal nature of the everyday lived experience and ask how the everyday use of social networking and online publishing technologies might be useful to local communities in ways beyond the remit of traditional discussions about local news and democracy. We also seek to address the issues of concern to commentators and policymakers by examining the viability of the fictive hyperlocal publisher as a figure on which to base our hopes that local democracies can once again be enriched by vibrant, pluralistic, local media ecologies.

Through extensive empirical research, case studies and interviews, we tell the story of the decline of the local press and the rise of hyperlocal journalism in the UK – a story that is not uncommon to many Western media systems. Along the way we draw attention to the excellent work done by hyperlocals to hold local power to account, to tackle local corruption and to give voice to those too often ignored by mainstream media. Yet we seek to challenge the view that hyperlocal journalism only matters when it is doing that kind of journalism. Rather, our aim here is to identify why the stuff in-between – the banal and everyday – matters just as much in creating value for those communities which benefit from having a hyperlocal journalist on their patch.

Structure of this book

In chapter 1 we outline our theoretical framing, drawing, as one might expect in a discussion about the ability of local journalism to hold power to account, on ideas of the public sphere. However, we also discuss perspectives of the 'everyday' and argue that framing hyperlocal journalism as a cultural practice offers a useful theoretical lens. In the two chapters that follow we chart in detail the decline of mainstream local journalism from the perspective of a single region. Chapter 2 looks at the political economy of local and regional news journalism in South Wales, and chapter 3 then offers a detailed case study of what happens to local news and local citizens when a town is left without any local newspaper. Chapter 4 shifts the gaze to hyperlocal journalism, looking at the scale and scope of the practice in the UK and what kind of news it covers. Drawing on extensive research, we map out how hyperlocal performs against normative expectations of local journalism. In chapter 5 we look at the motivations and practices of hyperlocal journalists, while in chapter 6 we offer three case studies based on close observation of hyperlocal newsrooms. Chapter 7 examines and discusses the evidence for the sustainability of hyperlocal news operations. Finally, we conclude with some reflections on the potential for hyperlocal publishing to reinvigorate local journalism with a fresh authentic approach.

References

Ali, Christopher (2017) *Media Localism: The Policies of Place*. Urbana: University of Illinois Press.

BBC (2017) Why no-one heard the Grenfell blogger's warnings [Online]. *BBC*. Available at: www.bbc.co.uk/news/stories-42072477 [Accessed 2 December 2017].

Beckett, Charlie (2010) *The Value of Networked Journalism*. London: London School of Economics and Political Science.

Bourdieu, Pierre & Passeron, Jean-Claude (1996) Introduction: Language and relationship to language in the teaching situation. In: Bourdieu, P., Passeron, J.-C., De Saint Martin, M. & Teese, R. (eds) *Academic Discourse: Linguistic Misunderstanding and Professorial Power*. Stanford, CA: Stanford University Press, pp. 1–34.

Bruns, Axel (2010) Citizen journalism and everyday life: A case study of Germany's myHeimat.de. In: Franklin, B. & Carlson, M. (eds) *Journalists, Sources, and Credibility: New Perspectives*. Abingdon: Routledge, pp.182–194.

Bruns, Axel, Wilson, Jason A. & Saunders, Barry J. (2008) Building spaces for hyperlocal citizen journalism. Paper presented at Association of Internet Researchers 2008: Internet Research 9.0: Rethinking Community, Rethinking Place, Copenhagen, Denmark, 15–18 October. Available at: http://eprints.qut.edu.au/15115/ [Accessed 20 May 2016].

Carnegie UK Trust (2014) *The Future's Bright – The Future's Local*. Dunfermline: Carnegie UK Trust.

Castells, Manuel (2012) *Networks of Outrage and Hope: Social Movements in the Internet Age*. Cambridge: Polity.

Department for Culture, Media and Sport, Department for Business Innovation and Skills (2009) *Digital Britain*. London: The Stationery Office.

Downie, Leonard & Schudson, Michael (2009, November/December) The reconstruction of American journalism [Online]. *Columbia Journalism Review*. Available at: http://archives.cjr.org/reconstruction/the_reconstruction_of_american.php [Accessed 20 November 2017].

Feller, Grant (2017, 23 June) Why I know the Grenfell Tower disaster could have been prevented [Online]. *Huffington Post*. Available at: www.huffingtonpost.co.uk/grant-feller/grenfell-tower-prevented_b_17243118.html [Accessed 20 January 2018].

Fenton, Natalie, Freedman, Des, Curran, James & Couldry, Nick (2010) *Independently Funded News Consortia – A Submission to DCMS*. London: Goldsmiths Leverhulme Media Research Centre, Goldsmiths, University of London.

Firmstone, Julie & Coleman, Stephen (2015) Rethinking local communicative spaces: Reflecting on the implications of digital media and citizen journalism for the role of local journalism in engaging citizens in local democracies. In: Nielsen, R. K. (ed.) *Local Journalism: The Decline of Newspapers and the Rise of Digital Media*. Oxford: I. B.Tauris, pp. 117–139.

Flouch, Hugh & Harris, Kevin (2010a) *London's Digital Neighbourhoods Study: Typology of Local Websites*. London: Connected London.

Flouch, Hugh & Harris, Kevin (2010b) *The Online Neighbourhood Networks Study – the Future for Citizen-run Neighbourhood Websites*. London: Connected London.

Fröhlich, Romy, Quiring, Oliver & Engesser, Sven (2012) Between idiosyncratic self-interests and professional standards: A contribution to the understanding of participatory journalism in Web 2.0. Results from an online survey in Germany. *Journalism*, Vol. 13, No. 8, pp. 1041–1063.

Goode, Luke (2009) Social news, citizen journalism and democracy. *New Media & Society*, Vol. 11, No. 8, pp. 1287–1305.

Grenfell Action Group (2016) KCTMO – Playing with fire! [Online]. Available at: https://grenfellactiongroup.wordpress.com/2016/11/20/kctmo-playing-with-fire/ [Accessed 1 December 2017].

Harcup, Tony (2006) The alternative local press. In: Franklin, B. (ed.) *Local Journalism and Local Media: Making the Local News*. London: Routledge, pp.129–139.

Harcup, Tony (2016) Alternative journalism as monitorial citizenship? A case study of a local news blog. *Digital Journalism*, Vol. 4, No. 5, pp. 639–657.

Hess, Kristy (2012) Breaking boundaries. *Digital Journalism*, Vol. 1, No. 1, pp. 48–63.

Hess, Kristy & Waller, Lisa (2016) Hip to be hyper: The subculture of excessively local news. *Digital Journalism*, Vol. 4, No. 2, pp. 193–210.

Hyperlocal Alliance (2013) Definition of hyperlocal [Online]. Available at: http://hyperlocalalliance.org.uk/wiki/definition-of-hyperlocal/?action=diff&post_type=incsub_wiki&left=749 [Accessed 6 April 2013].

ICNN (2017) About Independent Community News Network [Online]. Available at: https://www.communityjournalism.co.uk/icnn/ [Accessed 20 Janauary 2018].

John, Philip (2011, 2 February) The problem with the word "hyperlocal" [Online]. *Wannabe Hacks*. Available at: https://web.archive.org/web/20170630103923/http://www.wannabehacks.co.uk/2011/02/02/philip-john-the-problem-with-the-word-hyperlocal/ [Accessed 20 January 2018].

Jones, Sally (2014) Gendered discourses of entrepreneurship in UK higher education: The fictive entrepreneur and the fictive student. *International Small Business Journal*, Vol. 32, No. 3, pp. 237–258.

Jurkowitz, Mark (2014, 26 March) *The Growth in Digital Reporting*. Washington, DC: Pew Research Center. Available at: www.journalism.org/2014/03/26/the-growth-in-digital-reporting/ [Accessed 1 November 2015].

Local Web List (2015) Inclusion criteria [Online]. Available at: http://localweblist.net/inclusion-criteria/ [Accessed 29 July 2015].

Meese, Emma (2017, 18 July) ICNN – The Independent Community News Network now open for members [Online]. *Cardiff University Centre for Community Journalism*. Available at: https://www.communityjournalism.co.uk/icnn/icnn-the-independent-community-news-network-now-open-for-members/ [Accessed 20 January 2018].

Metzgar, Emily T., Kurpius, David D. & Rowley, Karen M. (2011) Defining hyperlocal media: Proposing a framework for discussion. *New Media & Society*, Vol. 13, No. 5, pp. 772–787.

Moore, Martin (2014) *Addressing the Democratic Deficit in Local News through Positive Plurality. Or, Why We Need a UK Alternative of the Knight News Challenge*. London: Media Standards Trust.

Moore, Martin (2015) Plurality and local media. In: Barnett, S. & Townend, J. (eds) *Media Power and Plurality: From Hyperlocal to High-Level Policy*. Basingstoke: Palgrave Macmillan UK, pp.65–82.

Nesta & Kantar Media (2013) *UK Demand for Hyperlocal Media Research Report*. London: Nesta.

Ofcom (2009) *Local and Regional Media in the UK*. London: Ofcom.

Ofcom (2012) *Communications Market Report 2012*. London: Ofcom.

Oliver, Laura (2008, 12 December) Third of local newspapers to have disappeared between 2002 and 2013, says Enders chief [Online]. *journalism.co.uk*. Available at: www.journalism.co.uk/news/third-of-local-newspapers-to-have-disappeared-between-2002-and-2013-says-enders-chief/s2/a533054/ [Accessed 24 March 2012].

Perrin, William (2017) Hyperlocal blog can help hold power to account in tower block blaze [Online]. *Talk About Local*. Available at: https://talkaboutlocal.org.uk/hyperloca

l-blog-can-help-hold-power-to-account-in-tower-block-blaze/ [Accessed 2 December 2017].

Preston, Peter (2017, 2 July) A functioning local press matters: Grenfell Tower showed us why [Online]. *The Guardian*. Available at: https://www.theguardian.com/media/2017/jul/02/grenfell-tower-local-newspapers-authority-journalism [Accessed 2 December 2017].

Radcliffe, Damian (2012) *Here and Now: UK Hyperlocal Media Today*. London: Nesta.

Radcliffe, Damian (2015) *Where Are We Now? UK Hyperlocal Media and Community Journalism in 2015*. London: Nesta.

Royal Commission on the Press (1977) *Periodicals and the Alternative Press*. London: H. M. Stationery Office.

Schaffer, Jan (2007) *Citizen Media: Fad or the Future of News? The Rise and Prospects of Hyperlocal Journalism*. College Park, MD: J-Lab–The Institute for Interactive Journalism.

Sharman, David (2015, 10 June) City daily is no longer "paper of record" admits publisher [Online]. *holdthefrontpage.co.uk*. Available at: www.holdthefrontpage.co.uk/2015/news/daily-no-longer-its-citys-paper-of-record-admits-regional-publisher/ [Accessed 20 June 2016].

Siles, Ignacio & Boczkowski, Pablo J. (2012) Making sense of the newspaper crisis: A critical assessment of existing research and an agenda for future work. *New Media & Society*, Vol. 14, No. 8, pp. 1375–1394.

Talk About Local (2011) FAQ – What is Talk About Local? [Online]. Available at: http://talkaboutlocal.org.uk/faq/ [Accessed 2 December 2015].

van Kerkhoven, Marco & Bakker, Piet (2014) The hyperlocal in practice. *Digital Journalism*, Vol. 2, No. 3, pp. 296–309.

Williams, Andy, Barnett, Steven, Harte, Dave & Townend, Judith (2014) *The State of Hyperlocal Community News in the UK: Findings from a Survey of Practitioners* [Online]. Available at: https://hyperlocalsurvey.files.wordpress.com/2014/07/hyperlocal-community-news-in-the-uk-2014.pdf [Accessed 12 May 2015].

1

HYPERLOCAL NEWS IN CONTEXT

In this chapter, we set out the theoretical framing for our study of hyperlocal news. Such a framing is partly an examination of the ways in which hyperlocal news might be considered within traditional notions of the democratic roles of journalism, and partly based on rationalist conceptions of citizenship. Yet we also draw on ideas from a cultural studies perspective to examine the value of the more banal aspects of hyperlocal journalism and, in doing so, seek to frame it as an emergent cultural practice. Recent work by Kristy Hess and Lisa Waller (2016) argues for resituating the debate about hyperlocal news within a different framework from that which has most occupied journalism scholars to date. We therefore consider the extent to which we might see the role of hyperlocal news operations as a set of practices that extend beyond 'news'. We begin by looking at scholarly concerns over the impact a declining local press has on democracy before arguing that hyperlocal news is situated at the juncture of alternative and bourgeois pubic spheres. Finally, we look at how theories of the everyday could be particularly important in describing those aspects of the civic and community value of hyperlocal news content which fall outside, or on the margins of, the traditional foci of public sphere or democracy-oriented theories.

The crisis in local news

Chris Morley (2013), a senior officer in the National Union of Journalists and a former local journalist, argues that the "havoc" wreaked by media owners wanting to extract as much economic value as possible from a declining local press means that the case should be made for local newspapers to be seen as community assets, which would allow them to be 'rescued' by citizens under the 2011 Localism Act. Without a robust local press, who will do the job of "holding the rich, powerful and those with vested interest to scrutiny and account in the public good, while

16 Hyperlocal news in context

standing up for those that do not have a voice?" (Morley 2013). Morley's community-led vision of local journalism's future reveals, as does much of the commentary around hyperlocal, attitudes to the role of local newsmaking in the public sphere. He isn't the first to lament the "apparently remorseless advance of the market as the arbiter of the nature, the content, the form, the labour relations and mode of production and the ownership of the local press" (Franklin and Murphy 1998: 22). In their account of scholarship about the "crisis" in the newspaper industry (a crisis of declining audiences and income streams), Siles and Boczkowski note that a lack of empirical studies has not stopped academics stating "that the crisis has had negative implications for democracy because it undermines the watchdog role traditionally played by the press and its significance as a vehicle for free speech" (2012: 1380). The public interest value of news is often viewed through the prism of its relationship to democracy (McNair 2009). Key to this is the idea that representative democracy enables good government most effectively if citizens' decisions are based on accurate and reliable (and, where necessary, oppositional) information (Chambers and Costain 2000; Habermas 1989).

McNair identifies four principal (and interrelated) democracy-enabling roles for the news. He sees news: as a source of accurate information for citizens; as a watchdog/fourth estate; as a mediator and/or representative of communities (a role which can help with community cohesion); and as an advocate of the public in campaigning terms (McNair 2009: 237–240). The value of local news has been defined similarly. Bob Franklin argues that "local newspapers should offer independent and critical commentary on local issues, make local elites accountable, [and] provide a forum for the expression of local views on issues of community concern" (2006b: xix). However, numerous studies have found the ongoing crisis in the UK news industry is endangering the 'localness', quality and independence of local news (Fenton 2011; Franklin 2006a; Howells 2015). These studies find that as revenues fall and staff are cut, workloads increase, mainstream local news relies more on official sources and PR, and only a very narrow range of sources are routinely cited (Davis 2008; Franklin and Murphy 1998; Howells 2015; O'Neill and O'Connor 2008; VanSlyke Turk and Franklin 1987). This news becomes less local in focus as editions are cut, high-street offices are closed, and use of cheap news agency filler becomes more prevalent (Davies 2008; Franklin 2011; Hamer 2006; Williams and Franklin 2007). This has all led to increasing concerns about the industry's ability to play its democracy-enabling roles.

That the UK local, regional and national news media face a deep and continuing crisis and that this is having detrimental effects on news is now widely accepted (we offer a detailed account and case study of this in the next two chapters). Newspaper publishers have traditionally made their money in two principal ways: by selling news to us and by selling our attention to advertisers. But advertisers have left newspapers in numbers, large increases in audience figures for online news have not been translated into profits, and revenues at most major local and regional news publishers in the UK have been hit hard (Freedman 2010; Williams and Franklin 2007; Williams 2012). Many advertisers no longer find subsidising the production of local and regional news to be as profitable as previously and are, quite understandably, migrating to other more lucrative outlets such as online search engines, social networks and classified advertising websites (Fenton 2008; Freedman 2010: 37–39; Mintel 2013). At the same time, many readers no longer feel inclined to pay up front for news, and this has had very marked effects on the profits companies can make from newspaper sales. Even though most major industry players report growing advertising profits from online news and expanding audiences for their websites, they have yet to formulate a reliable business model to compensate for the significant revenue losses caused by the ongoing collapse of print (Greenslade 2009; Mintel 2013; Williams 2012). The impacts of such significant changes in the local and regional news industry have arguably been exacerbated by the business strategies pursued by the dominant UK newspaper publishers for much of the last two decades. The most challenging market conditions are a relatively recent phenomenon brought about by the large local and regional newspaper publishers pursuing cost-cutting measures to increase profits in the short term and failing to invest significantly in their journalism even while profits were very high between the late 1990s and mid 2000s (Franklin 2005, 2006a; Freedman 2010; Williams 2012). The publishers' unrelenting pursuit of profit has had worrying impacts on the quality and independence of local news.

Harrison (1998), echoing others' findings (Franklin and Murphy 1998; VanSlyke Turk and Franklin 1987), reported that local newspapers' reliance on sources in local government was very high, even going as far as to suggest that the growing power imbalance between local media and local governments means that "local newspapers are unlikely to be able to perform their role as 'principal institutions of the public sphere'"(Harrison 1998: 161). O'Neill and O'Connor (2008) provide the most detailed investigation into patterns of source access to local news. They found that local and regional journalists in the North of England relied very heavily on a relatively small range of official sources, usually those with the most resources to devote to media relations and the production of effective "information subsidies" (Gandy 1982) to journalists (O'Neill and O'Connor 2008). The police, court officials, local government, businesses and those who run public services were quoted the most often, and very few members of the public or local activists were cited at all (O'Neill and O'Connor 2008: 491–492). They also note with alarm that the majority of stories (76 per cent) relied on single sources, with less than a quarter of stories employing secondary sources who may provide alternative, opposing or complementary information to that provided by primary sources (O'Neill and O'Connor 2008: 492). This suggests a local press that takes too much information on trust, is too uncritical and provides readers with limited access to the range of (often competing) voices and perspectives actually present in local public debates.

Scholars have reached similar conclusions about the range of topics covered by UK local newspapers. In-depth coverage of local politics and the governance of local communities has gradually given way to a more tabloid-oriented spread of news (Franklin 2005). Franklin uses data from content analysis and interviews with

18 Hyperlocal news in context

journalists to chart a move towards an increased emphasis on news about entertainment, consumer issues and human interest stories (2006a: 12). Specifically in relation to the coverage of politics, there have also been shifts away from hard news topics often associated with information that equips readers to be informed local citizens. Since the mid 1980s the local press in the UK has reduced coverage of local elections, has produced fewer election stories with distinct local angles, and has had a "growing emphasis on trivial and entertaining coverage rather than a sustained discussion of policy concerns" (Franklin *et al.* 2006: 257).

The public sphere

It's unsurprising, given this rather gloomy picture of the decline of the mainstream local press (a picture we add to in the next two chapters), that Habermasian notions of the public sphere have been invoked by scholars seeking to understand the emerging phenomenon of hyperlocal news. Normative ideals about how citizens should be able to participate in decision-making in society are articulated by Habermas in his key work, *The Structural Transformation of the Public Sphere* (1989, originally published in 1962 in German). He details the development of a bourgeois public sphere: "the sphere of private people come together as a public" (Habermas 1989: 27). Within this specific historical phase and place (the 16th to 18th centuries in Western Europe), it was possible for citizens to use the "coffee houses, the *salons*, and the *Tischgesellschaften* (table societies)" (Habermas 1989: 30, his italics) and engage in wide-ranging discussions about art, literature and "common concerns" (36). In essence, subjects that lay previously only within the domain of the church or state came within the domain of groups of private citizens who represented the 'public': "the issues discussed became 'general' not merely in their significance, but also in their accessibility: everyone had to be able to participate" (Habermas 1989: 37). This in turn prepared the way for "human self-determination and political emancipation" (Hohendahl and Silberman 1979: 90). Habermas spends some time discussing the role of the media in the public sphere. He charts the way in which the 18th-century press shifted from being primarily carriers of information to being editorialising vehicles through which the public were able to make their contribution felt in the public sphere: "the editorializing press as the institution of a discussing public was primarily concerned with asserting the latter's critical function" (Habermas 1989: 184).

However, with the establishment of the 'state' and its increasing influence, the press was left to focus on profit-making, with the result that by the Victorian period, its editorial freedom had become an illusion and newspapers more readily reflected the commercial interests of their owners, whilst doing their best to shape 'public opinion'. This illusion is at its most rampant in the era of mass media, Habermas (1989) argues. State intervention in electronic media (that is, the development of state broadcasters for television and radio in many Western countries) combined with the development of public relations as a practice results in a kind of 'dumbing-down' of the public sphere and a giving way to the logic of late capitalism: "because private enterprises evoke in their customers the idea that in their consumption decisions they act in their capacity as citizens, the state has to 'address' its citizens like consumers" (Habermas 1989: 195). Ultimately, he argues, "the communicative network of a public made up of rationally debating private citizens has collapsed" (Habermas 1989: 247). Indeed, the Habermasian view of the role of the media in advanced capitalist societies is ultimately a discussion of its responsibility for the "refeudalisation of the public sphere" (Habermas 1989: 195).

For many scholars, hyperlocal journalism can potentially fulfil the role of rejuvenating a 'denigrated' public sphere whose journalism is "turning people off citizenship rather than equipping them to fulfil their democratic potential" (McNair 2000: 8). Moreover, as Luke Goode argues, there is an inevitability about citizen journalism initiatives feeding the democratic imagination, "because it fosters an unprecedented potential, at least, for news and journalism to become part of a conversation" (2009: 1294). For Chen *et al.*, hyperlocals "serve not only as a traditional information source but also as a forum for ongoing discussion of local affairs and a mechanism for building and strengthening relationships among local residents" (2012: 932). James Curran notes that the "divergence of approach between liberal and radical perspectives [on the public sphere] also give rise to different normative judgements about the practice of journalism" (1991: 32). Liberal-plural judgements certainly seem to infuse the current discussion on hyperlocal, essentially seeing it as playing a useful role in the democratic functioning of society, where it can seemingly help citizens to engage with local democracy and understand the political alternatives facing them: "it is clear that the hyperlocal news sector has a considerable contribution to make to media provision, plurality of voice, democratic scrutiny, accountability and information provision at a local level" (Carnegie UK Trust 2014: 13).

David Baines (2010) draws on Habermas for his study of a commercial web-based hyperlocal initiative in the UK. The intention was to create a "putative public sphere" (Baines 2010: 584) to support the development of an 'informed' citizenry (drawing on Schudson 1999: 123). Baines emphasises the "glocalised" nature of being on the Internet, where one has the potential not just to make local connections but also to draw on many previously unavailable sources of information:

> In a "glocalised", networked society, even relatively isolated communities will have a large range of networks and sources of information, from direct social interaction, business, professional and civic contacts and customers; to regional, national and global networks occupying numerous channels of communication, some one way, most two way.
>
> *(2010: 584)*

Yet when set against this idealised public sphere, the commercial hyperlocal offering comes up short, failing to meet the "monitorial" needs of citizens and neglecting to engage with global perspectives (Baines 2010: 590). Metzgar *et al.*

20 Hyperlocal news in context

also draw on Habermas to reflect on the role of the interactive technology employed by hyperlocal sites (2011: 784), while Steven Barnett and Judith Townend draw on and adapt Curran's (1991) formulation of the "classical liberal" theory of a free press when isolating the "informing, representing, campaigning, and interrogating" of those in power as key democratic roles for news against which hyperlocal content can be measured (Barnett and Townend 2015: 335). They come to the conclusion that hyperlocal journalism has the potential to "fulfil the journalistic norms for contributing to local democratic engagement" (Barnett and Townend 2015: 344).

Karin Wahl-Jorgensen (2007: 13–15) outlines the many criticisms of Habermas' work, in particular noting that his idealised notion of the public sphere tends to exclude women and the poor, and their concerns. It also presumes that actors in the public sphere have a shared sense of the 'public good' rather than holding ferociously onto their own points of view. Essentially, it ignores the messiness of real debate, she argues. Nancy Fraser, however, states that although Habermas' work "needs to undergo some critical interrogation and reconstruction" (1990: 57), it is an "indispensable resource" (56). She makes the case that the Habermasian view that a multiplicity of publics "is necessarily a step away from, rather than toward, greater democracy" is flawed (Fraser 1990: 62). Rather, both in egalitarian, multicultural societies and in more stratified societies, her reconceptualising of the public sphere as a space of multiplicity and with less divide between 'public' and 'private' can better show "how inequality affects relations among publics in late capitalist societies, how publics are differentially empowered or segmented, and how some are involuntarily enclaved and subordinated to others" (Fraser 1990: 77).

Alternative public spheres

In later reviewing his key work, Habermas acknowledges many of his critics and concedes that understanding the complexity of the public sphere requires acknowledgement of 'alternative institutions', which would include not only 'independent media' but other forms of informal gatherings "outside of the state and the economy" (Habermas 1992: 453). He makes a contrast between the powerful role that 'citizen movements' played in the overthrow of totalitarian regimes in Eastern Europe and the more complex picture in the West:

> This is the question of whether, and to what extent, a public sphere dominated by mass media provides a realistic chance for the members of civil society, in their competition with the political and economic invaders' media power, to bring about changes in the spectrum of values, topics, and reasons channelled by external influences, to open it up in a critical way, and to screen it critically.
>
> *(Habermas 1992: 455)*

This reconfiguring by Habermas is critical. How can ideas counter to the mainstream in society be articulated when media systems are dominated by private interests in the West? John Downing, in his forensic study of the anti-nuclear alternative press in West Germany, argues that scholars need only look at the way in which popular culture is developed and positioned in relation to 'mass' culture to see "the existence and productivity of an alternative public realm" (1988: 169). The anti-nuclear media represented an example of a particularly vigorous and flourishing alternative public realm, argues Downing. He is keen to ensure that the reader understands that the original German word for realm/sphere, *Öffentlichkeit*, suggests "movement, activity and exchange" (Downing 1988: 168) more than it does a boundary, which might be inferred from the English words. Thus, he articulates the alternative public sphere's relationship to and influence on the 'official' public sphere. Alternative public spheres offer opportunities for "experiences, critiques and alternatives" (Downing 1988: 168) to be developed.

How do these positions then create an impact in the mainstream? John Downey and Natalie Fenton (2003) pick up this concern, drawing on ideas of "counter-public" spheres. Their claim is that the relationships between the "common domain" and the "advocacy domain" need to be better understood as the points of breakthrough (from the latter to the former). It is these moments that provide "the opportunity for ideological claims to be displaced, ruptured or contested" (Downey and Fenton 2003: 200). They propose that a study of the virtual counter-public sphere (which in 2003 would have been an emerging but vibrant space for alternative ideas) would allow us to see whether "the mass-media public sphere will become more open to radical opinion as a result of the coincidence of societal crises and the growth of virtual counter-public spheres" (Downey and Fenton 2003: 199).

Importantly for this study, there is precedent in examining the value of alternative media scenes in the UK. Tony Harcup draws on Habermas to articulate the practices and histories that make up a "plebeian public sphere" (2013, drawing on Negt and Kluge 1983). In contrast to the notion of the increasingly homogenised public sphere that Habermas initially described, Harcup pinpoints moments where alternative media flourished in the UK. In particular, he covers similar ground to that discussed by the Comedia group (Comedia 1984; Landry *et al.* 1985), who examined the failure of a large number of alternative press titles of the 1970s and early 1980s. They note the tendency for workers in small, radical organisations to "exploit their own labour to a high degree" (Landry *et al.* 1985: 97). Further, in doing so, such organisations played an unintended role in shaping mainstream media output:

> The "alternatives" have produced something which has the chance of commercial viability, the "majors" move in and "sign up" the producers, who then leave the sector … . [T]he alternative sector … continually functions as a kind of unpaid "Research and Development" for the major commercial companies.
>
> *(Landry* et al. *1985: 97)*

Ultimately, the potential for radical, marginal projects to develop a "Gramscian political strategy" (Landry *et al.* 1985: 97) – that is, to develop a sufficient economic base in order to navigate their own way to sustainability – is undone: "marginality becomes a self-fulfilling prophecy" (98). However, Harcup explicitly critiques this view and sees this moment as evidence of alternative media's ability to create alternative public spheres to compete with "the dominant hegemonic public sphere" (2013: 78).

Throughout his work, Harcup draws heavily on the idea of alternative public spheres, arguing their importance despite the often small audiences for the media they produce. His empirical work draws on his own experience as an alternative media producer to claim that alternative media may offer the possibility of "subverting the dominant discourse by providing access to alternative voices, alternative arguments, alternative sets of 'facts', and alternative ways of seeing" (Harcup 2003: 371). In a series of interviews with journalists who had experience of working in both mainstream and alternative journalism, Harcup found that there was much "crossover of ideas, content, style, and, not least, people" (2005: 370). Further research in 2011, this time interviewing a group of "alternative media practitioners", has led him to conclude that the value of this alternative public sphere lies in providing a benchmark against which citizens can measure mainstream output (Harcup 2011: 27) and, importantly, create spaces that are "less male, less bourgeois and less dominated by the market" (17).

Geopolitical counter-spheres

Though alternative public spheres are most often spoken of as serving societal groups defined by class or identity (such as feminists or the black community) and which are in opposition to the prevailing "dominant" public sphere (Fraser 1990: 67), there are hints in the literature that geographically defined public spheres may also exist in some kind of interrelational aspect to the national public sphere defined by Habermas. For example, some researchers have put forward the notion of geographical divisions of the public sphere, or geopolitical counter-spheres to the public sphere, which serve publics with certain geopolitical interests or commonalities (Downey and Fenton 2003; Koopmans and Erbe 2004; Somers 1993: 588–589). For Koopmans and Erbe (2004), there is a case to be made for a European public sphere that exists in a layer outside the national public sphere and corresponds with the focus of different mass media. They envisage the public sphere in a series of concentric circles, like a cross-sectioned onion, with the national media at the centre and various rings they call international "intraspheres" outside it, such as the European Union, NATO, and even other nations; they also incorporate "intersphere" communication occurring between the spheres. For other commentators, the existence of local public spheres is clear. Conboy examines the history of local newspapers and notes the interrelations between local news and local politics: "Local political factions throughout the country used the local press as a battleground for the hearts, minds, not to mention wallets of the local population so that the national public was increasingly complemented by a series of local publics" (2005: 9).

Chris Atton's work (specifically across three key books: Atton 2002, 2004; Atton and Frederick 2008) is focused on articulating the value of the alternative public sphere as a model for understanding the alternative media practices of new social movements. Atton is concerned with proposing a new model for understanding alternative media that addresses two key questions: "What is radical about the ways in which the vehicle (the medium) is transformed? And: What is radical about the communication processes (as instances of social relations) employed by that media?" (2002: 24). The alternative media 'field' therefore is one of "process and relation" (Atton 2002: 30). As Christian Fuchs points out, "alternative media at the form level of the products have a radical potential if they transcend their societal context and have the potential to subvert experience" (2010: 188). However, at the level of content, such media might have a more direct critical political engagement: "[It] shows suppressed possibilities of existence, describes antagonisms of reality and potentials for change, questions domination, expresses the standpoints of oppressed and dominated groups and individuals" (Fuchs 2010: 189).

Atton presents a typology for understanding alternative media, split between products (content, form, reprographic innovations) and processes (distribution, social relations, communication processes). Atton makes the case that applying such a model to alternative media operations "avoids homogenizing alternative and radical media as the media of radical politics, of publications with minority audiences, of amateur writing and production" (2002: 29). Atton (2002: 30) notes how better understandings of "active" and "mobilised" audiences means that simply seeing alternative media texts as vehicles for disseminating non-mainstream messages is insufficient. Instead, we need to consider how the media, in their organisation and in their textual norms, have the potential to be transformed through "wider social participation in their creation, participation and dissemination" (Atton 2002: 25). In turn, wider participation can not only transform the media themselves but can also lead to transformations of social relations (Atton 2002: 25).

In this sense, Atton offers a potential route to seeing value in hyperlocal as an alternative media movement. While in chapter 4 of this book we will identify hyperlocal's similarities to mainstream local media in terms of form, its production processes (examined in chapters 5 and 6) may well offer a challenge to those emerging in an increasingly conglomerated and streamlined local media industry. Although Christian Fuchs is concerned that "small-scale local alternative projects will develop into psychological self-help initiatives without political relevance" (2010: 189), we should not dismiss the potential of hyperlocal's alternativeness so easily. Instead, it can be seen to form part of a wider alternative media 'field' that, as Atton notes, consists of a range of cultural practices which are diverse but share in common "extremes of transformation in products, processes and relations" (2002: 30). The products, processes and relations inherent in hyperlocal journalism are discussed throughout this book, and in many instances they stand in stark contrast to those within mainstream media.

Between bourgeois and alternative, private and public

To some extent, ideas of the public sphere are useful in creating a space in which it is possible to study the value of emerging practices such as hyperlocal news production in the context of the contribution they make to dealing with the "crisis" in local journalism that so concerns Chris Morley (2013). Of course, for it to play any effective role, there needs to be sufficient evidence that hyperlocal media has impact; which is to say that it is actually used by citizens (discussed in chapter 3). But it is clear that discussions about the decline of the press certainly have a distinctly Habermasian feel to them, and the appearance of hyperlocal media operations has some commentators idealising their role within a bourgeois public sphere: "I do think the growing belief in hyperlocal media needs much more thought, especially in Britain. We have fractured communities here and there is an urgent need to find some glue" (Greenslade 2007). Perhaps seeing past this hyperbole requires us to examine hyperlocal as a challenge from the private sphere to public agendas and as a continuation of existing alternative media practices, maybe as part of the subaltern public sphere and a field of cultural production in and of itself. Negt and Kluge argue that assimilation into dominant practices is an inevitable process in the development of "proletarian" public spheres and that to be truly alternative is to resist the organisational norms of the bourgeois public sphere:

> The proletarian public sphere which comes about through the use of its own forms of organisation not only binds together truly proletarian interest and experiences, but concentrates them as a specific stage in the proletarian public sphere which also differentiates itself externally from bourgeois forms of the public sphere.
>
> *(1983: 93)*

In this sense, to reject the norms associated with the organisation of journalism (if not always its form) might situate the practice of hyperlocal within the alternative public sphere. In taking this position, we can widen the scope of our study so that we might see the forms of value generated by hyperlocal as extending beyond merely what it can do for journalism and journalism's 'mission'. Chris Atton's work, in arguing for an examination of process and product, and seeing the value in each (2002: 29), provides a route for us to consider hyperlocal outside this narrow framing and support this book's intention to look at the wider range of potential value generated. The opportunity here, then, is to situate this study of hyperlocal in the context of a post-industrialised era of journalism, where technology has given "everyone" (Hartley 2009: 154) the required agency to act as producers.

But for many scholars, it is the "problematically blurred" (Livingstone 2005: 164) line between the public and private spheres that is a cause for concern. Habermas had himself lamented the way the media had become the conduit between the private and the public sphere: "The problems of private existence are to a certain degree absorbed by the public sphere; although they are not resolved under the supervision of the publicist agencies, they are certainly dragged into the open by them" (1989: 172). Livingstone argues that the debate around the impact of new technology tends to be polarised. Participation in the public sphere means being "connected" and "engaged", whereas the private sphere connotes "withdrawal or isolation" (Livingstone 2005: 170). As danah boyd (2014) also notes in her work with teenagers, it's in the private sphere that identity is constructed and social connections are made, outside of the public gaze. There is value in online seclusion, argues Livingstone: "rather than stressing the problem of withdrawal or isolation from community and political participation, the activities these terms characterise can be re-described as independence or even resistance" (2005: 170). The space between the private and public spheres is a site of struggle, she argues (using children's media as her example). That is, the struggle between resisting the individualising effects of the market on the private sphere and the desire for greater participation, through new media, in public debate.

Hyperlocal news as cultural practice

The value of invoking commonly held and widely used theoretical benchmarks for a healthy news media is clear. There are many existing studies of mainstream local news which employ the same, or similar, theoretical models, and operationalising them in a new and developing sphere of news production allows scholars to compare the value of emergent cultural forms with what has gone before as well as what is disappearing in the mainstream provision of local news. They also allow scholars to add empirical weight to the (often un-evidenced) assertions of commentators about the value of hyperlocal news. However, the dangers of an over-reliance on these theoretical frames include, for instance, the risk of missing new values or problems when applying well-worn theories to newer digital media.

Zizi Papacharissi (2010b) argues that the development of the Internet as a public space doesn't necessarily mean that the concept of the Habermasian public sphere is the best way to understand and critique it. Such critiques tend to ignore what she calls the "in-between" (Papacharissi 2010b: 244) nature of online digital spaces. Instead, she requires us to consider the ways in which the private sphere has become a vital site of study, as it is here that the private connected citizen is most active: "Whereas in the truest iterations of democracy, the citizen was enabled through the public sphere, in contemporary democracy, the citizen acts politically from a private sphere of reflection, expression, and behaviour" (Papacharissi 2010b: 244). Comments on blogs, YouTube videos, interactions on social networks, even 'lurking' online are all examples of a private sphere that is now networked and as a result is "empowering, liquid and reflexive" (Papacharissi 2010b: 244). Papacharissi (2010a) also articulates the value of personal blogging as an aspect of communications operating in the private sphere. It is the connectedness that bloggers have with others in the networked private sphere that makes them powerful, along with their use of personal narratives about public issues (a feature of the "new narcissism", as she calls personal blogging): "for citizens of developed and contemporary democracies, net-based technologies provide the tools with which to challenge what is defined as private and what is defined as public" (Papacharissi 2010a: 152). The result she argues is "broadening and overlapping private and public agendas" (Papacharissi 2010a: 149).

Kristy Hess and Lisa Waller make a similar claim about the value of taking the perspective of the personal in their argument that we should see the production of the "personalised spaces" of "hyperlocal subculture" not simply as an attempt to replace non-viable forms of mainstream local journalism, but rather examine it as a "marginalised practice" (2016: 206) in much the same way that one might study subcultures. They argue that scholars need a "greater focus on the social and cultural dimensions of hyperlocal news alongside its economic and political importance" (Hess and Waller 2016: 206). Such a shift might allow for the ability to theorise the value of productive acts of media creation and better understand issues of sustainability. In this regard scholars should seek to understand hyperlocal news production as "non-normative ... , a resistance to massification; generating an authentic – sometimes confronting – sense of style" (Hess and Waller 2016: 194). Hess and Waller use this approach to conjecture on the failures of networked or franchised hyperlocal operations set up by larger commercial media companies. It may be that these companies simply failed to understand the culture of hyperlocal: "Conceptualizing hyperlocal as 'excessively local' points to a celebration of the uniqueness of a given place and highlights the problem with trying to bottle hyperlocal culture and sell it as a template to distribute across mass audiences" (Hess and Waller 2016: 204). The subcultural lens allows them to see "the discomforting spectacle of outsiders trying too hard to fit in" (Hess and Waller 2016: 194). Ultimately, Hess and Waller argue that it is timely to "take a step back and view hyperlocal not as a product or object, but as a cultural phenomenon" (2016: 194). The focus of hyperlocal on the "excessively" local means that the "types of news featured in many hyperlocal publications provide a challenge to the very nature of news itself" (Hess and Waller 2016: 201).

Metzgar *et al.* also see the need to look beyond the narrow confines of the discussion to date about the value of hyperlocal as journalism and see it as part of a broader set of changes to local communications systems: "HLMOs [Hyper Local Media Operations] are about both stepping into the breach left by the retrenchment of local news operations and the exploitation of the tools available to the former audience" (2011: 782). In general, Metzgar *et al.*'s upbeat assessment of the potential of the Internet is widely shared by other academics. The sense that digital technologies afford everyone the ability to participle and, therefore, the potential to collaborate underpins the writings of authors such as Jenkins (2006), Shirky (2008, 2010) and Leadbeater (2008). Shirky (2010) argues that the "cognitive surplus" we have as a result of less time spent engaging with mainstream media (specifically television) is now put to use in large collaborative projects (he cites Wikipedia) that would have been unimaginable in the pre-Internet age. John Hartley suggests similarly that the Internet has now made it possible for "everyone" to be a journalist: "journalism has transferred from modern expert system to contemporary innovation system – from 'one to many' to 'many to many' communication" (2009: 152), and thus journalism research needs to take account of such practices and to take account of the "everyday". Hartley points out the issues that come into play when everyone is a journalist (issues of access, quality, truth, organisation of content, amongst others), but he stresses that the expansion of journalism beyond professional journalism is already happening and is changing both form and practice: "user-led innovation will reinvent journalism, bringing it closer to the aspirational ideal of a right for everyone" (2009: 162).

Hartley (2009) goes on argue that it is these affordances offered by digital technologies that call for new perspectives to be brought to the study of journalism. In order to understand this impact, he suggests we turn to cultural studies' interest in aspects of everyday cultural life rather than to journalism studies' interest in "producer and practice" (Hartley 2009: 155). Bill Reader suggests that cultural studies offers a flexible approach to the study of journalism practices in communities due to its "open-ended, yet still empirical, approach to investigating the interactions between community culture and journalism" (2012: 109). Given the near saturation of digital capture and publishing devices (which is to say, smartphones) that we can carry with us nearly everywhere we go, the extent to which these devices become ways in which 'everyone' can capture and curate the 'everyday' needs some further thought. We now inhabit a digital world saturated with images and updates from ordinary citizens. As Ben Highmore argues: "'saturation' could be seen as a cognate term for the everyday: when something reaches saturation point it has bled into the everyday, set up home there, colonised the domestic realm" (2010: 115). No topic seems too banal for us as we seemingly photograph and record everything around us. This abundance of 'everything' goes well beyond what Hartley imagines as the circulation of opinion on "blogs, websites, SMS and the like" (2009) and extends to the whole realm of social networking sites as posts, stories, (often temporary on services such as Snapchat), comments, curated lists, hashtagged conversations. How this 'everything' reshapes journalism needs a framing beyond that of the public sphere; rather, "this is the terrain that a cultural theory of journalism needs to investigate" (Hartley 2009: 160). Similarly, Chris Atton argues that we must study "the banality of the internet and of the everyday practices that construct it and its relations to the wider world" (2004: 7). He makes the case that it is the "significant everyday" that is of value to the cultural studies ethnographer interested in understanding how "the possibilities for meaning are organised" (Atton 2004: 8).

Distraction, habit and everyday 'banal' activism

Ben Highmore is amongst those scholars who have taken an interest in the role that technology plays in the everyday. He discusses the everyday, distracted way in which media is consumed and engaged with in the digital age. Like much else that happens in the home, media consumption is formed out of habit, which by its very nature also leaves space for surprise: "Habit, it may seem obvious to say, is the essential ingredient of ordinary life: without it there would be no room for day-dreaming, no space for the new" (Highmore 2010: 124). Habit – operating as it does in the realm of the almost unthinking – can free us up to better appreciate the points of "rupture" (here Highmore draws on Rancière). We are primed for such moments, he argues, because so much of what we do is relegated to motor-based habit. Thus, we are ready for the exceptional which may come in the form of memorable encounters with media texts that act to disrupt our distracted state (Highmore gives examples from listening to music and watching television).

Other scholars have also focused on habit and the "grindingly ordinary" (Shove 2003: 1), which can offer insight into societal concerns about inequality or, in the case of work by Elizabeth Shove (2003, 2009; Shove *et al.* 2012) and Sarah Pink (2012), about the environment. Shove *et al.* (2012) outline an approach for the study of everyday activities, habits as such, that examines the ways in which these move from a pattern to a performance and, ultimately, constitute a practice. Her contribution to theories of practice is to de-emphasise the role of individual taste or behaviour and instead see individuals as "hosts" of habitual practices (Shove *et al.* 2012: 7). Such practices are "provisional but recognisable entities composed of also recognisable conventions, images and meanings; materials and forms of compe-tence" (Shove 2009: 18). Further, such practices are dynamic. Over time, "the meanings and purposes of the practice and its characteristics [are] reconfigured" (Shove *et al.* 2012: 8). Shove is less concerned with activism than with how these practices constitute new patterns of consumption. By contrast, Sarah Pink's work focuses on how a study of the everyday can reveal points of resistance and discusses the extent to which new media can facilitate critique. Sarah Pink argues that the everyday "is neither static nor necessarily mundane, and to understand activism we need to recognise that it not only involves dramatic public actions but is also embedded in ordinary ways of being" (2012: 14).

Pink asks that we rethink "digital media through a theory of place" (2012: 131). She draws on work by Ingold, who describes the notion of a meshwork – how knowledge about place comes together through a process of wayfaring: "places, then, are like knots, and the threads from which they are tied are lines of wayfar-ing" (2009: 33). Places are not strictly geographic; rather, they are distinguished by movement (Ingold uses the term 'inhabitants' rather than 'locals'). Pink uses Ingold's concept – the idea of "interwovenness" and "relatedness" rather than "connectedness" – to argue that we must approach place as an abstract concept: "Ingold's work allows us to both appreciate the idea of place as unbounded and open … and to understand human perception and movement as central to the process of place" (Pink 2012: 26). In this sense, the digital plays a role in a "meshwork", rather than a network. Pink wants us to explore the way the mesh-work is "lived, represented and experienced, through the multisensory, experi-ential, embodied and everyday practice" (2012: 129). As we use digital technology on an everyday basis, whether to record the extraordinary or the banal, what matters is its journey through the meshwork and the degree to which it contributes to a sense of place. Pink then is arguing that 'placemaking' happens as much through the ways in which people utilise online social technologies as through embodied actions and experiences. People utilise these media in a multifaceted way on an everyday basis: switching between platforms, reading from a wide range of sources, making contributions (about 'everything') in social media updates or in posting photographs. Shaun Moores makes a similar case, arguing we should "understand everyday media uses by considering them alongside other social practices today, rather than as isolated activities" (2012: x). He calls for a renewed interest in seeing movement as part of a richer understanding of ways in which media technologies and texts are put to use. Such views prompt us to rethink our approach to a study of online activism, argues Pink: "Contemporary social media platforms and the technologies through which we access them make digital activism interweave with our everyday media practices and the environment in which we participate" (2012: 131).

The banality of online activism

While Pink and Moores seek to focus our attention on the activist value of everyday media use, John Postill (2011), through his examination of the use of the Internet in a suburb of Kuala Lumpur, Malaysia, is concerned that researchers see value in how the Internet brings to the fore the everydayness of citizens' concerns. His study of Subang Jaya in Kuala Lumpur notes a "vibrant Internet scene" (Postill 2008: 422) that contributes to an active culture of participation and debate amongst residents on matters that are of concern only to that specific locality. However, he notes how since the 1990s the Internet's increasing 'localness' (how, over time, the huge increase in users has meant more users at a local level) has created a problem for researchers: "the challenge is how to keep track of the fast pace of technological change while avoiding the default position whereby a seemingly stationary 'local community' is assumed to be impacted upon by 'global' technologies" (Postill 2011: 11).

He critiques the tendency for researchers to oversimplify the notions of 'network' and 'community' as "vague notion[s] favoured in public rhetoric, not … sharp analytical tool[s]" (Postill 2008: 421). They have had "troubled careers as anthropological concepts" (Postill 2011: 12), saddled with normative, idealised notions of democracy and empowerment. He argues instead that we need to pay attention to the ways in which "people, technologies and other cultural artefacts are co-producing new forms of residential sociality in unpredictable ways" (Postill 2008: 426). Postill utilises Bourdieu's notion of field theory, allowing for the examination of relations between social agents who might be competing for the same public rewards (2011: 16). This allows Postill to study the detail of everyday engagement between citizens and those in positions of power. A number of other researchers (Benson 2006; Couldry 2003; Schultz 2007; Willig 2013) have also made use of field theory to examine the "invisible structures of power and recognition" (Willig 2013: 384) that shape the field of journalism. The work contributes

30 Hyperlocal news in context

to a shift away from the newsroom-centricity (Wahl-Jorgensen 2009: 22) of so much work in journalism studies, arguing that there has been a methodological presumption that the practice of doing journalism only takes place in specific 'fields' (such as newsrooms), which are then bound by cultures, power relations, unspoken rules and the like. These fields are sites of research that sit in contrast to other fields (such as the home) whose practices, culture and politics are therefore marginalised. These researchers note that whilst anthropology has undergone its 'reflexive turn' and interrogated established notions of what constitutes its field, the anthropology of journalism has only just begun that process as it reacts to the deinstitutionalisation and de-professionalisation of news and information provision (Wahl-Jorgensen 2009: 22).

Postill (2008, 2011) argues that an advantage of drawing on Bourdieu's notion of fields is "that it is a neutral, technical term lacking the normative idealism of both public sphere and community" (Postill 2008: 418). In essence, it allows us to see participants in local online activism as social agents who might be competing for the same public rewards (Postill 2011: 16). Ultimately, like Sarah Pink, Shaun Moores and Chris Atton, he is frustrated at the lack of attention to the ways in which everyday use of Internet technologies might be used to support change at the local level. There is much value, he claims, in studying "emerging forms of residential sociality linked to "banal activism" – the activism of seemingly mundane issues such as traffic congestion, waste disposal and petty crime" (Postill 2008: 419). He makes the case that with very few exceptions, "banal activism has been neglected by internet scholars" (Postill 2008: 419). We believe that given the focus of much hyperlocal news on such banal, everyday issues, and taking into account its propensity for co-creation and collaboration with community members in the act of media production, this theoretical perspective provides a useful focus for the research we set out here.

The value of everyday digital participation

We might think of the conceptual framings of the everyday as a way to consider how citizens put the Internet and social networking technologies to use as tools for participation. Perhaps the banal way in which we record the everyday, almost on a kind of autopilot, might constitute a practice in and of itself. Such a practice would obviously be dynamic – the unwritten rules of participation are changing all the time and the line between habit and cultural practice is becoming increasingly fuzzy – but it could be argued that it has the potential to engender a form of 'quiet' or 'slow' activism through its politicisation of the banalities of everyday living in localities. This might allow us to think beyond producer/audience divides and the degree to which everyday use of technology allows for participation. Susan Forde points out that "the internet has provided this potential to empower audiences, and to reinforce the suspension of the audience-producer barrier" (2011: 46). Forde draws on significant primary research to make the point that simple audience/producer divides are increasingly difficult to make. In analysing community radio audiences in Australia, she finds that: "it was in fact the simple, local, community-connectedness of an outlet that engaged its audiences and indeed, made its audiences members feel like they, too, could be part of the station's programming" (Forde 2011: 91). However, she does make the distinction between these forms of participation and the traditional role of the alternative media as "watcher" of mainstream media; that is, as a vehicle for addressing misrepresentation and revealing its ideologies as opposed to explicitly facilitating "the extensive involvement of 'ordinary' people" (Forde 2011: 45).

By thinking about the 'everyday', we have the potential to consider new ways in which we might frame hyperlocal as a practice that emerges not simply from a set of societal ideals that then informs and shapes a set of professional norms (that is to say, the profession of journalism as underpinned by notions of democracy). Rather, hyperlocal might also be thought of as a citizen-led practice that disrupts the assumptions inherent in journalism's norms. The theoretical framings of the everyday that we have focused on in this section have concerned themselves with the ways in which capitalist societies function to disguise our subjugation to the means of production, yet our developing 'habit' of using social media on an everyday basis has the potential to emerge as a practice that offers insight into life in localities and works against this subjugation. Such insights are often not those moments of disruption, conflict or extraordinariness that would most interest the established mainstream media. Instead, they act as glimpses into the banal and everyday ways in which people connect to spaces (from nostalgic discussions about the local park to word-of-mouth recommendations for restaurants) or to each other. We might conceive of this as a practice through which everyday activism takes place, a practice that has the potential to be a "methodical confrontation of so-called 'modern' life" (Lefebvre 1991: 251). In this study, this allows us to address the role of the citizen producing information about their localities through hyperlocal publishing in greater detail and to pay attention to information creation practices that sit outside well-established, normative journalistic practices.

Journalism and citizenship

In his article entitled 'Things I Wish I'd Known Before I Became a Citizen Journalist', Barry Parr, a journalist who set up a hyperlocal site for a coastal community in California, notes that the gatekeeping role in journalism had all but disappeared: "every citizen journalist is also a citizen publisher" (2005). Parr argues that his citizen journalism activity both ties him to the community and, in turn, ties them to each other. Yet he has a discomfort with the way in which the concept is expressed in commentary: "It implies that the roles of citizen and journalist are separate, and I'm some weird sort of hybrid. All journalists are citizens, aren't we?" (Parr 2005). Luke Goode (2009) outlines the various positions taken in academic literature towards the role citizens play in journalism. On the one hand, they are framed to represent a kind of 'postmodern' journalism where the process of crowdsourcing and collaboration produce fluid meanings and unfixed outcomes. In contrast, "there remains a tendency to invoke a modernist, heroic narrative" (Goode 2009: 1290). Goode argues that citizens now have the chance to involve themselves in many areas of the newsmaking process, not just in content creation but also "rating, commenting, tagging and reposting" news stories on mainstream news websites and dedicated social news services (2009: 1290). Jane Singer recognises these actions as "two-step gatekeeping" whereby editors make initial editorial decisions but the user can then "upgrade or downgrade the visibility of that item for a secondary audience" (2014: 67). Goode claims we can consider such actions to be a kind of "metajournalism", thus allowing us to situate our analysis of the citizen as journalist "within a framework of *mediation*" (2009: 1291, his italics).

Yet a broader articulation of the citizen's role in journalism inevitably meets resistance. Brian McNair (2012) focuses on how journalists and media organisations need to form a rearguard action in the face of a threat to their trusted position. Whilst acknowledging that institutions should embrace user-generated content, McNair argues that it should remain a news source and that the act of "critical, creative thinking" is very much one only trained journalists can carry out (2012: 87). Nothing less than the "survival" of journalism is at stake, he claims. Gary Hudson and Mick Temple offer an equally acerbic critique in their essay "We Are Not All Journalists", arguing that many academics are "stretching the concept of journalism to extremes" (2010: 66) by claiming that any 'user' who generates news content is therefore a journalist. Kevin Barnhurst claims that this "fear" around the rise of the citizen journalist is built around the notion of active citizenship as a failed endeavour in the eyes of journalists and political scientists: "it imagined an unreachable ideal that ignored how people enact citizenship in daily life and devalued their political passions" (2013: 218). The lofty stance taken by journalists "guaranteed that citizens would fail" (Barnhurst 2013: 218). This position also ignores the role citizens have long played in news production, with local community columns written by lay reporters, bulging letters pages and other contributions by local activists, photographers, poets and others forming a welcome staple of local newspapers for many decades (Howells 2015). Perhaps the commercial threat of this free or cheap content to many professional journalists' jobs is what changed the attitudes of many of them to what has latterly been labelled – with emphasis on the stigma of the label – 'user-generated content'.

Encouraging 'active' citizenship

The sense that journalism is looking down its nose at citizens is endorsed by Justin Lewis, who argues that "citizenship is implicated in the discourse of news but in forms that are neither enticing nor engaging, and never centre stage" (2006: 312). The news industry is 'top-down', therefore the citizen is more likely than not positioned as recipient or consumer, allowed a voice only through the 'vox pop'. Lewis (2006) and Barnhurst (2013) share the concern that without a shift in journalism's form, 'active' citizenship will fail to flourish. To a degree, Lewis argues for that shift to be towards the everyday: "the focus on the spectacular rather than the typical – endemic in news coverage of crime, for example – rarely implicates citizenship in useful or informative ways" (2006: 315). The ideal of the active citizen is explored by Tony Harcup, who argues that while alternative media is awash with examples of this being fostered, it remains "little discussed within mainstream literature about relationships between journalism and politics" (2011: 15). To be active requires both agency and participation, according to Harcup. He draws on the work of feminist political theorist Chantal Mouffe, who claims that "a radical, democratic citizen must be an active citizen, somebody who acts as a citizen, who conceives of herself as a participant in a collective undertaking" (Mouffe in Harcup 2011: 17). The possibility of active citizenship is that it opens up opportunities for alternative voices in the public sphere. Harcup makes it clear that alternative media has a central role to play:

> It is by encouraging and reflecting a culture of participation that alternative media projects can be seen as supportive of active citizenship; and it is by being participatory forms of media that such projects themselves constitute a form of active citizenship.
>
> *(2011: 27)*

Harcup later goes on to ask the question: "To what extent can an engagement with alternative journalism foster active citizenship?" (2016: 681). Drawing on his audience study of a hyperlocal website in Leeds, he notes the valuable role that this website plays in holding local power to account. However, although the audience self-identifies as active, he questions whether "some people choose to consume alternative journalism not as an integral part of their civic activism but as an alternative to engaging in civic activism at all" (Harcup 2016: 681).

The citizen as participant and as consumer

Studies of citizen-led, participatory and user-generated content (UGC) initiatives or experiments (Bruns *et al.* 2008; Chen *et al.* 2012; Fröhlich *et al.* 2012) have tended to emphasise the effective role played by engaging citizens in media-making experiences and their subsequent positive impact on the public sphere. Wardle and Williams (2010), in research examining the use of UGC at the BBC in 2007 (see also Wahl-Jorgensen *et al.* 2010; Wardle and Williams 2008), argue that their work contains a lesson for journalism studies scholars. They note the positive impact of UGC initiatives but claim that a redefining of terms would help "to further understand the relationship which exists between audiences and media producers in terms of 'Audience comment', 'Audience content', 'Collaborative content' and 'Networked journalism'" (Wardle and Williams 2010: 786). Axel Bruns (2008) emphasises the role that content production plays in enhanced citizenship. He describes the ability to create and share online content as "produsage": "the capacity to be an active produser … equates increasingly with the capacity for active, participatory citizenship" (Bruns 2008: 339). He cites citizen journalism as a key

34 Hyperlocal news in context

example of how produsage behaviour "can be seen to help build the capacities for active forms of cultural and democratic citizenship" (Bruns 2008: 398). In examining the culture of groups of "produsers", Bruns argues that social capital plays a key role: "sustained and constructive participation enables the accumulation of positive social capital" (2008: 341). José van Dijck's essay on new approaches to studying UGC sees a problem in current academic approaches to the practice: "conceptually and methodologically, media scholars will need to devise new ways to assess content trends across these new production platforms" (2009: 55). However, John Hartley sees the potential of participatory forms of journalism as examples of "user-led innovation" that will reshape and even undermine commercial models of public service journalism (2009: 162).

Hartley discusses notions of citizenship throughout much of his work on media audiences. In large part, he focuses on consumption practices and the ways in which citizenship is mediated (Hartley 1987, 2002b). He notes the tensions inherent in the debate about the citizen's position between political sovereignty and consumer sovereignty (Hartley 2002a). The former is enacted through the choices we make in elections, whereas the latter "suggests that our choices as consumers are our primary means of exerting influence over the market" (Hartley 2002a: 37). Hartley rejects the divide between the two and argues that "consumption" is a vital concept in understanding how citizenship works: "our cultural consumption, and in particular our media consumption teach us about our society and to how to act in it" (2002a: 37). Nick Couldry makes a similar point in arguing that there is value in examining "the possibilities for more dispersed symbolic production (image-making, information distribution) embedded within new models of consumption" (2004: 24). He argues that we might find what he describes as the "dispersed citizen" by examining "websites or portals that collect information for consumption and civic activism on a relatively local scale" (Couldry 2004: 25). Couldry makes an explicit call for researchers to recognise that there are "new contexts of public communication and trust" (2004: 26), contexts that may include consumption practices as well as explicit citizenship practices. He makes clear his object of study: "the productive and distributional potential of the internet is central" (Couldry 2004: 26).

Towards creative – 'silly' – citizenship

Couldry's later research (2006) into the ways in which citizens connect through their media consumption is an attempt to look for "cultures of citizenship". He draws on an analytical model by Peter Dahlgren, who argues that modern citizenship in democracies is "multi-dimensional and protean" (2003: 159). In suggesting an analytical framework to allow analysis of citizens' political involvement and use of media, Dahlgren wants us to consider how civic engagement happens in the everyday through cultural expression and engagement: "civic culture … is anchored in the practices and symbolic milieu of everyday life" (2003: 152). Dahlgren argues that this "civic culture" is important for democracy and comprises six interlocking processes (values, affinity, knowledge, practices, identities and discussion). He is optimistic about the role the Internet might play in strengthening civic culture: "looked at from the standpoint of any and all of our six dimensions, there are clear alternatives emerging on the Internet" (Dahlgren 2003: 165). Couldry critiques aspects of Dahlgren's model, but uses it in his 2006 qualitative exploration of how people engage through media with the world around them. To a degree, there seems to be a 'culture' of citizenship evidenced in the way people talk about aspects of their cultural consumption or even in the way they talk about their work. However, he does not find much evidence of connectedness happening through the media: "we did not find any case where this sense of collective connection through media – important pleasure though it may be, we make no judgement on that – connected with any discussion, action or thought about issues of public concern" (Couldry 2006: 334).

John Hartley (2010) argues for a shift in thinking that requires us to consider citizenship through an individual's media consumption, focusing on their capacity to create and distribute media using online platforms. This DIY/DIWO (Do It Yourself/Do It With Others) citizenship is "more individuated and privatised than previous types, because it is driven by voluntarist choices and affiliations, but at the same time it has an activist and communitarian ethic, where 'knowledge shared is knowledge gained'" (Hartley 2010: 240). To a degree, Hartley argues, we have arrived at a point where the importance of "silly citizenship" (Hartley 2010) should not be underestimated – 'silly' being a way to describe the often bizarre mix of cultural mash-ups and seemingly frivolous dance videos that have become extremely popular on YouTube. Around such creative content, communities (usually of interest rather than geographic) come together and "self-organise and self-represent, and act both culturally and politically, without bearing the weight of 'standing for' the whole society" (Hartley 2010: 240). Such frivolity perhaps shows the limitations of understanding the public sphere only in a narrow Habermasian sense: "While it may not look very much like the Habermasian public sphere, it is clearly attracting the attention of those who are notoriously hard to reach by traditional technologies of citizenship" (Hartley 2010: 241).

Creating value for citizens

Whilst journalism has always sought input from citizens, there is recognition by both academics and the media themselves that the relationship is changing. The Internet-based resources available to the citizen with which they can be both producer and gatekeeper are striking in their ease of use and their potential impact, which, as Goode (2009) points out, is impact in terms of reaching audiences and also in exerting editorial control. Doubts may remain amongst professionals about how to best make use of citizen-created content, but it has become clear that managing and verifying such material is something mainstream media organisations now have to incorporate into their production processes. In some ways, the relationship between the citizen and the journalism industry has become increasingly complex and messy.

36 Hyperlocal news in context

How citizenship is expressed online ranges from more direct expressions of political or advocacy blogging ("writer-gatherers" as Couldry 2010 calls them) to acts of consumership. Indeed, if we were to see such value in consumer choice as an important aspect of citizenship, then we might regard those more commercially orientated local hyperlocal websites as serving a useful citizenship function; that is, the act of buying locally, prompted by geo-aware applications, as a form of enacting local civic duty (perhaps in turn being activist by resisting the lures of more corporate 'chain' offerings online or in shopping malls). Wider online participation has also led to greater cultural expression outside mainstream media channels and certainly outside what we might regard as the norms of journalistic practices. Perhaps it has indeed become 'sillier' (Hartley 2010), more memetic in nature, becoming remixed and remediated along the way. Yet our concern here ultimately echoes that of Tony Harcup, who argues that "the production of alternative and participatory forms of media" (2011: 15) is one of the ways in which active citizenship is enacted. His view is that in turn this may well foster active citizenship in the wider population. Whilst his later case study (Harcup 2016) has him doubting this view a little, it is clear he sees value in alternative local media publications as making an important contribution to the public sphere.

Conclusion

As we outlined in the introduction, the definition of 'hyperlocal' is somewhat contested with practitioners seemingly keen to emphasise their community credentials (Hyperlocal Alliance 2013; Talk About Local 2011), while investors seek to broaden the pool of potential operations by including "organisations with a background in local broadcasting, local newspapers and local authorities" (Nesta and Kantar Media 2013: 3). Scholarly interest has tended to focus on the viability of hyperlocal in filling the 'democratic deficit' that results when local newspapers withdraw titles from localities and so reduce the plurality of news sources that citizens have access to. Some research suggests it may not be able to fulfil this role, with work by Kurpius et al. (2010) and van Kerkhoven and Bakker (2014) casting doubt on hyperlocal's ability to contribute to the democratic deficit over the long term because of its economic precariousness. Yet the interest in ensuring community voices are heard in the public sphere persists, and hyperlocal media continues to present itself as a ready-made solution to policymakers and other news media (BBC 2015).

In our overview of debates about the public sphere, we drew on work by Chris Atton (2002) to argue that hyperlocal might usefully be seen as an alternative media practice. Yet we must recognise that its form can feel closer to personal blogging and could be an effective example of the networked private sphere reshaping "what is defined as private and what is defined as public" (Papacharissi 2010a: 152). As we will examine in further detail later, hyperlocal media seems to be both stubbornly independent and stubbornly non-lucrative despite the scale of investment to date (Geels 2013). These factors could be seen as valuable markers of its alternativeness and of activity in the private domain.

The development of social networking technologies, whose use is now widespread amongst a broad range of age and socio-economic groups, has for some academics prompted a renewed interest in the 'everyday'. Sarah Pink (2012) and others (e.g. Postill 2011) are interested in how such technologies make us rethink our understanding of place and how the 'banal' is now foregrounded and put to use in holding local power to account. To an extent, this allows us to consider the role of this digital 'everyday' as a counter-hegemonic one, pushing back against dominant representations of place that come through mainstream media (Parker and Karner 2011). As we will see in later chapters, hyperlocal producers are confronted daily with the noisy banality of their local areas, almost struggling to keep it at bay in the social media spaces they manage. This raises the question of what value is created for citizens by their greater participation in the production of information.

We began this chapter by offering an overview of scholarly concerns about the decline of the local press. The degeneration of the public sphere and the potential democratic deficit that arises is the focus of the next two chapters as we examine the political economy of local and regional journalism in one area of the UK.

References

Atton, Chris (2002) *Alternative Media*. London: Sage.

Atton, Chris (2004) *An Alternative Internet*. Edinburgh: Edinburgh University Press.

Atton, Chris & Hamilton, James Frederick (2008) *Alternative Journalism*. London: Sage.

Baines, David (2010) Hyper-local: Glocalised rural news. *International Journal of Sociology and Social Policy*, Vol. 30, No. 9–10, pp. 581–592.

Barnett, Steven & Townend, Judith (2015) Plurality, policy and the local. *Journalism Practice*, Vol. 9, No. 3, pp. 332–349.

Barnhurst, Kevin G. (2013) "Trust me, I'm an innovative journalist," and other fictions. In: Peters, C. & Broersma, M. J. (eds) *Rethinking Journalism: Trust and Participation in a Transformed News Landscape*. London: Routledge, pp. 210–220.

BBC (2015) BBC seeks views of community news websites and bloggers [Online]. Available at: www.bbc.co.uk/mediacentre/latestnews/2015/hyperlocal [Accessed 29 July 2015].

Benson, Rodney (2006) News media as a "journalistic field": What Bourdieu adds to new institutionalism, and vice versa. *Political Communication*, Vol. 23, No. 2, pp. 187–202.

boyd, danah (2014) *It's Complicated: The Social Lives of Networked Teens*. New Haven, CT: Yale University Press.

Bruns, Axel (2008) *Blogs, Wikipedia, Second Life, and Beyond: From Production to Produsage*. New York: Peter Lang.

Bruns, Axel, Wilson, Jason A. & Saunders, Barry J. (2008) Building spaces for hyperlocal citizen journalism. Paper presented at Association of Internet Researchers 2008: Internet Research 9.0: Rethinking Community, Rethinking Place, Copenhagen, Denmark, 15–18 October. Available at: http://eprints.qut.edu.au/15115/ [Accessed 20 May 2016].

Carnegie UK Trust (2014) *The Future's Bright – The Future's Local*. Dunfermline: Carnegie UK Trust.

Chambers, S. & Costain, A. N. (2000) *Deliberation, Democracy, and the Media*. Oxford: Rowman & Littlefield Publishers.

Chen, Nien-Tsu N., Dong, Fan, Ball-Rokeach, Sandra J., Parks, Michael & Huang, Jin (2012) Building a new media platform for local storytelling and civic engagement in ethnically diverse neighborhoods. *New Media & Society*, Vol. 14, No. 6, pp. 931–950.

Comedia (1984) The alternative press: The development of underdevelopment: Comedia. *Media, Culture & Society*, Vol. 6, No. 2, pp. 95–102.

Conboy, Martin (2005) The print industry – yesterday, today, tomorrow: An overview. In: Keeble, R. (ed.) *Print Journalism: A Critical Introduction*. Abingdon: Routledge, pp. 3–20.

Couldry, Nick (2003) Media meta-capital: Extending the range of Bourdieu's field theory. *Theory and Society*, Vol. 32, No. 5–6, pp. 653–677.

Couldry, Nick (2004) The productive "consumer" and the dispersed "citizen". *International Journal of Cultural Studies*, Vol. 7, No. 1, pp. 21–32.

Couldry, Nick (2006) Culture and citizenship: The missing link? *European Journal of Cultural Studies*, Vol. 9, No. 3, pp. 321–339.

Couldry, Nick (2010) New online news sources and writer-gatherers. In: Fenton, N. (ed.) *New Media, Old News: Journalism & Democracy in the Digital Age*. London: Sage, pp. 138–153.

Curran, James (1991) Rethinking the media as a public sphere. In: Dahlgren, P. & Sparks, C. (eds) *Communication and Citizenship: Journalism and the Public Sphere in the New Media Age*. London: Routledge, pp. 27–57.

Dahlgren, Peter (2003) Reconfiguring civic culture in the new media milieu. In: Corner, J. & Pels, D. (eds) *Media and the Restyling of Politics: Consumerism, Celebrity and Cynicism*. London: Sage, pp. 151–171.

Davies, Nick (2008) *Flat Earth News*. London: Vintage.

Davis, Aeron (2008) Public relations in the news. In: Franklin, B. (ed.) *Pulling Newspapers Apart: Analysing Print Journalism*. Abingdon: Routledge, pp. 272–281.

Downey, John & Fenton, Natalie (2003) New media, counter publicity and the public sphere. *New Media & Society*, Vol. 5, No. 2, pp. 185–202.

Downing, John D. (1988) The alternative public realm: The organization of the 1980s anti-nuclear press in West Germany and Britain. *Media, Culture & Society*, Vol. 10, No. 2, pp. 163–181.

Fenton, Ben (2008) Bad ad news ripples across the sector [Online]. *Financial Times*. Available at: www.ft.com/cms/s/0/3d73394e-46e3-11dd-876a-0000779fd2ac.html [Accessed 2 December 2015].

Fenton, Natalie (2011) Deregulation or democracy? New media, news, neoliberalism and the public interest. *Continuum*, Vol. 25, No. 1, pp. 63–72.

Forde, Susan (2011) *Challenging the News: The Journalism of Alternative and Community Media*. Basingstoke: Palgrave Macmillan.

Franklin, Bob (2005) McJournalism: The McDonaldization thesis and the UK local press. In: Allen, S. (ed.) *Journalism: Critical Issues*. Milton Keynes: Open University Press, pp.137–150.

Franklin, Bob (2006a) Attacking the devil? Local journalists and local newspapers in the UK. In: Franklin, B. (ed.) *Local Journalism and Local Media: Making the Local News*. London: Routledge, pp. 3–15.

Franklin, Bob (2006b) *Local Journalism and Local Media: Making the Local News*. London: Routledge.

Franklin, Bob (2011) *Sources, Credibility and the Continuing Crisis of UK Journalism*. London: Routledge.

Franklin, Bob & Murphy, David (1998) *Making the Local News: Local Journalism in Context*. London: Routledge.

Franklin, Bob, Court, Geoff & Cushion, Stephen (2006) Downgrading the "local" in local newspapers' reporting of the 2005 UK general election. In: Franklin, B. (ed.) *Local Journalism and Local Media: Making the Local News*. London: Routledge, pp. 256–269.

Fraser, Nancy (1990) Rethinking the public sphere: A contribution to the critique of actually existing democracy. *Social Text*, No. 25–26, pp. 56–80.

Freedman, Des (2010) The political economy of the "new" news environment. In: Fenton, N. (ed.) *New Media, Old News: Journalism and Democracy in the Digital Age*. London: Sage, pp. 35–50.

Fröhlich, Romy, Quiring, Oliver & Engesser, Sven (2012) Between idiosyncratic self-interests and professional standards: A contribution to the understanding of participatory journalism in Web 2.0. Results from an online survey in Germany. *Journalism*, Vol. 13, No. 8, pp. 1041–1063.

Fuchs, Christian (2010) Alternative media as critical media. *European Journal of Social Theory*, Vol. 13, No. 2, pp. 173–192.

Gandy, Oscar H. (1982) *Beyond Agenda Setting: Information Subsidies and Public Policy*. New York: Ablex Publishing Corporation.

Geels, Kathryn (2013, 15 November) Destination local: A new competition and new opportunities [Online]. *Nesta* [Blog]. Available at: www.nesta.org.uk/blog/destination-local-new-competition-and-new-opportunities [Accessed 15 November 2015].

Goode, Luke (2009) Social news, citizen journalism and democracy. *New Media & Society*, Vol. 11, No. 8, pp. 1287–1305.

Greenslade, Roy (2007, 12 July) The peoples' papers? A new view of hyperlocal media [Online]. *The Guardian*. Available at: www.guardian.co.uk/media/greenslade/2007/jul/12/thepeoplespapersanewview [Accessed 26 March 2013].

Greenslade, Roy (2009, 24 September) British journalism is in crisis, but we are doing too little to save it? [Online]. *The Guardian*. Available at: www.guardian.co.uk/media/greenslade/2009/sep/24/downturn-mediabusiness [Accessed 2 March 2015].

Habermas, Jürgen (1989) *The Structural Transformation of the Public Sphere: An Inquiry into a Category of Bourgeois Society*. Cambridge: Polity.

Habermas, Jürgen (1992) Further reflections on the public sphere. In: Calhoun, C. J. (ed.) *Habermas and the Public Sphere*. Cambridge, MA: MIT, pp. 421–461.

Hamer, Martin (2006) Trading on trust: News agencies, local journalism, and local media. In: Franklin, B. (ed.) *Local Journalism and Local Media: Making the Local News*. London: Routledge, pp.210–218.

Harcup, Tony (2003) "The unspoken – said": The journalism of alternative media. *Journalism*, Vol. 4, No. 3, pp. 356–376.

Harcup, Tony (2005) "I'm doing this to change the world": Journalism in alternative and mainstream media. *Journalism Studies*, Vol. 6, No. 3, pp. 361–374.

Harcup, Tony (2011) Alternative journalism as active citizenship. *Journalism*, Vol. 12, No. 1, pp. 15–31.

Harcup, Tony (2013) *Alternative Journalism, Alternative Voices*. London; New York: Routledge.

Harcup, Tony (2016) Asking the readers: Audience research into alternative journalism. *Journalism Practice*, Vol. 10, No. 6, pp. 680–696.

Harrison, Shirley (1998) The local government agenda: News from the town hall. In: Franklin, B. & Murphy, D. (eds) *Making the Local News: Local Journalism in Context*. London: Routledge, pp. 150–162.

Hartley, John (1987) Invisible fictions: Television audiences, paedocracy, pleasure. *Textual Practice*, Vol. 1, No. 2, pp. 121–138.

Hartley, John (2002a) *Communication, Cultural and Media Studies: The Key Concepts*. London: Routledge. Hartley, John (2002b) *Uses of Television*. London: Routledge.

Hartley, John (2009) *The Uses of Digital Literacy*. St Lucia, Qld.: University of Queensland Press.

Hartley, John (2010) Silly citizenship. *Critical Discourse Studies*, Vol. 7, No. 4, pp. 233–248.

Hess, Kristy & Waller, Lisa (2016) Hip to be hyper: The subculture of excessively local news. *Digital Journalism*, Vol. 4, No. 2, pp. 193–210.

Highmore, B. (2010) *Ordinary Lives: Studies in the Everyday*. Abingdon: Routledge.

Hohendahl, Peter Uwe & Silberman, Marc (1979) Critical theory, public sphere and culture: Jürgen Habermas and his critics. *New German Critique*, No. 16, pp. 89–118.

Howells, Rachel (2015) *Journey to the Centre of a News Black Hole: Examining the Democratic Deficit in a Town with No Newspaper*. PhD Thesis, Cardiff University.

Hudson, Gary & Temple, Mick (2010) We are not all journalists now. In: Monaghan, G. & Tunney, S. (eds) *Web Journalism: A New Form of Citizenship?* Eastbourne: Sussex Academic Press, pp.63–76.

Hyperlocal Alliance (2013) Definition of hyperlocal [Online]. Available at: http://hyperloca lalliance.org.uk/wiki/definition-of-hyperlocal/?action=diff&post_type=incsub_wiki& left=749 [Accessed 6 April 2013].

Ingold, Tim (2009) Against space: Place, movement, knowledge. In: Kirby, P. W. (ed.) *Boundless Worlds: An Anthropological Approach to Movement*. New York: Berghahn Books, pp. 29–44.

Jenkins, H. (2006) *Convergence Culture: Where Old and New Media Collide*. New York: New York University Press.

Koopmans, Ruud & Erbe, Jessica (2004) Towards a European public sphere? Vertical and horizontal dimensions of Europeanized political communication. *Innovation: The European Journal of Social Science Research*, Vol. 17, No. 2, pp. 97–118.

Kurpius, David D., Metzgar, Emily T. & Rowley, Karen M. (2010) Sustaining hyperlocal media. *Journalism Studies*, Vol. 11, No. 3, pp. 359–376.

Landry, Charles, Morley, David, Southwood, Russell & Wright, Patrick (1985) *What a Way to Run a Railroad: An Analysis of Radical Failure*. London: Comedia.

Leadbeater, Charles (2008) *We-think: Mass Innovation, Not Mass Production: The Power of Mass Creativity*. London: Profile Books.

Lefebvre, Henri (1991) *Critique of Everyday Life, Volume 1*. London: Verso.

Lewis, Justin (2006) News and the empowerment of citizens. *European Journal of Cultural Studies*, Vol. 9, No. 3, pp. 303–319.

Livingstone, Sonia (2005) In defence of privacy: Mediating the public/private boundary at home. In: Livingstone, S. (ed.) *Audiences and Publics: When Cultural Engagement Matters for the Public Sphere*. Changing Media – Changing Europe, Vol. 2. Bristol: Intellect Books, pp.163–185.

McNair, B. (2000) *Journalism and Democracy: An Evaluation of the Political Public Sphere*. London: Routledge.

McNair, Brian (2009) Journalism and democracy. In: Wahl-Jorgensen, K. & Hanitsch, T. (eds) *The Handbook of Journalism Studies*. London: Routledge, pp. 237–249.

McNair, Brian (2012) Trust, truth and objectivity: Sustaining quality journalism in the era of the content-generating user. In: Peters, C. & Broersma, M. J. (eds) *Rethinking Journalism: Trust and Participation in a Transformed News Landscape*. London: Routledge, pp.75–88.

Metzgar, Emily T., Kurpius, David D. & Rowley, Karen M. (2011) Defining hyperlocal media: Proposing a framework for discussion. *New Media & Society*, Vol. 13, No. 5, pp. 772–787.

Mintel (2013) Regional Newspapers – UK – March 2013 [Online]. Available at: http://aca demic.mintel.com/display/638001/ [Accessed 2 December 2015].

Moores, S. (2012) *Media, Place and Mobility*. Basingstoke: Palgrave Macmillan.

Morley, Chris (2013) How regional media companies brought themselves down [Online]. Available at: www.uk.coop/makethenews/newslibrary [Accessed 21 August 2013].

Negt, Oskar & Kluge, Alexander (1983) The proletarian public sphere. In: Mattelart, A. & Siegelaub, S. (eds) *Communication and Class Struggle, Vol. 2*. New York: International General, pp. 92–94.

Nesta & Kantar Media (2013) *UK Demand for Hyperlocal Media Research Report*. London: Nesta.

O'Neill, Deirdre & O'Connor, Catherine (2008) The passive journalist: How sources dominate local news. *Journalism Practice*, Vol. 2, No. 3, pp. 487–500.

Papacharissi, Zizi (2010a) *A Private Sphere: Democracy in a Digital Age*. Cambridge: Polity.

Papacharissi, Zizi (2010b) The Virtual Sphere 2.0: The Internet, the public sphere and beyond. In: Chadwick, A. & Howard, P. N. (eds) *Routledge Handbook of Internet Politics*. Abingdon: Routledge, pp.230–245.

Parker, David & Karner, Christian (2011) Remembering the Alum Rock Road: Reputational geographies and spatial biographies. *Midland History*, Vol. 36, No. 2, pp. 292–309.

Parr, Barry (2005) Things I wish I'd known before I became a citizen journalist [Online]. *Nieman Reports*. Available at: www.nieman.harvard.edu/reports/article/100568/Things-I-Wish-Id-Known-Before-I-Became-a-Citizen-Journalist.aspx [Accessed 15 October 2013].

Pink, Sarah (2012) *Situating Everyday Life: Practices and Places*. London: Sage.

Postill, John (2008) Localizing the Internet beyond communities and networks. *New Media & Society*, Vol. 10, No. 3, pp. 413–431.

Postill, John (2011) *Localizing the Internet: An Anthropological Account*. Oxford: Berghahn Books.

Reader, Bill (2012) Drawing from the critical cultural well. In: Reader, B. & Hatcher, J. A. (eds) *Foundations of Community Journalism*. Thousand Oaks, CA: Sage, pp.109–123.

Schudson, Michael (1999) What public journalism knows about journalism but doesn't know about "public". In: Glasser, T. L. (ed.) *The Idea of Public Journalism*. London: Guilford Press, pp.118–133.

Schultz, Ida (2007) The journalistic gut feeling. *Journalism Practice*, Vol. 1, No. 2, pp. 190–207.

Shirky, Clay (2008) *Here Comes Everybody: The Power of Organizing Without Organizations*. London: Allen Lane.

Shirky, Clay (2010) *Cognitive Surplus: How Technology Makes Consumers into Collaborators*. New York: Penguin.

Shove, E. (2003) *Comfort, Cleanliness and Convenience: The Social Organization of Normality*. Oxford: Berg.

Shove, E. (2009) Everyday practice and the production and consumption of time. In: Shove, E., Trentmann, F. & Wilk, R. (eds) *Time, Consumption and Everyday Life: Practice, Materiality and Culture*. Oxford: Berg, pp. 17–34.

Shove, E., Pantzar, M. & Watson, M. (2012) *The Dynamics of Social Practice: Everyday Life and How it Changes*. London: Sage.

Siles, Ignacio & Boczkowski, Pablo J. (2012) Making sense of the newspaper crisis: A critical assessment of existing research and an agenda for future work. *New Media & Society*, Vol. 14, No. 8, pp. 1375–1394.

Singer, Jane B. (2014) User-generated visibility: Secondary gatekeeping in a shared media space. *New Media & Society*, Vol. 16, No. 1, pp. 55–73.

Somers, Margaret R. (1993) Citizenship and the place of the public sphere: Law, community, and political culture in the transition to democracy. *American Sociological Review*, Vol. 58, No. 5, pp. 587–620.

Talk About Local (2011) FAQ – What is Talk About Local? [Online]. Available at: http://talkaboutlocal.org.uk/faq/ [Accessed 2 December 2015].

van Dijck, José (2009) Users like you? Theorizing agency in user-generated content. *Media, Culture & Society*, Vol. 31, No. 1, pp. 41–58.

van Kerkhoven, Marco & Bakker, Piet (2014) The hyperlocal in practice. *Digital Journalism*, Vol. 2, No. 3, pp. 296–309.

VanSlyke Turk, Judy & Franklin, Bob (1987) Information subsidies: Agenda-setting traditions. *Public Relations Review*, Vol. 13, No. 4, pp. 29–41.

Wahl-Jorgensen, Karin (2007) *Journalists and the Public: Newsroom Culture, Letters to the Editor, and Democracy*. Cresskill, NJ: Hampton.

Wahl-Jorgensen, Karin (2009) On the newsroom-centricity of journalism ethnography. In: Bird, S. E. (ed.) *The Anthropology of News and Journalism*. Bloomington, IN: Indiana University Press, pp. 21–35.

Wahl-Jorgensen, Karin, Williams, Andrew & Wardle, Claire (2010) Audience views on user-generated content: Exploring the value of news from the bottom up. *Northern Lights: Film and Media Studies Yearbook*, Vol. 8, No. 1, pp. 177–194.

Wardle, Claire & Williams, Andrew (2008) *ugc@thebbc – Understanding its Impact upon Contributors, Non-contributors and BBC News*. Cardiff: Cardiff School of Journalism, Media and Cultural Studies.

Wardle, Claire & Williams, Andrew (2010) Beyond user-generated content: A production study examining the ways in which UGC is used at the BBC. *Media, Culture & Society*, Vol. 32, No. 5, pp. 781–799.

Williams, Andy (2012) The crisis in the Welsh media and what to do about it. *Cyfrwng: Media Wales Journal*, Vol. 10, pp. 71–80.

Williams, Andrew & Franklin, Bob (2007) *Turning Around the Tanker: Implementing Trinity Mirror's Online Strategy* [Online]. Cardiff: Cardiff School of Journalism, Media and Cultural Studies. Available at: http://image.guardian.co.uk/sys-files/Media/documents/2007/03/13/Cardiff.Trinity.pdf [Accessed 2 December 2015].

Willig, Ida (2013) Newsroom ethnography in a field perspective. *Journalism*, Vol. 14, No. 3, pp. 372–387.

2

THE WITHDRAWAL OF LOCAL AND REGIONAL NEWS JOURNALISM

In this chapter, in order to situate the emergent field of hyperlocal news more fully in its economic and industrial contexts, we outline the context of newspaper decline that has been a precursor to the rise of hyperlocal media in the UK. We examine the current state and recent historic decline of established commercial local and regional news media in the UK via a detailed case study of South Wales, which has experienced a hollowing out of its local media to a degree that is comparable to other developed democratic nations. We draw on Welsh, UK and international research, news industry company accounts, trade press coverage and first-hand testimony from journalists. With specific reference to the case study of the company Media Wales (and its UK parent Trinity Mirror, renamed Reach plc in May 2018) – the dominant publisher of local and regional news in the country – we provide a critical analysis which charts changes in business models, the related withdrawal of established local journalism from Welsh communities, and the detrimental effects of this retreat on the provision of high-quality and independent local news which is reflective of local communities and produced in the public interest. We begin by providing contextual information about Wales and its news media in general before examining the case of Media Wales specifically. We then outline key findings about the recent rise of hyperlocal community news and conclude by outlining current gaps in the evidence base and suggesting priorities for future research.

National and international newspaper decline

Newspaper circulations in Europe and America are declining across all sectors of the industry. It is tempting to explain this trend with reference solely to the rise of digital technology, particularly the Internet, and the ready availability of online news since the mid 1990s. However, circulation decline predates by many decades the structural changes triggered by new digital technologies. This has been a long, slow fall that has its roots in the 1960s but which, thanks to the continuation of high levels of profits due to buoyant advertising revenues and the willingness of newspaper owners to cut costs, has until recent times kept newspaper profits largely insulated from its effects. Until the 1990s the decline was largely ignored by newspaper owners and journalists (Cole and Harcup 2010: 178; Picard 2010: 17). When the Internet's emergence began to be felt by the print industry after 2000, alarm started to take hold (Cole and Harcup 2010: 179). The downturn provided by the 2008 recession merely accelerated the effects (Cole and Harcup 2010; Nielsen and Levy 2010: 4–12; Picard 2010: 19–20).

There's no doubt that the structural decline witnessed in recent decades has partly been caused by the advent of digital media platforms. Both advertisers and audiences have been tempted away from newsprint by new media as well as online offerings of traditional publishers (Nielsen and Levy 2010: 7–8; Phillips and Witschge 2012; Picard 2010: 21). But this is not a wholly new phenomenon – new and disruptive technologies have challenged existing news hierarchies before as other formats, cumulatively, took their toll on reader numbers. As Black notes, "each period of English newspaper history can be presented as one of transformation, shifts in content, production, distribution, the nature of competition, and the social context" (2001: 1). In particular, television, and later the explosion in the number of available channels, took readers away from newspapers. Where television penetration in UK homes in 1956 was 36.5 per cent, by 2013 it was 96.7 per cent (Broadcasters Audience Research Board 2014), and the number of channels had risen from 2 in 1954 to 527 in 2013 (House of Lords Communications Committee 2010; Ofcom 2014). News is now available 24 hours a day on rolling news channels or the Internet and is more available, immediate and prevalent than it has ever been before (Phillips and Witschge 2012: 8).

Alongside the Internet and other competing media, other, more urbane, reasons for the decline in newspaper circulations have been noted. These are largely symptomatic of cultural and social shifts which exist outside the control of the newspaper industry. Commuting habits (Anderson *et al.* 2007: 26), changing working hours, an increase in office workers and the move away from daily convenience shopping have all impacted on newspaper buying habits. Some of the "facts that drove purchase … [such as] late racing results or cricket scores" are no longer published, because late editions have been scrapped in favour of overnight printing in centralised printing hubs (Preston 2009: 14). Picard (2010: 21) notes that the emergence of more choice for consumers, through emergent technologies, including radio, television and the Internet, has pulled audiences to a mix of other media for their news and entertainment. Meyer calls this a "media overload problem" (2009: 12), contending that the surplus of news and entertainment available on multiple channels and across multiple media consumes and therefore dilutes the attention of the audience and fragments it (see also Anderson *et al.* 2007; Phillips and Witschge 2012).

These factors have thereby combined to pull readers away from the paid-for news in newspapers and divided the mass readership that existed during most of the

19th and 20th centuries into many small groups of audiences, a process of audience fragmentation. Through the Internet, anyone with a computer can access most newspapers, radio stations and television channels in the world as well as the many millions of websites that also offer news (raw or in aggregate), information, entertainment, opinion, marketing, advertising and retail. This has produced an audience of browsers, who are adept at surfing the net, using multiple news sources across many different formats, and who are also able to consume information directly from sources such as government websites or eyewitnesses on social media. This is seen by some scholars to offer a new dawn of civic and democratic participation as there is now a wealth of opportunities to receive, create and interact with information as well as to link with vast networks of people (Gillmor 2008; Shirky 2008). However, many empirical studies cast doubt on this hypothesis. For example, though the Internet offers vast quantities of news, it is not used mainly for this purpose. Instead, television is often cited as the main source of news for most people around the world (Curran and Witschge 2010), and a recent Ofcom study confirmed television is still the UK's biggest news source, though it reported a 3 per cent decrease in television's prevalence in 2014 compared to the previous year and a 9 per cent growth in the use of digital platforms in the same period (Ofcom 2014a).

There are four factors that continue to limit take-up of digital news or access to news online. First, it remains the case that linguistic, literacy and cultural factors exclude many potential users of the Internet (Curran and Witschge 2010; Mitchelstein and Boczkowski 2010: 1088) – for example, those who cannot read or those who do not speak the dominant language (English). Second, there are some who cannot access the Internet because they cannot afford to do so or because, due to their socioeconomic status, they are not "equipped with additional tools to be more active citizens" (Papacharissi 2002: 15). Third, as discussed above, many people have limited time available to search out alternative points of view, to cross-check what they read or to refer to raw data online: the Ofcom research shows rather that most people continue to gather news at mainstream websites such as the BBC website/app (59 per cent) or other well-known news sources (Ofcom 2014). Indeed, other studies of online traffic have similarly found a large audience concentration among a handful of established websites with a smaller portion of the audience scattered among a large number of much smaller news outlets (Hindman 2009). Fourth, online news itself has been found to be narrow in scope and agenda (Lee 2007; Phillips 2012) with "content online … increasingly more homogenous" (Mitchelstein and Boczkowski 2010: 1090), prompting some scholars to suggest that public messages are still reaching mass audiences because of the increasing tendency of the many news outlets to run similar content (Coleman and McCombs 2007) or even "cannibalise" one another's content (Phillips 2011). Though the public agenda may arguably be served under these conditions, with important messages possibly getting out to a large proportion of the audience, there are consequent problems with a lack of multiplicity and alternative viewpoints feeding into the narrative.

Local and regional news in South Wales

We find a useful case study in Wales, which shares many of the democratic and political structures of Western democratic nations, while suffering particularly from homogenous newspaper ownership, severe cuts and closure across the industry, and a weak presence in national UK-based media. As a nation within the UK, Wales has a semi-autonomous devolved assembly (the National Assembly for Wales) with the power to make some legislation and having responsibility for the administration of areas of public life such as health and education. The population of Wales is just over 3 million, with the majority living in the largely urban South East (as distinct from the more rural areas of West, Mid and North Wales). Its capital, Cardiff (estimated pop. 361,468 in 2016), is surrounded by nine other densely populated local government districts, including two smaller cities (Swansea to the West and Newport to the East) and many neighbouring small towns and villages with a further combined population of 1,202,634 (StatsWales 2016). Cardiff, as the seat of government and the principal cultural and economic hub, has the highest concentration of news media and is home to the main offices of national public service broadcaster BBC Wales as well as the largest commercial newspaper company in Wales, Media Wales.

Media Wales publishes more news, owns more outlets and employs more journalists than any other local news provider in Wales. Its flagship title is the *Western Mail* (which mainly serves South Wales). It also produces daily newspapers in Cardiff, the *South Wales Echo*, and Swansea, the *South Wales Evening Post*, and a national weekend title, *Wales on Sunday*. The *Post* was acquired in 2015 when parent company Trinity Mirror, previously the fifth-largest UK local news publisher, bought out the fourth largest, Local World. As well as these, it owns a diminishing group of weekly newspapers in the surrounding post-industrial South Wales Valleys. Elsewhere, the company also owns the *North Wales Daily Post* and the West Wales weekly *Llanelli Star*, and the weekly *Carmarthen Journal*. Aside from a number of free fortnightly newspapers (also, in the main, produced by Trinity Mirror), most of these publications have for decades stood virtually alone in their local media markets, which have essentially been local advertising monopolies with next to no local news plurality. This has historically been a factor in keeping revenues and profits high as circulations continue to fall; but fragmentation and increased competition in local media markets since the rise of digital news means that this period is now drawing to a close. The company also publishes a large national news website, WalesOnline.co.uk, which aggregates coverage from journalists based around the country (mainly the South and West, but principally Cardiff). Notably, the centralisation of most of Media Wales' local and regional digital news on this site means that individual newspaper titles owned by the firm tend to have no branded online presence. For instance, if you live in a town served by Media Wales, in most cases you don't have a news site dedicated to your area and must access local news online by navigating the complex architecture of this centralised site.

The commercial press (and its associated online content) is by far the dominant provider of local news, but consumption of such news has traditionally not been very widespread compared with that of either nationally focused news about Wales or UK national news. For instance, local and regional newspaper circulation has been very low compared with that of UK national titles – 85 per cent of papers bought in Wales are UK nationals produced in England and composed of news about England (Thomas 2006: 49). Broadcast news in Wales is dominated by the daily televised public service provision of BBC Cymru Wales and its main commercial rival, ITV Cymru Wales. However, both of these broadcasters are Welsh-national in approach, so they cannot really be seen as local, or even regional, news providers. The same can be said of the BBC's Radio Wales, but BBC Wales' online news is less nationally focused, allowing audiences to view and navigate news pieces relevant to five Welsh regions. Despite this broad limitation, in the absence of a strong local and regional newspaper sector, the national broadcasters remain a crucial source of daily news and information about Welsh politics and Welsh life. As such, they enjoy reasonably high audience figures, with the BBC's flagship early evening news programme attracting an average audience of 293,000 in 2014, and ITV's attracting 181,000 (IWA 2015: 35–36).

Since 2015 a limited amount of local television news has been produced by small Welsh providers in Cardiff and Swansea in South Wales and Mold in North Wales under the Local Digital Programme Services Scheme. These outlets are mainly funded by public money diverted ('top-sliced') from the UK national BBC budget, and they are accessible on digital television set-top boxes or live online. The channels are guaranteed funding for three years in return for a commitment to produce 20 hours of local programming which is shared with the BBC. However, the owners of the channels in Cardiff and Swansea have, respectively, cut back on this commitment after funding ended or applied to do so ahead of the three-year deadline (Thomas 2018). Commercial local radio in Wales, as in the rest of the UK, previously provided substantial amounts of locally produced news by well-staffed teams of local journalists; but after years of consolidation and disinvestment made possible by the ever greater relaxation of regulation, very little radio news is now produced locally, and local radio journalism staffing levels have decreased substantially (McDonald and Starkey 2016). The local radio industry is currently lobbying the UK government to complete a promised "switchover" from analogue to the (even more) lightly regulated digital radio (DAB) where companies will be able to drop "all remaining local content" (IWA 2015: 108).

Wales is a bilingual nation with two official languages; virtually everyone speaks English, and 19 per cent of the population speaks Welsh (StatsWales 2011). In South Wales between 10 and 15 per cent are Welsh speakers, but this rises to as high as 65 per cent in North West Wales (StatsWales 2011). The Welsh-language broadcaster S4C produces daily bulletins which blend Welsh-national, UK-focused and international news. The BBC also runs a Welsh-language radio station, Radio Cymru, and a Welsh-language news website, Cymru Fyw ('Wales Live'; www.bbc.co.uk/cymrufyw), whose annual budget in 2014 was £399,000 (roughly a quarter of the budget of its English-language equivalent). A "unique feature" of Wales' media ecosystem is a series of DIY newspapers, produced, printed and distributed by the community, called the "papurau bro, Welsh-language community newspapers" (Thomas 2006: 54). Initially arising from a period of intense Welsh-language advocacy activism in the early 1970s, there are now 58 such publications, which allow local citizen journalists to record daily life among the Welsh-speaking communities they serve (Williams and Harte 2016). These outlets mainly include stories about local residents (e.g. notable achievements, births, marriages and deaths, often in the form of reports from readers) along with articles about local clubs, societies and cultural events (Thomas 2006: 54–55). In their focus on community coverage and human interest stories and with the participatory nature of their production, these outlets are valuable agents of community representation and social cohesion. However, only rarely do they cover political and civic life, campaign or seek to hold elite local actors to account.

The decline of Welsh local and regional newspapers

Echoing UK trends, the recent history of established, professional Welsh newspaper journalism has been one of ever greater consolidation and decline. In 1985, there were 1,687 local newspapers in the UK; by 2005 this had fallen by almost a quarter to 1,286 (Franklin 2006). By 2015 the figure stood at 1,100, a drop of more than a third over 30 years, with a quarter of those lost being paid-for newspapers (Ramsay and Moore 2016). The same research found only a very small number of new local titles launched over the same period. Industry executives have downplayed these figures, arguing that most of the closures were of free and weekly titles and that previous, more extreme, predictions (e.g. Enders Analysis 2011) had "blown [the problem] out of proportion" (Sweney 2015). The loss of more than a third of local titles, however inaccurate previous predictions may have been, is not something to be dismissed easily. Communities in Wales, from Port Talbot in the South to Wrexham in the North, have lost news outlets. As we will argue in the next chapter, which focuses on the closure of the weekly *Port Talbot Guardian*, such a loss can have profound and wide-ranging effects on the quantity and quality of information circulated in local public debate and the consequent ability of citizens to navigate community, civic and democratic life.

But closures only tell us part of the story of the decline of professional commercial journalism. A less dramatic and visible, but equally disturbing, trend can be found in across-the-board falls in Welsh newspaper circulations, which have been declining since the 1950s, but more sharply in recent years. Between 2008 and 2015: the *Daily Post*'s circulation declined 33 per cent (from 36,432 to 24,485); the *South Wales Echo* lost 60 per cent of readers (from 46,127 to 18,408); and the *South Wales Evening Post*'s sales fell by 46 per cent (from 51,329 to 27,589) (IWA 2015: 62). A longer-term view of circulation decline is evident in Figure 2.1, which charts average six-monthly circulation of the *Western Mail* since the turn of the century.

Withdrawal of local and regional news journalism 49

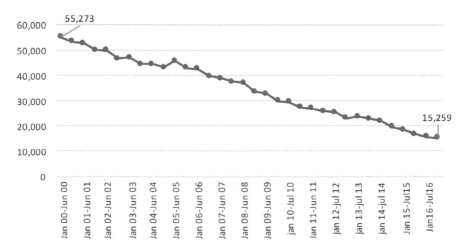

FIGURE 2.1 Average six-monthly circulation of the *Western Mail*
Source: Audit Bureau of Circulations

This data shows that South Wales' flagship newspaper lost almost three-quarters of its audited circulation between the years 2000 and 2016. This is alarming for numerous reasons, but most immediately because print circulation revenues still remain very important to the balance sheets of major local news publishers and because of the likely continued decline in the perceived value of print among advertisers as audiences continue to shrink (there will come a time when reaching relatively small printed newspaper audiences no longer benefits advertisers). The *Western Mail* has consistently lost around 10,000 daily sales every four or five years over the last two decades; if this trend continues, there will be no readers left by the early to mid 2020s.

In Wales, as elsewhere, daily newspaper circulations have suffered steeper declines than weekly paid-for newspapers, while weeklies showed comparative resilience until the early to mid 2000s (Williams and Franklin 2007: 28). In Port Talbot, for example, the *Guardian* had returned relatively stable circulation figures and profits until the mid 2000s. However, after harsh cuts, disinvestment in human resources and corresponding cuts to the quality and localness of news, its circulation halved between 2000 and 2009 (Williams and Franklin 2007: 27). As we will discuss in more detail in the next chapter, when the paper closed citizens lost a newspaper of record, their primary source of day-to-day information about how to navigate civic and community life. So far, closures in Wales have been limited to free and weekly papers, but the effects of losing one of the larger daily newspapers in this way could be even more serious and wide-ranging.

Decreasing local news revenues

As it has elsewhere, Welsh local news has traditionally sustained itself in two main ways: by selling news products to the public and by selling the public's attention to advertisers. Both of these principal revenue streams are now under threat and have substantially decreased. UK local newspaper advertising income fell by an average of 6.6 per cent annually over the period from 2009 to 2013; the drop included both display and classified advertising, with classified ad expenditure – previously a staple of the local newspaper sector – falling 63 per cent between 2007 and 2012 (Ramsay and Moore 2016). As we have seen, at the same time as advertising revenues have fallen, there have been drastic reductions in revenues from sales of printed news and no widespread adoption of paid content strategies for digital local news (Greenslade 2009; Mintel 2013; Williams 2013). Revenues from the local press, which has always been more reliant on advertising income than cover price, have declined significantly and, in some cases, have more than halved (Picard 2008). This trend has altered the traditional balance of revenue streams, and insiders at Media Wales have reported that by 2016 the main source of the *Western Mail*'s revenue had become its cover price, overtaking advertising income for the first time.

In one detailed (and extreme) local case study, Perch (2015) showed that annual revenues at the English regional daily *Leicester Mercury* sank from £59 million to just £16 million between 1996 and 2011. Declining newspaper circulations have also served to depress the price newspapers can charge for advertising, and the declines in editorial quality associated with subsequent staff cuts have led to what has been described as a "suicide spiral" (Rosenstiel and Mitchell 2004: 87), which continues apace throughout the UK.

Media Wales' revenues and profits over the last two decades offer a useful, and broadly representative, case study to explore analogous trends in Wales and the wider UK (see Figure 2.2). Between 1999 and 2005 revenues grew steadily by almost £15 million, and profitability soared. This was largely down to a combination of still very high print advertising revenues, sustained cuts to the editorial

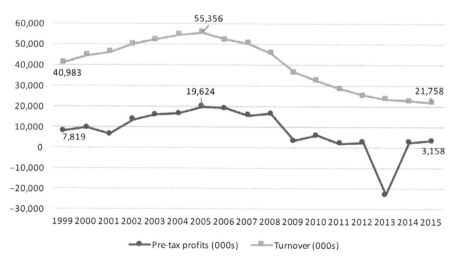

FIGURE 2.2 Turnover and profitability at Media Wales, 1999–2015
Source: Media Wales/Western Mail and Echo (2000–2015)

workforce (in common with other major publishers) and successive restructuring exercises carried out in order to save money and maintain high profits. Profit margins in the period 2002–2008 hovered between 27 and 36 per cent (Media Wales/Western Mail and Echo 2000–2015), which, as National Union of Journalists (NUJ) General Secretary Michelle Stanistreet has observed, made the company among the "most profitable companies in Wales of any kind, let alone the media industry" (National Union of Journalists 2012).

The 2008 financial crisis led to a long advertising recession and a slump from which the local news industry has yet to emerge. Revenues at Media Wales fell by more than 50 per cent against the high-water mark of 2005, and profits shrank. Notably (excepting 2013),[1] relatively high profit margins were still maintained at between 6 and 18 per cent. This might pale in comparison with previous figures, but relative to other sectors and industries this is still high and reflects the way in which the company has continued to implement cuts and consolidate its costs throughout this turbulent period.

The withdrawal of professional journalism

In Wales, as elsewhere, there has been a steady withdrawal of established professional journalism from newsrooms and communities after decades of redundancies, staff cuts and recruitment freezes. This is arguably the most concerning consequence of the collapse in the regional and local news business model, and the most alarming cost of the strategies pursued by big publishing companies to deal with it. This withdrawal has almost certainly been hastened and intensified by large publishers' decisions to maintain high profits to fund regular shareholder dividends.

There are no reliable figures to determine exact longitudinal staffing trends, but from the fragmentary existing research, it is clear that in Wales, as throughout the UK, the human resources of the local news industry have been decimated. An NUJ Commission on multimedia in 2007 found that "there had been editorial job cuts at 45 per cent of titles since online operations were introduced" (Freedman 2010: 41). The publishers' trade body, the News Media Association (NMA), has (perhaps understandably) since stopped publishing statistics on industry job losses, but figures cited by Nel (2010) suggest there was a 14 per cent contraction in the number of local and regional press jobs between 2002 and 2007, a fall from 13,020 to 11,230. By October 2015 the Press Gazette estimated, based on analysis of selected companies' staffing levels reported to Companies House, that the number of professional journalists employed in the local press was about half of what it had been before the 2008 recession. A report by Oliver and Ohlbaum Associates Ltd in 2015 appears to substantiate Press Gazette estimates, stating that Trinity Mirror reduced its workforce by 47 per cent between 2008 and 2013, with other large industry players Johnston Press and Archant cutting by 46 per cent and 27 per cent, respectively.

Studies of specific local media systems over longer periods shed further light on the nature and scale of this problem. Howells (2015) found that the two largest regional news organisations in South Wales were staffed by almost 1,000 editorial and production employees in the year 2000, but by 2014 this had shrunk to under 300. Similarly, the Leicester Mercury Group employed 581 staff in 1996, but only 107 by 2011 (Perch 2015).

At Media Wales[2] (see Figure 2.3) there were almost 700 editorial and production staff in 1999 (Williams 2013), but by 2015 this had shrunk by over 85 per cent, with the company employing only 100 (Media Wales/Western Mail and Echo 2000–2015). This means that local communities in Cardiff and the surrounding areas (a combined population of over a million people) are currently being served by 85 per cent fewer journalists and production staff than in 1999; in the commercial newspaper sector, for every ten reporters (or subeditors or designers) working in the region at the turn of the millennium, only one and a half remain. In 2013, there were more people employed in administration, sales and distribution combined at Media Wales than journalists putting together two dailies, seven weeklies, one Sunday and the biggest news website in the country. The *Western Mail*'s chief reporter and NUJ activist Martin Shipton (2011) has been particularly critical of his company's online strategy:

> Companies saw the Internet as a means to make advertising revenue without the expense of producing and distributing newspapers. When the revenues failed to materialise at anywhere near the hoped-for rate, they resorted to the only tactic they could think of: slashing labour costs and harming their papers in the process. Thus will the downward spiral continue until there is nothing left to cut.

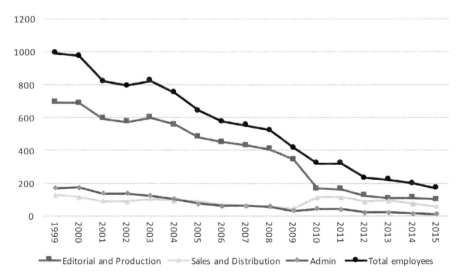

FIGURE 2.3 Staffing levels at Media Wales, 1999–2015
Source: Media Wales/Western Mail and Echo (2000–2015)

The weekly newspapers serving the post-industrial South Wales Valleys, known collectively as the Celtic Weeklies, have been particularly neglected. These once proud and well-resourced local institutions had accessible offices on the high street, each staffed by teams that included an editor, a small full-time reporting staff, photographers and administrators. By 2011, after a series of redundancies and the closure of the Port Talbot and Neath *Guardian* titles, Press Gazette (2011) reported that only six senior reporters and five trainees remained to produce seven titles. After several further rounds of cuts, all of the local offices have been closed (leaving these areas to be covered remotely, from a geographical and a cultural distance, in Cardiff). No titles have dedicated editors, and all seven weekly papers, along with their associated online news outputs, are produced by just 3.5 journalists, meaning there are now more newspaper titles than reporters at the Celtic Weeklies.

The future is digital, yet digital revenues remain low

Since the advent of digital news, many advertisers have deserted newspapers, preferring the cheaper and more targeted services offered by digital intermediaries such as search sites (principally, but not only, Google), social networking platforms (principally, but not only, Facebook) and a range of competitor online classified advertising sites (Fenton *et al.* 2010; Meikle and Young 2011). At the same time, fragmented audiences have moved in increasing numbers to the non-linear consumption of digital news. When reading digital news, they often do so on social media platforms or on news aggregation sites rather than directly from local news sites themselves (Doyle 2013; Freedman 2010).

These trends, combined with declining print news audiences, have led Trinity Mirror, in common with almost all other local news publishers, to prioritise the web at the expense of print in their business strategies. This model has led to impressive audience growth (albeit from a very low base) in the readership of Wa lesOnline.co.uk, which has increased average daily unique readers from 34,000 to 390,000 in just seven years (see Figure 2.4). However, large increases in audiences for UK local and regional online news have not translated into anything approaching profits equivalent to those lost due to declining print titles. We have already seen how falling revenues combined with a mini-max editorial approach (which maximises profits, and dividends to shareholders, while minimising investment) has led to the loss of many hundreds of journalists in South Wales. The data presented so far, though, does not show where the revenues to pay the remaining workforce come from. Media Wales do not differentiate in annual accounts between revenues earned from digital and print, but these figures are indicated in the group accounts published by parent company Trinity Mirror.

Figure 2.5 shows the proportion of revenues derived from printed news and from digital news at Trinity Mirror's Regionals and Publishing divisions between 2003 and 2016.[3] The large dark area represents the percentage of revenues derived from newspaper circulation and printed advertising; the slim light area, the proportion obtained from digital advertising. Media Wales has (as is common in the

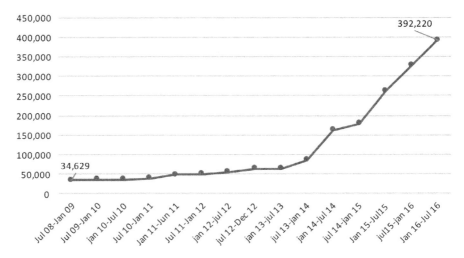

FIGURE 2.4 WalesOnline.co.uk average daily unique users, 2008–2016
Source: Audit Bureau of Circulations

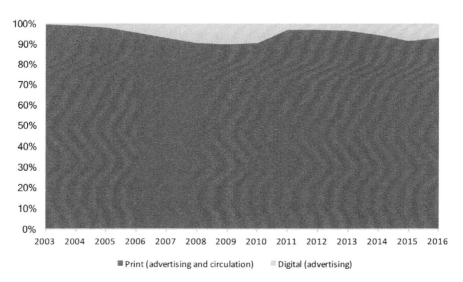

FIGURE 2.5 Trinity Mirror Regionals/Trinity Mirror Publishing revenue breakdowns by platform, 2003–2016
Source: Trinity Mirror

sector) prioritised digital, web-first editorial strategies since the mid 2000s. But this graph underlines the still relatively low economic value of online news compared with print. Despite print's decline and its near-universal displacement as a corporate priority, it still pays for the majority of the workforce. Given that declining revenues from print have been such a large factor in the hollowing out of newsrooms to date, it seems likely that we will lose many more journalists before a more sustainable balance between income streams and staffing levels can be found. This is likely to have many and far-reaching consequences on the working conditions and practices of those journalists who remain, as well as the future quality of local news.

Declining media plurality

The loss of newspapers adds to the existing concerns around a lack of local media plurality caused by publishers' quests for consolidation and greater economies of scale. UK media regulator Ofcom states that "plurality matters because it makes an important contribution to a well-functioning democratic society … through **informed citizens** … and **preventing too much influence over the political process**" (Ofcom 2012: 6, emboldening in the original). Yet the UK's local media markets are far from plural. In 1992 there were 200 companies publishing local newspapers in the UK. By 2005 this had fallen to just 87, with 8 companies owning 80 per cent of UK titles (Williams and Franklin 2007). By 2015 ownership had further consolidated, with 6 companies owning 80 per cent of titles and only 62 companies owning at least one daily or weekly newspaper (Media Reform Coalition 2015). Trinity Mirror's 2016 acquisition of Local World saw the UK's fourth-largest publisher buy out the fifth largest, leading to further consolidation and efficiency savings. Over two-thirds of the UK's Local Authority Districts (LADs), more than half of all parliamentary constituencies, and 56 per cent of the population are not served by a dedicated daily newspaper, and almost half of all LADs are served by just one publisher (Ramsay and Moore 2016). These headline data do not take into account the loss of intra-company plurality caused by moves to make journalists, previously dedicated to one title, produce news which is repurposed across numerous news outlets owned by the same company.

Diversity of news provision is generally seen as desirable because it limits the power and influence of news company owners. But equally important, in the local context, diverse news ecosystems may serve to limit the dominance of particular business models and their associated editorial priorities and practices. Wales' biggest local media plurality problem may not lie in the risk that Trinity Mirror's CEO might wish to exert undue influence over Welsh political life, but instead in the fact that his company's cost-cutting, high-output, consolidating and synergistic approach to its business means that almost all Welsh journalists in the commercial sector now work in similar ways, producing similar kinds of news while working under similarly difficult conditions and constraints. Without competition from others with different editorial and commercial priorities, local news owners have the luxury of being able to dominate local information systems with minimal outlay on news content; investment in news quality is not incentivised when you are the only player in town.

Does news have less civic value?

It should be noted that many of the trends discussed above – including diminishing resources, centralisation, convergence and increasing workloads – were already in evidence before the growth of online news and had led scholars to reach consistently gloomy conclusions about UK local newspaper coverage of local democracy. Between the mid 1980s and the mid 2000s the local press in Wales suffered a "collapse" in news about local elections, producing fewer election stories with distinct local angles and reducing "sustained discussion of policy concerns" in favour of "trivial and entertaining" coverage (Franklin *et al.* 2006: 257). In-depth news about local politics and the governance of local communities gradually gave way to a more tabloid-orientated spread of news, where emphasis on entertainment, consumer issues, and human interest stories increased, while coverage of democracy and public life decreased (Franklin 2006). Outside of election times, as journalistic workloads rose, mainstream local news came to rely more on official sources and public relations, the result being that only a very narrow range of community voices tend to be routinely cited about a limited variety of issues (Davies 2008; Franklin 1988; O'Neill and O'Connor 2008; VanSlyke Turk and Franklin 1987).

Harrison, echoing other studies, has found local newspaper reliance on sources in local government to be very high, even going as far as to suggest that the growing power imbalance between local media and local governments means that "local newspapers are unlikely to be able to perform their role as principal institutions of the public sphere" (1998: 161). O'Neill and O'Connor (2008), ten years later, found that local and regional journalists relied very heavily on a relatively small range of official sources, usually those with the most resources to devote to public relations. They also note with alarm that the majority of stories (76 per cent) relied on single sources, with less than a quarter of articles employing secondary sources, who may provide alternative, opposing or complementary information to that provided by primary sources.

The future of digital local news in the public interest

There is comparatively little research into the UK local news sector post 2008. This is concerning because if a growing number of first-hand critical accounts of digital local newsroom life from journalists are to be believed, many of the trends identified here have both intensified and transformed. Common predigital critiques of tabloidisation, or the 'dumbing down' of journalism (Franklin 2005), have taken new form with the rise of online local news and the need to attract audiences on a variety of platforms and to encourage them not only to read the news, but to share it among their own networks as well (Tandoc Jr and Jenkins 2017). A common theme in such accounts is anxiety about a perceived overemphasis on the production of clickbait articles such as odd-numbered listicles, the need for which is driven by the currently dominant high-volume, quick-turnaround digital editorial strategy. The listicle is only one of the innovations which have a potentially detrimental effect on the quality and independence of Welsh digital local news, but it has come to act as an emblem in wider debates around standards and quality in online local news.

Paul Rowland, then online editor at Media Wales (and now editor-in-chief), presented his experiences of creating shareable 'online content' on WalesOnline.co. uk at an industry conference (McNally 2014). He described an epiphany in which he recognised the shareability of light-hearted listicles after a humorous article entitled "14 Welsh place names with no (English) vowels", playing on a stereotyped notion of the impenetrability of the Welsh language, went viral. Some journalists didn't "get it", he said, implying some resistance among the staff. But the piece was "shared in a way we hadn't had anything shared before" (McNally 2014). Such stories, frequently based around telling of jokes, strategic employment of emotion or use of stereotypes about local or national identity, and often devoid of information in the public interest, have since become a mainstay of the news site's output. This approach has caused concern among some journalists working at Media Wales, in common with many others across the UK who doubt the broader sustainability of the current online business model and lament the perceived fall in editorial quality and standards that has accompanied it. Using discourse which seems to tacitly accept the misgivings of some among his critics, Rowland added: "Some people would say it's not journalism, but who says we have to do journalism all the time anyway? What we have to do is fit what our audience wants" (McNally 2014).

A number of factors combine to inform a click-led editorial policy, which necessitates a very high volume of stories be produced each day to satisfy demand from online advertisers. Due to the continued decline in the value of print advertising and stark falls in revenues from printed newspaper circulations, almost all major local and regional news publishers have prioritised increasing advertising revenues from digital news. But whereas in the predigital age, newspaper companies enjoyed high print advertising revenues from a series of largely discrete, secure regional advertising monopolies, the digital advertising market has been much less hospitable. Google and Facebook, who specialise in targeted advertising based on valuable search and social media user data (usually unavailable in such richness of detail to news publishers), continue to dominate the sector, with credible estimates suggesting that they will capture over 70 per cent of all money spent on display advertising in the UK by 2020 (Jackson 2016).

Useful insights into how these changes affect journalism practice and news content can be gleaned from increased industry-wide debate covered in the trade press as well as the steady drip, drip of critical first-hand confessional, satirical and campaigning accounts from serving or former local journalists. From the newspaper editor who reflected on his redundancy in the form of an odd-numbered listicle (Ponsford 2016b) to the "heartbroken" award-winning local news journalist who quit his job because of perceived falling print and online editorial standards (Ponsford 2016a), many local journalists fear that public interest news is being squeezed out by the need to attract website traffic. Managers, such as Trinity Mirror's David Higgerson (2015), contend that their editorial strategy is simply about "understanding what audiences want" and that such fears are unfounded. But others, such as CEO Simon Fox have given mixed messages, both downplaying the existence of a local-news-related democratic deficit and lamenting

58 Withdrawal of local and regional news journalism

perceived pressure on newspaper publishers to do something about it. Shipton cites Fox's comment, made at a Media Wales staff briefing in 2014, that the problem with "this democratic deficit stuff" is that "it doesn't get enough clicks" (Shipton 2015). A year later, when asked to respond to the BBC's plans for its nascent Local Democracy Reporter Scheme, Fox replied that as Trinity Mirror sees it, "there isn't a democratic deficit" (Turvill 2015).

There is, as yet, little empirical evidence about shifting local news editorial and commercial practices and their likely effects on community and democratic life in Wales and the wider UK. Research is needed into the developing balance (or not) between entertainment and public interest news in digital local news in general. A more specific area of inquiry entails fresh analysis of developing trends in local 'churnalism' (e.g. reliance on powerful official sources with well-funded and efficient public relations teams; the influence of a growing army of local public relations consultants with an evolving appreciation of what kinds of tailored information subsidies journalists need in the 21st-century digital local newsroom). There is also a need to explore more deeply the related realm of local native advertising, and the potential of innovations in advertorial content, which may be further blurring the already fuzzy boundaries between marketing and editorial at a time when media companies are facing very tough commercial challenges.

Another potential area of inquiry is into the effects on local advertising of the near-universal introduction of complex and expensive automated, centralised, programmatic online advertising systems. Just as over the last two decades major local news publishers have cut editorial costs (and staff) by centralising production of news, the same is now happening in their advertising departments. Local news publishers make much of their contribution to local consumers, local businesses and the broader local economy through hosting local ads. But programmatic advertising systems require high levels of expertise on the client side as well as the resources to engage with complex, competitive centralised bidding systems. This may be leading to decreasingly local advertising content, especially among smaller advertisers, which mirrors the de-localisation of news online. In a further area for future research, it is as yet unclear how companies like Trinity Mirror have innovated in their practices to incorporate the commercial exploitation of data about audience engagement with online advertising, and research is needed into the potential and actual effects of changing commercial practices on the commodification and privacy of digital news audiences. A clearer area of concern has also emerged in the use of real-time audience metrics on the click rates of individual news pieces in order to motivate (or discipline) journalists and promote newsroom competition. Future research will need to determine whether such performance-related data, with its near-exclusive emphasis on what digital audiences want and are willing to share, might further de-prioritise the production and consumption of news which many in the audience might not at present be interested in, but which is nonetheless squarely in the public interest. Again, the dominant publishers are insistent that these fears are unfounded, but previous experience suggests the need for independent researchers to monitor closely what they do, as well as what they say.

The rise of independent hyperlocal news

The decline of traditional local news appears to have encouraged a layer of entrepreneurial news providers. In addition to the established papurau bro, there are around 40 hyperlocal news outlets providing printed and/or online news across Wales (Meese 2017), run by a mixture of citizen and professional journalists. In Wales, as elsewhere, most hyperlocals are volunteer led and do not seek to make money, although a growing number of publishers could be described as small-scale local news entrepreneurs, earning enough revenues to pay themselves and, in some cases, a small staff. Notable examples of economically viable hyperlocal news outlets in Wales include Wrexham.com and the *Caerphilly Observer* (and the associated CaerphillyObserver.co.uk). Wrexham.com is a general local news website funded by online advertising, updated daily and serving a large town in North Wales (pop. 61,603). It began as a volunteer-run local bulletin board, and since its launch as a news site in 2011 it has grown into a small local news business which generates enough revenues to pay two journalists, whose output is supplemented by occasional work with local freelancers. Notably, it reaches a larger online audience than its Trinity Mirror-owned competitor LeaderLive.co.uk, the digital arm of the *Wrexham Leader* newspaper (Wrexham.com n.d.). The *Caerphilly Observer* is a fortnightly free newspaper with a print run of 10,000, and free daily news website with 30,000 monthly unique users, serving a small market town in the valleys north of Cardiff (pop. 41,402) (CaerphillyObserver.co.uk 2017). It started out in 2011 as a news website supported by enough online advertising to pay the wages of its editor and sole contributor. It grew steadily and went into print in 2013, and the increased advertising revenues afforded by the new print audience now pays the wages of three journalists and one part-time advertising salesperson. Although print and Internet advertising is still the dominant revenue stream among hyperlocals, others exist (such as crowdfunding, audience membership or co-operative structures, grant money from charities or foundations, and cross-subsidy with more lucrative forms of employment), and most of those who wish to make money employ a mixture of revenue streams (Williams and Harte 2016).

Later in this book we will explore the wide range of issues facing the emergent hyperlocal sector from a variety of perspectives and experiences. However, many of the trends discussed here, both positive and negative, are crystallised in the story of the town of Port Talbot and what happened as a result of the closure of the local newspaper and the development of a worker-owned co-operative hyperlocal news outlet, the Port Talbot Magnet (of which Howells was the main contributing editor and manager). These are examined in detail in the next chapter.

Notes

1 The sharp drop in profits in 2013 reflects a huge, group-wide devaluation of the company's intangible assets, which includes things like relationships with advertisers, the value of the company's brand, etc. These had previously been significantly overvalued by the company.

60 Withdrawal of local and regional news journalism

2 These figures are average weekly full-time-equivalent posts reported in audited annual accounts and represent the most reliable indicator of staffing level changes over time. The 'Editorial and Production' category includes journalists but also staff in other production roles (such as designers, layout specialists and subeditors). Figures for news journalists alone are not published.
3 In 2011/12 Trinity Mirror changed its divisional structure, which means this graph shows data relating to Trinity Mirror Regionals (a now defunct arm of the company composed of only local/regional newspapers and websites) between 2003 and 2010, and to Trinity Mirror Publishing (a new division combining all national and local/regional newspapers and websites) between 2011 and 2016. Although the graph refers to two different corporate entities (the former representing local and regional news outlets only, and the latter to regional, local and UK national news outlets, its common focus is on the proportion of revenues derived from printed and digital news is what we seek to highlight here.

References

Anderson, Peter J., Weymouth, Anthony & Ward, Geoff (2007) The changing world of journalism. In Anderson, P. J. & Ward, G. (eds) *The Future of Journalism in the Advanced Democracies*. Aldershot: Ashgate Publishing, pp. 17–38.

Black, Jeremy (2001) *The English Press 1621–1861*. Stroud: Sutton Publishing.

Broadcasters Audience Research Board (2014) Television ownership in private domestic households 1956–2013 (millions) [Online]. Available at: www.barb.co.uk/resources/tv-fa cts/tv-ownership?_s=4: [Accessed 20 January 2018].

CaerphillyObserver.co.uk (2017) Advertise with us [Online]. Available at: www.caerphil lyobserver.co.uk/advertise/ [Accessed 1 December 2017].

Cole, Peter & Harcup, Tony (2010) *Newspaper Journalism*. Journalism Studies: Key Texts. London: Sage.

Coleman, Renita & McCombs, Maxwell (2007) The young and agenda-less? Exploring age-related differences in agenda setting on the youngest generation, baby boomers, and the civic generation. *Journalism & Mass Communication Quarterly*, Vol. 84, No. 3, pp. 495–508.

Curran, James & Witschge, Tamara (2010) Liberal dreams and the Internet. In: Fenton, N. (ed.) *New Media, Old News*. London: Sage, pp. 102–118.

Davies, Nick (2008) *Flat Earth News*. London: Vintage.

Doyle, Gillian (2013) *Understanding Media Economics*. London: Sage.

Enders Analysis (2011) Competitive pressures on the press: Presentation to the Leveson Inquiry [Online]. Available at: http://webarchive.nationalarchives.gov.uk/ 20140122145147/http://www.levesoninquiry.org.uk/wp-content/uploads/2012/07/Cla ire-Enders-Competitive-pressures-on-the-press.pdf [Accessed 1 December 2017].

Fenton, Natalie, Metykova, Monika, Schlosberg, Justin & Freedman, Des (2010) *Meeting the News Needs of Local Communities*. London: Media Trust.

Franklin, Bob (1988) *Public Relations Activities in Local Government: A Research Report*. London: Charles Knight Publishing.

Franklin, Bob (2005) McJournalism: The local press and the McDonaldization thesis. In: Allen, S. (ed.) *Journalism: Critical Issues*. Milton Keynes: Open University Press, pp. 137–150.

Franklin, Bob (2006) Attacking the devil? Local journalists and local newspapers in the UK. In: Franklin, B. (ed.) *Local Journalism and Local Media: Making the Local News*. London: Routledge, pp. 3–15.

Franklin, Bob, Court, Geoff & Cushion, Stephen (2006) Downgrading the "local" in local newspapers' reporting of the 2005 UK general election. In: Franklin, B. (ed.) *Local Journalism and Local Media: Making the Local News*. London: Routledge, pp. 256–269.

Freedman, Des (2010) The political economy of the "new" news environment. In: Fenton, N. (ed.) *New Media, Old News: Journalism and Democracy in the Digital Age*. London: Sage, pp. 35–50.

Gillmor, Dan (2008) *We the Media: Grassroots Journalism by the People, for the People*. Sebastopol, CA: O'Reilly Media.

Greenslade, Roy (2009, 24 September) British journalism is in crisis, but we are doing too little to save it [Online]. *The Guardian*. Available at: www.guardian.co.uk/media/greensla de/2009/sep/24/downturn-mediabusiness [Accessed 2 March 2015].

Harrison, Shirley (1998) The local government agenda: News from the town hall. In: Franklin, B. & Murphy, D. (eds) *Making the Local News: Local Journalism in Context*. London: Routledge, pp. 150–162.

Higgerson, David (2015) Why audience targets can be good for journalism [Blog]. Available at: https://davidhiggerson.wordpress.com/2015/06/11/why-audience-targets-can-be-good-for-journalism/ [Accessed 1 December 2017].

Hindman, M. (2009) *The Myth of Digital Democracy*. Princeton, NJ: Princeton University Press.

House of Lords Communications Committee (2010) British television. In: *The British Film and Television Industries*. London: The Stationery Office, pp. 41–55.

Howells, Rachel (2015) *Journey to the Centre of a News Black Hole: Examining the Democratic Deficit in a Town with No Newspaper*. PhD Thesis, Cardiff University.

IWA (2015) *Wales Media Audit: 2015*. Cardiff: Institute of Welsh Affairs.

Jackson, Jasper (2016, 15 December) Google and Facebook to take 71% of UK online ad revenue by 2020. *The Guardian*. Available at: https://www.theguardian.com/media/2016/dec/15/google-facebook-uk-online-ad-revenue [Accessed 1 December 2017].

Lee, Jae Kook (2007) The effect of the Internet on homogeneity of the media agenda: A test of the fragmentation thesis. *Journalism and Mass Communication Quarterly*, Vol. 84, No. 4, pp. 745–760.

McDonald, Katy & Starkey, Guy (2016) Consolidation in the UK commercial radio sector: The impact on newsroom practice of recent changes in regulation, ownership and local content requirement. *Radio Journal: International Studies in Broadcast & Audio Media*, Vol. 14, No. 1, pp. 123–135.

McNally, Paul (2014, 20 February) Lessons learnt from Media Wales "journey to shareability" [Online]. *newsrewired.com*. Available at: https://www.newsrewired.com/2014/02/20/lessons-learnt-from-media-wales-journey-to-shareability/ [Accessed 1 December 2017].

Media Reform Coalition (2015) *Who Owns the UK Media?*London: Media Reform Coalition.

Media Wales/Western Mail and Echo (2000–2015) Annual Reports and Financial Statements.

Meikle, Graham & Young, Sherman (2011) *Media Convergence: Networked Digital Media in Everyday Life*. Basingstoke: Palgrave Macmillan.

Meese, Emma (2017) The Centre for Community Journalism and its work. Evidence submitted to National Assembly for Wales' Culture, Welsh Language, and Communications Committee Inquiry into News Journalism in Wales. Available at: http://senedd.assembly. wales/documents/s63457/ [Accessed 24 March 2018].

Meyer, P. (2009) *The Vanishing Newspaper: Saving Journalism in the Information Age*. Columbia, MO: University of Missouri Press.

Mintel (2013) Regional Newspapers – UK – March 2013 [Online]. Available at: http://aca demic.mintel.com/display/638001/ [Accessed 2 December 2015].

Mitchelstein, Eugenia & Boczkowski, Pablo J. (2010) Online news consumption research: An assessment of past work and an agenda for the future. *New Media & Society*, Vol. 12, No. 7, pp. 1085–1102.

National Union of Journalists (2012, 6 July) Future of Welsh newspapers in crisis, Michelle Stanistreet warns [Online]. Available at: https://www.nuj.org.uk/news/future-of-welsh-newspapers-in-crisis-michelle-stanistreet-warns/ [Accessed 1 December 2017].

Nel, Francois (2010) *Laid Off: What Do UK journalists Do Next*. Preston: University of Central Lancashire andjournalism.co.uk. Available at: https://www.journalism.co.uk/up loads/laidoffreport.pdf

Nielsen, Rasmus Kleis & Levy, David A. L. (2010) The changing business of journalism and its implications for democracy. In: Nielsen, R. K. & Levy, D. A. L. (eds) *The Changing Business of Journalism and its Implications for Democracy*. Oxford: Reuters Institute for the Study of Journalism, pp. 3–15.

O'Neill, Deirdre & O'Connor, Catherine (2008) The passive journalist: How sources dominate local news. *Journalism Practice*, Vol. 2, No. 3, pp. 487–500.

Ofcom (2012) *Measuring Media Plurality: Ofcom's Advice to the Secretary of State for Culture, Olympics, Media and Sport*. London: Ofcom.

Ofcom (2014) *News Consumption in the UK: 2014 Report*. London: Ofcom.

Oliver & Ohlbaum Associates Ltd (2015) *UK News Provision at the Crossroads: The News Market in the 21st Century and the Likely Implications for the BBC's Role* [Online]. Available at: www.newsmediauk.org/write/MediaUploads/PDF Docs/OandO_NMA_-_UK_ news_provision_at_the_crossroads.pdf [Accessed 20 January 2018].

Papacharissi, Zizi (2002) The virtual sphere: The Internet as a public sphere. *New Media & Society*, Vol. 4, No. 1, pp. 9–27.

Perch, Keith (2015) The collapse of the business model of regional newspapers has been far greater than previously stated. Paper presented at Future of Journalism, Cardiff University, 24 September.

Phillips, Angela (2011) Journalists as unwilling "sources": Transparency and the new ethics of journalism. In: Franklin, B. & Carlson, M. (eds) *Journalists, Sources and Credibility: New Perspectives*. New York: Routledge, pp. 49–60.

Phillips, Angela (2012) Faster and shallower: Homogenisation, cannibalisation and the death of reporting. In: Lee-Wright, P., Phillips, A. & Witschge, T. (eds) *Changing Journalism*. Abingdon: Routledge, pp. 81–98.

Phillips, Angela & Witschge, Tamara (2012) The changing business of news: Sustainability of news journalism. In: Lee-Wright, P., Phillips, A. & Witschge, T. (eds) *Changing Journalism*. Abingdon: Routledge, pp. 3–20.

Picard, Robert G. (2008) Shifts in newspaper advertising expenditures and their implications for the future of newspapers. *Journalism Studies*, Vol. 9, No. 5, pp. 704–716.

Picard, Robert G. (2010) A business perspective on challenges facing journalism. In: Levy, D. A. L. & Nielsen, R. K. (eds) *The Changing Business of Journalism and its Implications for Democracy*. Oxford: Reuters Institute for the Study of Journalism, pp. 17–24.

Ponsford, Dominic (2016a, 2 August) Editor axed by Trinity Mirror uses odd-numbered listicle to reflect on an ignominious exit [Online]. *Press Gazette*. Available at: www.pressga zette.co.uk/editor-axed-by-trinity-mirror-uses-odd-numbered-listicle-to-reflect-on-an-ignominious-exit/ [Accessed 1 December 2017].

Ponsford, Dominic (2016b, 31 July) "Heartbroken" reporter Gareth Davies says Croydon Advertiser print edition now "thrown together collection of clickbait" [Online]. *Press Gazette*. Available at: www.pressgazette.co.uk/heartbroken-reporter-gareth-davies-says-croydon-advertiser-print-edition-now-thrown-together-collection-of-clickbait/ [Accessed 1 December 2017].

Press Gazette (2011, 8 August) Seven compulsory redundancies at Media Wales [Online]. Available at: www.pressgazette.co.uk/seven-compulsory-redundancies-at-media-wales/ [Accessed 1 December 2017].

Preston, Peter (2009) The curse of introversion. In: Franklin, B. (ed.) *The Future of Newspapers*. Abingdon: Routledge, pp. 13–20.

Ramsay, Gordon & Moore, Martin (2016) *Monopolising Local News: Is there an Emerging Local Democratic Deficit in the UK Due to the Decline of Local Newspapers?*London: Centre for the Study of Media, Communication and Power, Kings College.

Rosenstiel, Tom & Mitchell, Amy (2004) The impact of investing in newsroom resources. *Newspaper Research Journal*, Vol. 25, No. 1, pp. 84–97.

Shipton, Martin (2011, 3 September) Welsh civic engagement 6: Stuck with the media giants [Online]. *Institute of Welsh Affairs*. Available at: www.iwa.wales/click/2011/09/welsh-civic-engagement-6-stuck-with-the-media-giants/ [Accessed 1 December 2017].

Shipton, Martin (2015) Click targets, quality journalism and towards a media manifesto. Conference panel discussion, Who Will Pay for Welsh Journalism?University of South Wales, 7 November.

Shirky, Clay (2008) *Here Comes Everybody: The Power of Organizing without Organisations*. London: Allen Lane.

StatsWales (2011) Welsh speakers by local authority, gender and detailed age groups, 2011 Census [Online]. *Welsh Government*. Available at: https://statswales.gov.wales/Catalogue/Welsh-Language/WelshSpeakers-by-LocalAuthority-Gender-DetailedAgeGroups-2011 Census [Accessed 1 December 2017].

StatsWales (2016) Population estimates by local authority and year [Online]. *Welsh Government*. Available at: https://statswales.gov.wales/Catalogue/Population-and-Migration/Population/Estimates/Local-Authority/populationestimates-by-localauthority-year [Accessed 20 January 2018].

Sweney, Mark (2015, 19 November) Johnston Press chief: Local newspaper closures blown out of proportion. *The Guardian*. Available at: https://www.theguardian.com/media/2015/nov/19/johnston-press-chief-local-newspaper-closures-blown-out-of-proportion [Accessed 1 December 2017].

Tandoc, Edson C., Jr & Jenkins, Joy (2017) The Buzzfeedication of journalism? How traditional news organizations are talking about a new entrant to the journalistic field will surprise you! *Journalism*, Vol. 18, No. 4, pp. 482–500.

Thomas, Huw (2018, 17 January) Call to safeguard Swansea's Bay TV's programme output [Online]. *BBC*. Available at: www.bbc.co.uk/news/uk-wales-42712000 [Accessed 20 January 2018].

Thomas, James (2006) The regional and local media in Wales. In: Franklin, B. (ed.) *Local Journalism and Local Media: Making the Local News*. London: Routledge, pp. 49–59.

Turvill, William (2015, 5 November) Trinity Mirror chief: "No democratic deficit" in local news and he doesn't want more BBC reporters in regions [Online]. *Press Gazette*. Available at: www.pressgazette.co.uk/trinity-mirror-chief-says-there-isnt-democratic-deficit-local-news-and-he-doesnt-want-more-bbc [Accessed 20 June 2016].

VanSlyke Turk, Judy & Franklin, Bob (1987) Information subsidies: Agenda-setting traditions. *Public Relations Review*, Vol. 13, No. 4, pp. 29–41.

Williams, Andy (2013) Stop press? The crisis in the Welsh media and what to do about it. *Cyfrwng: Media Wales Journal*, Vol. 10, pp. 71–80.

Williams, Andrew & Franklin, Bob (2007) *Turning Around the Tanker: Implementing Trinity Mirror's Online Strategy* [Online]. Cardiff: Cardiff School of Journalism, Media and Cultural Studies. Available at: http://image.guardian.co.uk/sys-files/Media/documents/2007/03/13/Cardiff.Trinity.pdf [Accessed 2 December 2015].

Williams, Andy & Harte, David (2016) Hyperlocal news. In: Witschge, T., Anderson, C. W., Domingo, D. & Hermida, A. (eds) *The SAGE Handbook of Digital Journalism*. London: Sage, pp. 280–293.

Wrexham.com (n.d.) About Wrexham.com [Online]. Available at: www.wrexham.com/about [Accessed 1 December 2017].

3

INSIDE A NEWS BLACK HOLE – CASE STUDY OF A TOWN WITH NO NEWSPAPER

In this chapter we take an in-depth approach to examining the consequences of the media decline we noted in chapter 2. We describe the effects of cuts and closures on the local news itself, ask if losing a local weekly newspaper matters to a town and its citizens, and examine whether and how local people might be affected by the withdrawal of traditional local journalism. We also draw on the experiences of a hyperlocal in attempting to address the provision of public interest news. The 2009 closure of the weekly newspaper the *Port Talbot Guardian* in the South Wales town of Port Talbot provided an opportunity to study the effects of the closure on local citizens. In response to the closure, co-author Howells co-founded and worked at the journalism co-operative Port Talbot Magnet, an online hyperlocal news service that latterly printed a periodic tabloid newspaper. As both a researcher and journalist, therefore, Howells gained invaluable insights into a post-newspaper community.

The closure of the *Port Talbot Guardian* came at a time when the threat of widespread newspaper closures had become a cause for concern. Claire Enders, for example, predicted that by 2014 the number of UK local and regional newspaper titles would halve, meaning around 650 closures (Brook 2009). However, there remained uncertainty about the potential damage should closures come to pass. Commentators worried that the lack of a local newspaper might affect civilians' ability to inform themselves, to participate in civic and democratic life, and to have their views aired and voices heard.

This chapter uses a mix of research methods to gain an understanding of the nature of what many commentators were calling the "news black hole" in Port Talbot (Moore 2010). An analysis of a large sample of local newspaper stories published between 1970 and 2015 by the two main Port Talbot newspapers, the weekly *Port Talbot Guardian* and the regional daily *South Wales Evening Post*, enabled a longitudinal understanding of the change in news content and quantity

66 Inside a news black hole

over time. The content analysis was supplemented by interviews with local news journalists who had worked as reporters or subeditors on the Port Talbot patch during these years. Additionally, a survey allowed an examination of how local people consumed news and discovered important information after the newspaper closure. Focus groups added to this picture, giving more nuanced detail about access to essential information and representation. Analysis of documentary evidence, statistics and polls was also carried out.

According to the 2011 UK Census, the town of Port Talbot has a population of 37,276, and the slightly larger Aberavon parliamentary constituency in which the town is located has a population of 66,133. Due to a concentration of heavy industry – including the UK's largest steelworks – and power stations and a busy stretch of motorway running on a large overpass through it, Port Talbot has repeatedly been found to be the most polluted urban site in the UK outside of London (Roberts 2014). It is a relatively young town: it was designated as the borough of Port Talbot – and officially named Port Talbot for the first time – as recently as 1925. Just a year before that, the *Port Talbot Guardian* was established as the local newspaper.

Decline, cuts and closures

Port Talbot has witnessed the same trends in newspaper circulation and revenue decline that have been seen across the majority of Europe and America. These can be understood as a long, slow downward spiral which has worsened since the wide take-up of digital technology in the late 1990s and has been compounded by the recession of 2008. Declines in newspaper circulations and revenues have led to job cuts and cuts to resources in order to maintain healthy profits, as discussed in chapter 2. In Port Talbot, the decline in journalist numbers between 1970 and 2010 is likely to have beeen as high as 90 per cent. In 1970 as many as 11 reporters worked across five newspapers, all of which had offices in the town. Forty years later, only two reporters remained, based in an office in Swansea ten miles away, working at the *South Wales Evening Post* across a much larger patch that also included the neighbouring towns of Neath and Pontardawe. Additionally, these reporters worked across an even larger territory when required:

> they're also doing a lot of Swansea stuff as well. So if you think you go from those numbers down to two reporters who are not based in the area and producing copy for other areas, you just can see why the local coverage is just a shadow of what it was.
>
> *(Post reporter from 1980s to 2000s)*

Coupled with this drop in staff numbers, the number of pages in newspapers rose steadily over the sample period. In 1970, the average number of pages in the *Post* was 11, while the *Port Talbot Guardian* averaged 16; by 2008 this had increased to 55 pages in the *Post* and 42 in the *Guardian*. Falling staff numbers are therefore set against rising page numbers, a trend towards falling human resources and increasing workloads that has been noted in several studies (e.g. Williams and Franklin 2007). The result was an increase in the number of stories a journalist was expected to write up during a shift. At the *Post*, there was a marked change in the language used by journalists, who no longer described how they had "worked on stories" as they had before the mid 2000s. Instead, they "filled shapes" (templated boxes that reporters were required to fill with the right number of words) or "wrote down-page" (smaller, less significant stories used to fill pages): "Weekends were particularly tough because there were only two of you on all the down-page. Once, there were two people [working at the weekend] and they had 70 shapes to fill the whole weekend, all down-pages" (*Post* journalist, 2000s).

The shift in these journalists' discourse away from an emphasis on the often intensely interactive craft of making news is towards a mechanistic process of news production as a process of meeting targets under intense time pressure, echoing Nick Davies' assessment of the newsroom as a "news factory" (2008: 113).

Of equal significance, however, was the closure of district offices, an overhead that could be easily cut by newspaper owners. However, district offices emerged from the research as significant resources for both reporters and local people. Reporters from the 1960s to the 1980s described offices operated by both the *Guardian* and the *Post* that were open to the public and in which three or four members of staff were the norm. From this convenient base, reporters were able to leave the office regularly to uncover, investigate or report on nearby stories. District offices were credited with being not only a source of news stories but also a way to filter out those with "a bee in their bonnet" (*Post* reporter, 1990s–2000s). According to one interviewee, free newspapers were given out to the local police and traffic wardens, which gave them an incentive to call in to the office, forming a regular and informal point of contact between them and the reporters and encouraging the flow of information between reporters and local figures.

District offices also meant reporters could respond more quickly to stories, ask face-to-face questions and get a more detailed understanding of an event. One *Post* reporter who worked there from the 1980s to the 2000s described an incident in Neath in the mid 1990s:

> There was one example where I'd heard that somebody had been knocked down by a bus in the bus station. So I walked out of the office, round the corner and had a look, yes you could see something was going on and you'd warn the news desk that there'd been an incident over the bus station, I'll find out more.

This was contrasted with a later experience:

> Now you've got to hope you can get hold of the police if they are there when you ring. You can't just walk out of the office and look any more because you're based in Swansea and you've got to drive into Neath and back.

68 Inside a news black hole

The possibility of such stories going unreported, or reported with only single or official sources, is higher if journalists cannot make it to the scene of an event, and this also makes scrutiny of the official version of events much more difficult. Once district offices closed, news was often covered using the quickest or most convenient means possible, and journalists working in the late 2000s and early 2010s spoke about telephones and social media as their main points of access to members of the public. A *Post* journalist who had worked there since the early 1980s said that by the 2000s, "they didn't like people going out of the office unless they were going on a defined page lead story. There became more of a dependence on rewriting handouts of all kinds".

The distance of journalists from their local patch did not go unnoticed by the community. The *Guardian* had once been based in Port Talbot, but this office was closed in the very late 1990s and staff moved to Neath. But in 2008, the *Guardian*'s Neath office closed, some staff were made redundant, and the remaining reporters moved to share the *Glamorgan Gazette*'s Bridgend office. A *Guardian* reporter from this time remembers community contact dropping:

> You're not there and they just think you don't care about the community if you're not there. I think we probably were [missing stories]. I think people just didn't know where to go. I think people were losing touch with the paper because we weren't there to keep touch.

When district offices had operated, journalists felt embedded in the town, and local people also felt this connection. Older residents, over the age of 60, participating in a focus group spoke about trusting journalists when they were based in the town because you could see them face-to-face and know who they were:

> You could speak to [journalists], you could go along and inevitably [the reporter would say,] "do you mind if I quote you?" and an article would be written, and you go ahead knowing that because I'm big enough and ugly enough, do it, but don't misquote.

As this suggests, journalists who were known to the community in this way were also picked up and corrected by the local community if they got details wrong. The stakes were much higher for journalists to represent their communities accurately, because they themselves were part of the community. Participants in another focus group, which was made up of activists and campaigners, also spoke of the importance of a continuing relationship with a known journalist and linked this to accuracy in reporting:

> With the *Guardian* I felt particularly with this one reporter we dealt with that you build up a relationship with and always speak to [them], it works well, but when there were two or three other reporters who came in who didn't know the background, it was a total mess. I found [some reporters] used to misquote

me terribly … someone else would come in who didn't know the previous history and so on … so in the end I said, 'I'm not going to have an interview on the telephone, tell me what you want and then I [will] write [you] an email'. I'd say, 'you can use anything you like from the email', and I found that worked a lot better.

Some journalists put this down to the newspapers' focus on the bottom line, acknowledging that "newspapers aren't supposed to be social in that sense. They've got to make money". But they also lamented this and were critical of the position cuts had left them in: "I think that the balance has to be right between making money and also representing an area, representing the people of an area, giving the people a voice. I think the balance went the other way" (*Post* reporter, 1980s–2000s). This distance from the community coupled with a gradual reduction in staff numbers and editorial budgets can be tracked in the news itself, impacting both the quantity and quality of news about Port Talbot, and this is discussed later in this chapter.

Plurality, diversity and rivalry

Before cuts began to take hold, the presence of up to five local newspapers in Port Talbot from the 1970s to 1990s ensured a diverse and competitive local media that offered a comparatively rich stream of news and multiple perspectives. This benefited citizens in several ways. First, the contrasting nature of the different titles in Port Talbot meant that the town was served by journalists working and writing in a variety of different ways (for a national daily and a regional daily as well as paid and free weekly titles). The *Post*, for example, was a daily publication which covered a wider geographical area and emphasised breaking news, while the *Guardian* was a weekly that focused on detail, depth and more complete coverage of the town. This meant that readers were able to access important news stories as they happened while also gaining access to the 'minutiae' of everyday life, covered as it was by the *Guardian*'s approach of reporting every piece of news, large and small, to create what one interviewee dubbed a "weekly bible". Another interviewee said that this coverage enriched the public sphere by offering many sides and arguments for public debate over a prolonged period, with opportunities for readers to engage in the debate through vibrant letters pages, which in turn supported a healthy local democracy:

> The paper was called the *Guardian* and many years later this phrase, "the guardians of democracy", came to my mind, and I think that's what they were. Anything the council started to do, hinted at doing, or anyone hinted at doing, that didn't meet favour with the community would get a massive airing. If there was a major news story, then it would be given full vent in the paper, and people would have the opportunity to write letters that would be

70 Inside a news black hole

amply displayed. The story would be covered from all angles, so it would be given a good shakedown.

(Guardian and Post *reporter, 1960s–1990s)*

Second, competition and rivalry between journalists working for different newspapers covering the same patch was seen by all interviewees as a motivating factor in finding new and original stories, in improving their work and in finding original angles from which to report. A reporter who worked in the area from the early 1990s to the late 2000s said,

> if there's no competition and there's no hunger for the story, you don't get the same feel for it. [In] every job you've got to have dedication and motivation and be focused and try to outdo everybody else; otherwise there's no point. You might just as well be making washers in a factory.

Numerous interviewees stressed that coverage of local government was often made sharper, more critical and more forensic by the presence of competitor local journalists in council meetings. Journalists at competing titles worked hard to find and protect exclusive stories. Indeed, it was a formal editorial rule at the *Guardian* that original content should feature on the front page. As one interviewee testified,

> If we beat the *Post* to something, we'd be absolutely chuffed, and also each week the front page of the *Port Talbot Guardian* had to be an exclusive. That just drives you to get things ... which reporters on the *Post* hadn't been doing.

Reporters also worked to cover local events or issues in a distinctive way, looking for angles or points of views that their competitors had not featured. Arguably, covering numerous versions of the same story from multiple different perspectives, and often in different ways, led to a richer public sphere.

Third, the benefit of plurality was evident in protecting or encouraging an increase in journalistic resources. The research revealed that the *Post* increased editorial resources when there was competition in the patch from other publishers. For example, the *Neath Port Talbot Courier* was introduced in the mid 1980s, as one interviewee stated, as a "reaction" to a *Guardian* relaunch, and it was then used as a commercial foil to the *Guardian*, becoming more resourced and having better quality when the *Guardian* was perceived to be more of a commercial threat and more fallow in years when the *Guardian* was less threatening. It was suspended around 2000, but finally relaunched in 2009 following the closure of the *Guardian*. As another interviewee noted, "they looked then and thought there was some potential, probably for advertising revenue more than anything because there was no weekly paper any more sucking up the available advertising cash". Equally, the competition that arrived with the launch of the hyperlocal news website Port Talbot Magnet was thought by some interviewees to have helped protect jobs at the *Post* and to have motivated the rivals to make more of an effort. As one reporter said,

> I felt like maybe [the *Post*] had got a bit lazy with trying to cover the area, and I also feel like when the Magnet started printing that [the *Post*] stepped up a bit of a gear, as though [the reporters] thought, "we've got to do something here".

It would be reasonable to assume that the *Post* might step in to fill the news gap that opened in Port Talbot in the wake of the closure of the *Guardian*, if only to benefit from the opportunities offered by an abandoned commercial territory. However, the number of *Post* stories decreased slightly after the closure (from 272 stories in 2008 to 232 in 2013), lending weight to the suggestion that rivalry and plurality fostered healthy competition and stimulated both publishers and reporters to increase their efforts. The closure removed this rivalry, and this may have allowed the *Post* to relax its efforts at a time when revenue declines and increasing workloads were making themselves felt across most local newsrooms.

Fourth, there was some evidence that community members seeking coverage also benefited directly from competition between titles. Interviewees suggested plurality made it difficult to ignore, or defer dealing with, local contacts with a story to tell. A reporter active in the 1960s and 1970s said that "when there were lots of newspapers, [people would] say, 'If you don't do something on it, I'm going to the *Guardian* or the *Post*' – and don't forget the [South Wales] *Echo* and the *Western Mail* had offices in Port Talbot". In such instances, competition gave members of the public increased leverage and influence when seeking representation in the local press. The voice and influence of citizens, however, diminished in the face of cuts and closures, as we discuss in the next sections of this chapter.

Quantity, quality and localness

As has already been discussed, the decline in the quantity of news about Port Talbot was a long and gradual process that began decades before the newspaper shut. Equally, cuts to staff, changes in reporting practices and the closure of district offices meant the quality of the news was also gradually eroded in several key areas. The closure of the *Port Talbot Guardian* was a definitive moment, however: this closure alone meant that Port Talbot lost as much as half its local news in 2009. However, the amount of news about Port Talbot had already fallen by 23.9 per cent before that – an aggregate loss of 66.3 per cent.

The content analysis of newspaper stories published between 1970 and 2015 in the *Port Talbot Guardian* and the *South Wales Evening Post* was designed to measure the quality of the news, three markers of which – localness, news topic and sources – are widely agreed to denote the presence of public interest or fourth estate journalism. A fourth measure, news trigger, sought to identify the origin of the story and how it may have come to the reporter's attention; for example, by attendance at council meetings, interviewing contacts, going to press conferences or receiving an official statement from a politician.

The analysis revealed declines across all of these markers. For example, the declining number of local citizens used as sources revealed a weakening in the ability of the local media to scrutinise news. Interviews had already revealed journalists had less time to investigate stories, were discouraged from leaving the office and began to rely more on "handouts", such as PR, or the easy flow of information traded on social media, with less time to check these stories for accuracy or to balance their stories by sourcing additional quotes. An increase in the number of 'single source' stories confirmed this narrative. Equally, the localness of stories diminished, especially with the number of Port Talbot sources that were quoted but also in the coverage of certain news topics that are linked to community cohesion or democracy. Local sports coverage, in particular, fell dramatically, and this can be linked to a community's sense of its own identity (see, for example, Frisby and Millar 2002; Jarvie 2003; Skinner et al. 2008).

One aspect of news reporting that is often used in discussions about public interest news is the reporting of local government. O'Neill and O'Connor point to reporting of local government as having "a profound impact on the public interest and the fourth estate role of the regional press" and were concerned to find only 9 per cent of the stories they coded in local newspapers in the north of England were from local government sources (2008: 494). In Port Talbot, only 6.2 per cent of stories were about the local council itself, but when public institutions such as health boards, hospitals, schools, the emergency services, public transport and utilities were included in the definition, the overall proportion stood at 22.4 per cent, suggesting the public interest duty is one taken seriously by local newspapers. In fact, the research noted an increase in reporting of local government and civic news which went from 14.8 per cent in 1970 to 27.1 per cent in 2013. However, the way these stories were covered also changed over time from an active, face-to-face style to a more passive style led by PR, as Figure 3.1 shows. Journalists' attendance at local council meetings, public meetings or political party meetings dropped from 45.6 per cent in 1980 to 4.7 per cent in 2013. Meanwhile the use of announcements and statements, press events and successes – all of which were most likely to

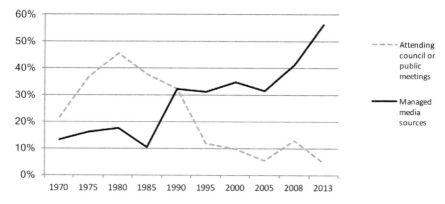

FIGURE 3.1 How Port Talbot's public interest news is covered, 1970–2013

be provided by PR sources – rose from 17.6 per cent in 1980 to 56.3 per cent in 2013.

Meanwhile, sources became less likely to be local and more likely to be higher in status. High-status sources included figures such as politicians, high-ranking civil servants, police officers, solicitors and other such authority figures. The use of such sources, which started at around 15 per cent in 1970, rose to around 28 per cent in 2000 and by a further 9 per cent to reach 37 per cent in 2013, while the use of low-status, citizen, sources increased by only 7 per cent in the same 2000–2013 period. This meant that the voice of local citizens became less likely to be featured in the local news, while paid officials and spokespeople from outside Port Talbot were much more likely to be given column inches. Commentators fear that the predominance of high-status sources

> influences both [the news story's] shape and its orientation, casually but irre-vocably promoting a particular perspective which often goes unchallenged if the balance which allegedly underpins the journalistic code of conduct is absent. Who is invited to speak as commentators on and in the news says crucially important things about who "counts" in society, whose voices have legitimacy and status.
>
> *(Ross 2007: 454)*

Equally, data for Port Talbot showed there was a diminishing local voice in the news – where local sources accounted for 60 per cent of the sample in 1980, this went down as low as 24.8 per cent in 2000, finishing at 44 per cent in 2013. Meanwhile sources located outside Port Talbot began as a minority – in 1975 as few as 6.7 per cent of stories carried quotes from people outside the town – but this grew exponentially across the sample, and non-local voices made up 60 per cent of the quotes in news stories in 2013. The effect appears to accelerate around the year 2000, after the closure of the district offices, suggesting the proximity of reporters to news events impacted on the localness of the news, as other studies have found (Martin 1988).

Informing, representing and scrutinising

Similar in many ways to the ideals of the public sphere, the normative ideals of journalism are that it should provide a platform for public debate, communicate any conclusions that arise and ensure the government takes account of these con-clusions (Curran and Seaton 1991: 277; Williams 1998: 4–5). News should also provide information and educate citizens to enable them to make informed deci-sions at election time (Curran and Seaton 1991: 278; Phillips and Witschge 2012: 4), champion the individual in the face of the "misdeeds of the powerful" (Curran and Seaton 1991: 278), provide an independent means by which different groups in society can communicate ideas and information to each other, and scrutinise those in power and call them to account (McChesney and Nichols 2010: 2). For

74 Inside a news black hole

McChesney and Nichols, the press should "regard the state secret as an assault to popular governance, watch the politically and economically powerful with a suspicious eye, ... recognize as [its] duty the informing and enlightening of citizens so that they may govern themselves" (2010: 2).

In addition to keeping people informed, McNair defines three other normative duties of journalism in relation to its democratic obligations: to scrutinise the powerful, in the form of a watchdog; to represent the views of the public and mediate between them and politicians; and to be a 'champion of the people', engaging in campaigns or taking sides in public debates (2009: 238–240).

An extension of the scrutiny function has also been suggested. In addition to the notion of the press as a watchdog that guards the public and 'barks' when it detects wrongdoing, some commentators have suggested the press acts as a kind of scarecrow, which, unlike a noisy dog that only barks when something is amiss, can prevent wrongdoing by its very presence. This so-called scarecrow journalism can be crucial to keeping public institutions in check:

> The fact that only a watchdog actively barks and the scarecrow does not bark does not always matter. Though the scarecrow "does nothing," its very existence, the very fact that the crows know it is out there, "watching," is often enough to constrain bad crow-like behaviour. And the same goes for journalism. The watchdog press, it must be admitted, barks only rarely. But the continuity of that press, the fact that it is "out there," is often enough to constrain bad behaviour on the part of powerful institutions.
>
> *(Anderson* et al. *2014: 54–55)*

Interviewees were certainly aware of this potential role, worrying that the absence of journalists from meetings after the *Guardian* closure meant planning decisions were being made behind closed doors by officers rather in the public forum of a meeting, or that big business could be pushing through an agenda without journalists questioning the official line being given out in press releases and challenging the official narrative. From the other side of the argument, one interviewee noticed that her presence at council meetings meant that "they all speak up, which is good, and you don't get the same old people speaking up all the time, which can be the case sometimes" (*Post* reporter, 2000s). We discuss the ability of Port Talbot's weakened journalism infrastructure to provide information, representation and scrutiny to citizens in the next section of this chapter.

Scrutiny

With so few journalists to operate either in the traditional role of the watchdog or the more recently defined role of the scarecrow, the duty has increasingly fallen to local people and, in particular, to a group of active and engaged citizens who have adopted the role of the "'armchair auditor', a citizen who browses government data to monitor its activities and hold it to account" (Frank *et al.* 2016: 4–5). Focus groups revealed a group of activists who worked hard to scrutinise the decisions of local politicians, planners or the Welsh Government or who attempted to hold agencies and companies to account over issues such as pollution and tourism. This group often found it difficult to access or verify information or even to discover which department or civil servant was responsible for a particular decision or that could answer their questions.

The opacity of institutions was discussed unprompted by participants in the focus groups. Participants felt institutions had confounded the public's ability to respond and said they did not feel those in authority were responsive to them. Several participants made the point that they had tried to complain or protest about an issue but had been pointed to another body. One summed up frustration at people's inability to access clear and useful local information:

> There's the blame game between our council and the Welsh Government. It's quite petty actually, because technically the council aren't responsible so they're not taking any rap for it at all but the Welsh Government are trying to pin it on the council as well. There's a really terrible piece [on the website] from the Trunk Road Agency where they're trying to say the council instigated the closure, which they have no power to do. So that's complete misinformation being put out by an official source and then reported on by the newspapers. It's a mess, but I think that's because the sources of information are completely messed up as well.

Traditionally, journalists would have been better placed than individual citizens to navigate confusing or opaque institutions. Journalists have historically been allowed privileged access to official institutions and are permitted to ask questions, and receive answers, that individuals find more difficult to access. Professional journalists, by their training, experience and knowledge, are at an advantage in scrutinising the complexities of government or government information. Additionally, through their access to a large audience, the information they transmit ensures clear messages are able to reach a large number of people, which is not the case for individuals or even opinion leaders in possession of the same knowledge.

Information and knowledge

It is perhaps ironic that scrutiny should be difficult for members of the public to attain in a new digital age which has often been assumed to offer a virtually endless supply of accessible information to all (Gillmor 2008; Shirky 2008). This is partly related to a problem with the flow of information in Port Talbot, as both focus groups and a survey of 350 local residents demonstrated. An essential component of a healthy democracy is said to include the normative ideal of an 'informed citizenry', with citizens able to make informed judgements come election time (Baresch *et al.* 2011). Anderson agrees: "high-quality, independent journalism which provides accurate and thoughtful information and analysis about current

76 Inside a news black hole

events is crucial to the creation of an enlightened citizenry that is able to participate meaningfully in society and politics" (2007: 65).

However, in our study of Port Talbot, there was evidence that local citizens were neither well informed nor particularly knowledgeable about local issues. Low levels of general knowledge about Port Talbot were revealed in the survey. Knowledge of the political landscape, particularly in naming candidates or policies, is a common method for measuring whether local people are well informed enough to be able to vote, and although such measures can be problematic when used in isolation, they can help add to an overall examination of how well informed the public is if we also examine the "broader discursive" evidence (Lewis 2001: 108). Even basic knowledge, such as the political persuasion of the con-stituency's MP, was relatively low in Port Talbot: only 56.6 per cent of people were able to answer correctly by naming Labour in spite of the party having held the constituency since 1922 and also controlling the local council. More detailed political knowledge was even less abundant: at the regional political level (i.e. the National Assembly for Wales), only 14.7 per cent of people were able to name a local or regional Assembly Member, while 11.0 per cent named someone incorrectly and 74.0 per cent said they did not know. Meanwhile, at the local political level (i.e. the local council), 27.5 per cent were able to name then-council leader Ali Thomas' job, while 0.5 per cent got it wrong and 72.0 per cent did not know. Political knowledge of this kind has often been found to be low (Lewis 2001: 108), and it is difficult to know how these data compare with results we might have got in pre-vious years, as data have not been collected at this local geographical level with any consistency.[1] What is noteworthy irrespective of longitudinal comparison, however, is the high proportion of "don't know" responses, which, as Page and Shapiro (1983) found, has been shown to correlate with low government responsiveness to public opinion; or put another way, "policy moves in harmony with opinion changes more often when 'don't know' survey responses are few" (Page and Shapiro 1992: 393).

Low levels of knowledge may be linked to relatively low local news consump-tion coupled with the problems with quality and quantity of available local news described in this chapter. In the survey, 20.2 per cent of Port Talbot residents said they watched Welsh regional television news at least once a week and 19.3 per cent, national news. This echoes findings in previous studies, which show televi-sion is the primary news source for most people (Thomas 2006: 7). Only 17.8 per cent of respondents said they read a local newspaper at least once a week, a finding echoed by the focus groups, where there were many discussions about why the majority had stopped reading, or didn't bother with, newspapers. Their reasons were varied, including convenience, cost, reporting styles and the lack of relevance or localness to their area. Many commentators pin their hopes on the news black hole being filled by the use of online news providers, but with only 10.4 per cent of local people saying they access local and national news in this way, this was not a dominant element of Port Talbot's news mix.

To measure information-seeking behaviour, the survey asked people whether they had sought local information related to a list of key topics: air quality (an ongoing and long-standing topic of concern in the town; Turner 2013), sport, travel updates, politics, council services, live theatre or music events, and crime. The majority of people in the town, a total of 64.3 per cent, said they had not looked for any information or news about key topics in the previous six months (n = 364). Of those that had, sport (32.6 per cent) and live events (24.7 per cent) were most often selected as the main topics of local interest. This suggests that people most actively look for news about local cultural events and not civic or political information. Local newspapers dedicated to a small geographic community often take a holistic approach to covering community life (see the discussion above of the *Guardian* as a local news 'bible'). In the past if these citizens had taken a dedicated local newspaper, or visited a local news website, to find out about sport or live music, there would have been a far higher likelihood of them also encountering news about local civic life, essential services or the environment. This kind of chance encounter with professionally produced news about Port Talbot is now much diminished.

However, there was significant evidence to support the idea that information was being discovered by chance as people stumbled upon changes, closures or events as they physically moved around the town. This was true even when media coverage preceding the event was relatively high. For example, one focus group participant said he had discovered the closure of Junction 41 of the M4 only when he tried to access the motorway one morning on his way to work and found it was closed. Another said he had found out about the closure when he read graffiti sprayed around the town. Others had only heard about a major open-air theatrical event when they went into town to shop and found their way barred.

There was a discussion of the merits of graffiti as a means of receiving news, as some of them had encountered local information this way, with one participant saying, "When it's actually tasteful and it's done correctly, graffiti can be a really good work and way of spreading news". This offers a fascinating insight into the way younger people relate to news and information. This group does not access traditional local news to the extent of older groups (e.g. 17.1 per cent of 18- to 30-year-olds, 39.1 per cent of 31- to 59-year-olds, and 53.2 per cent of over 60s read a local newspaper at least once a week), and they are more likely to use a more varied range of news and information sources – particularly online news and social media – than older groups. The focus group with the youngest participants advocated more use of public spaces to communicate essential information, and it also wished the media would be more transparent when referencing their sources. But these participants also demonstrated the highest levels of negativity, anger, resentment, powerlessness and cynicism and were least likely to access traditional media or, if they did, to trust it. Of all the groups, this was the only one which had nothing good to say about the town.

Social media was a dominant player in the news mix according to focus group participants, and many of them credit Facebook for alerting them to possible problems through digital contact with campaign groups or well-informed contacts. Even so, there was a high level of suspicion of the veracity of the information many were getting. Some participants were very clear about what they saw as the need for independent corroboration of such information that separates fact from hearsay. One commented, "All I read on Facebook is people's opinions on what's happening or a rumour they've heard in the shops, which isn't actually the truth of the situation. So you need something external".

A possible benefit of this trend, however, is the suggestion of a certain level of new media literacy, and this was also noted among all the age groups – all four groups seemed used to questioning all types of information and comparing different sources of information. They did not apply a simple binary in which information from journalists is trustworthy and that from a (potentially) self-interested institution or a friend or relative is not. Indeed, there were high levels of mistrust of mainstream news media, with allegations of bias levelled at journalists. For example, "It's like TV, you either believe what they say or you don't believe what they say. You've got to use your brain". This suspicion extended to all traditional media as well as some non-news sources such as the council website. All of this adds up to a widespread lack of trust in local information encountered online and an awareness of the need to verify sources and read widely from plural information sources. As one participant said,

> I look at Facebook – and I'm in a number of groups in Facebook. But those groups that interest me. If I want news about Port Talbot specific to things like bin collections and that sort of thing, I would go to the council website, which you would hope would be up to date; nine times out of ten it's not. I watch the BBC news. I don't trust it, but I think you've got to look across the board and use your own judgement as to what you think is right.

The results of an impoverished information flow in Port Talbot on local citizens are plain, however. Focus group discussions revealed extreme confusion and/or lack of knowledge about significant local developments, proposals and issues in the town. This confusion was sometimes founded on rumour and hearsay (indeed, the transcriptions of the focus groups yield much evidence of the rumour mill in action, as participants discussed important news and events in a somewhat circular manner, more often than not without the empirical anchor of verified facts). There were also signs of a lack of agency among many of the people interviewed in the focus groups, particularly the youngest group, in which there were several outward displays of anger as well as statements of hopelessness; for example, "What's the point? Nobody listens to us anyway". There was frustration and despondency about people's inability to affect their futures and, in some cases, their inability to protest against unwelcome developments or cuts because they were unaware of them until too late.

The evidence indicated Port Talbot citizens lacked enough credible, good-quality local news to enable them to be well informed. Furthermore, the opacity of institutions encountered by many is a barrier to them informing themselves about crucial issues by means other than traditional media. Even where the quality or quantity of news might be relatively high, this is not always enough to enable people to participate in local democracy. Information must be useful and timely in order to enable citizens to react, and too often it ticks neither box. A related problem to the quality of the information available is the possibility of unreported news. The Media Standards Trust's Martin Moore noted this problem in 2010 after discovering Europe's largest biomass energy plant had been given planning permission in Port Talbot, but also that it had received

> almost no coverage … in the news. Search for "Biomass Plant Port Talbot" on Google and you find fewer than 10 stories since the plant was given the go ahead in 2007 – including just two on BBC news online and three short pieces on Reuters. This is South Wales [the *Post*'s website], and Wales Online [the *Western Mail*'s website].
>
> *(Moore 2010)*

He set this against findings from the Institute of Welsh Affairs that more than 90 per cent of the Welsh population read national newspapers and that these have "virtually no Welsh content" (Davies and Morris 2008: 88–89) – also noting that no national newspapers have a correspondent based in Wales (Moore 2010).

More recently, the actor Michael Sheen noted this phenomenon in a Raymond Williams lecture entitled "Who Speaks for Wales?" (2017). Sheen listed several environmental issues that might have catastrophic consequences for local communities in Wales, but which had gone largely unreported: the Hazrem Environmental Ltd waste recycling plant in the Lower Sirhowy Valley, the dumping of radioactive mud in Cardiff Bay for the construction of Hinckley Point C, the proposed super-prison in Port Talbot, and contaminated water at Bofiscin Quarry. He said,

> These stories get bits of coverage here and there but they rarely break through. There just isn't the support for reporters to do the kind of long-form, in-depth investigative reporting that I know they feel many of these stories deserve. … The other aspect of all this that worries me is that when government is desperate to improve the economy and journalism is unable to give the powerful the scrutiny necessary, including powerful corporations and industry, then communities, often the poorer communities, can be left extremely vulnerable. … We have to be vigilant that it is not at the expense of communities who have already dealt with so much and whose voices can all too often either not be heard or too easily be drowned out.
>
> *(Sheen 2017)*

Representation and access to journalists

Alongside the weakened flow of information and a lack of access to adequate scrutiny, citizens in Port Talbot faced difficulty in gaining access to the pages of the local newspaper. Focus group participants said that they found it challenging to get

80 Inside a news black hole

their news and campaigns in the press, and one, a campaigner who as part of Port Talbot Residents Against Power Stations (PT-RAPS) had been a participant in public debate and community action against the new power plant, said that

> A lot was going on but the national newspapers just weren't interested. We tried really hard and they just weren't interested at all, even the *Western Mail* was a real struggle. We got two articles in the *Western Mail* but they just weren't interested; I think Port Talbot isn't on their radar; that's what I concluded.

This frustration about the remoteness of regional and national news outlets, and their unwillingness to cover some of the residents' concerns, was coupled with annoyance at the *Post* reporters' lack of attendance at grassroots events outside of more habitual working hours. This found expression in an attack on journalists' reluctance to attend events 'out of hours', and five activists from two separate campaigns mentioned specific incidents where this reluctance had affected news coverage, in one case resulting in the publication of a photograph so out of date that "there were a couple of people [in the photo] who were dead by then". The participant added, "That wasn't good, it reflects badly on the press". One active member of PT-RAPS said, "We found the *Post* journalists wouldn't work on a Saturday", and this is a problem because many of the campaigners were volunteering around their day jobs and so could only hold meetings or events out of normal working hours. Participants in the other focus groups complained events weren't being covered or that they didn't know what was going on, claiming that reporters "missed a lot of articles". This suggests that local people found difficulty engaging the increasingly remote traditional commercial media in telling their stories.

The consequences of the news black hole for local citizens

The problems faced by citizens in accessing three of the most basic tenets of fourth estate journalism – informing, representing and scrutiny of the powerful – have real-world consequences for local people. From basic difficulties such as planning a route to work in the face of major road closures to the imposition of large-scale energy projects with public health implications, citizens are facing difficulty living their lives without adequate, trustworthy information about local issues.

The effect of this damage to the flow of timely and useful information was difficult to miss in focus groups, with participants in all the age groups manifesting signs of frustration and some, even outright anger. The participants of the focus group for 18- to 30-year-olds appeared to be least engaged with traditional media and most negative about the town as a place to live, and this was the most volatile and outwardly angry of the groups. They spoke at some length about taking impulsive, potentially illegal direct action against a road closure, as the following exchange demonstrates:

MS1: I'd be very tempted to go up there with a disc cutter and just open [the barrier] up myself and then drive on it.

MS2: Need a revolution really but it's going to take violence for people to listen to it.

FS1: It doesn't always take violence.

MS2: A bit of a riot.

MS1: Yes, but in London there was all this big hoo-ha. They caused riots but they got what they wanted. They won't let that happen again.

INT: What did they want, what do you mean they got what they wanted?

MS2: The government listened, and they got a free telly [laughter].

MS2: The town's upset, they're just going to riot one day, everyone's just going to blow. I think everyone's going to get so angry they're just going to go …

FS1: It is going to get to that stage. I can see it getting to that stage very soon.

MS1: I'm going on Facebook after. I don't use Facebook but I'm going to have a go after. I'm going to start a riot.

The perception that direct, possibly violent, action is a viable option in a public sphere not served by healthy information flow, representation and scrutiny – together with the incorrect assumption of its effectiveness in other cases (e.g. implying that the London rioters "got what they wanted") – is worrying. One consequence of an ill-informed public could be an unstable public which feels it has no power in influencing decisions and therefore has only one option – aggression – if it wants to be heard. Research and analysis to explore the links between good public service news and young or disenfranchised groups should be a priority of future research. Ensuring the whole community continues to benefit from the fundamental features of fourth estate journalism – information, representation and scrutiny – must be a concern of journalists, researchers and policymakers alike.

Just as concerning are the visible cracks in democratic participation and engagement that must also be of concern to researchers and policymakers. Turnouts for elections at all levels were found to have been impacted, with signs that the public became disenfranchised around the same time district newspaper offices were closed. Studies into newspaper closures are few, but a handful of studies in America have found effects on democratic and civic markers following closures. Schulhofer-Wohl and Garrido's 2009 study of Cincinnati examined democratic behaviour following the closure of the *Cincinnati Post* and found lower election turnout rates and fewer candidates standing for office, and that incumbents were more likely to be re-elected following the closure, concluding that "newspapers – even underdogs such as the *Post*, which had a circulation of just 27,000 when it closed – can have a substantial and measurable impact on public life" (Schulhofer-Wohl and Garrido 2009, abstract). Gentzkow, *et al.* (2009) found election turnouts in US presidential elections were also affected by the presence or lack of newspapers. Shaker (2014) examined newspaper closures in Denver and Seattle along with data from the 2008 and 2009 Current Population Survey, finding a decline in civic engagement after the closures compared with civic engagement in other major American cities.

In the absence of census data or social surveys on civic engagement in the UK, analysis of election turnouts was the most accessible and replicable measure from the Schulhofer-Wohl and Garrido (2009) and Gentzkow et al. (2009) studies. In Port Talbot, turnouts in all three election types – general, local and National Assembly for Wales elections – showed decline when measured against UK or Wales turnout averages. Between the 1970 and 1999 local elections, turnout for the seats within the Aberavon constituency was an average of 2.45 percentage points above the UK average (see Figure 3.2), but this dropped from the 2004 elections onwards to 0.72 percentage points below the UK average. For general elections (see Figure 3.3), the turnout for Aberavon was an average of 1.17 percentage points above the UK average until the 2001 election: for elections from 2005 to 2015, this dropped to an average of 2.91 percentage points below the UK average. Similarly, Aberavon's turnout figures in the first National Assembly for Wales election in 1999 were 0.5 per cent above the Welsh average (Morgan 1999) but since then have dropped below the Welsh average by 0.35 per cent in 2003, 3.66 per cent in 2007 and 4.66 per cent in 2011.

It must be noted that the decline in voter turnout in Port Talbot did not happen after the *Guardian*'s closure in 2009, but much earlier, around the year 2000. This was an unexpected finding given the studies detailed above which noted declining civic and democratic engagement in local populations in the period immediately following newspaper closures (Gentzkow et al. 2009; Schulhofer-Wohl and Garrido 2009; Shaker 2014). This could suggest that the closure of district offices and the removal of embedded journalists from the community was of greater significance to local citizens than the closure of the weekly newspaper. The closure of district offices has already been identified by this research as a significant turning point in several key areas of news production, in terms of both quantity and quality, and it therefore seems possible these declines in voter turnout were closely

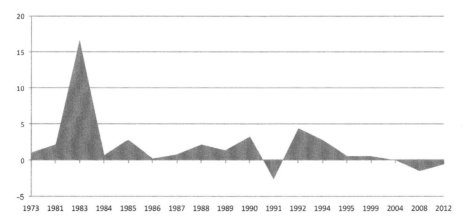

FIGURE 3.2 Percentage point difference in turnout average for local council elections compared with Wales average, 1973–2012

Source: Rallings et al. (2006)

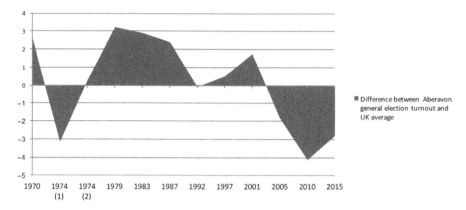

FIGURE 3.3 Percentage point difference in turnout average for general elections compared with UK average, 1970–2015
Source: Kimber (2012)

correlated with the closure of district newspaper offices and the withdrawal of journalists from the community.

Could a Port Talbot hyperlocal bridge the news black hole?

The discussion in this chapter has focused on the decline of local media and the consequences for citizens living in Port Talbot. While it is important to gauge the scope of the problem of news black holes, it is also helpful to examine potential solutions or interventions that may address elements of the democratic deficit. One such intervention was the founding of the Port Talbot Magnet, a co-operative hyperlocal news service that operated between 2009 and 2016.

The Port Talbot Magnet was started by a group of seven professional journalists (including one of the authors of this book, Rachel Howells) as an overt attempt to address a perceived news gap following the closure of the *Guardian*. These journalists were members of the nearby Swansea branch of the National Union of Journalists (NUJ) and had themselves faced the harsh realities of industry staff and budget cuts: all seven had been made redundant or lost freelance contracts in the preceding months. The service began as a small website run by volunteer journalists. Much of the first year was spent filling in grant application forms, but project funding remained elusive (though Howells was successful in applying for a funded PhD place at Cardiff University to carry out the study described in this chapter, which enabled her to continue working on the Magnet).

Following this failure to attract funding, the Magnet (Howells 2015) focused on developing its online presence, reporting on public meetings and quickly gaining a modest profile in the town. This was given a boost by a partnership with National Theatre Wales in 2011. Years of online reporting followed, with stories on the minutiae of Port Talbot life – the charity stunts, school musicals or new business openings – alongside reports on the more pressing issues facing the town, with campaigns, investigations, Freedom of Information requests, whistle-blowers' statements and council meetings all acting as triggers for news stories. The Magnet made overt attempts to carry out news reporting in the public interest by exposing injustice, fighting for answers to the community's questions and giving a voice and momentum to local campaigns in the same way their lost weekly paper, the *Guardian*, was once said to have done. Relations between reporters at the Magnet and rival journalists at the *Post* was largely cordial, though some animosity was noted and there was a rivalry between the two in trying to report unique stories.

However, stable revenue streams remained difficult to secure for the Magnet. Online advertising did not achieve large sums and attempts at crowdfunding were unsuccessful. Having mainly come from print backgrounds, the journalists on the Magnet's board were keen to relaunch a newspaper in the hope of securing stable advertising revenue. Experiments with print in 2012, including a profitable souvenir programme, solidified this resolve, and in 2013, with help from Carnegie UK Trust's Neighbourhood News scheme, the Magnet's online service was able to make the transition to print in the shape of a quarterly (later monthly) tabloid newspaper. An advertising salesperson was recruited on a commission-only basis, and the consequent revenue allowed the Magnet to pay freelance journalists, photographers and graphic designers for the first time, though this remained a periodic, rather than regular, feature of the Magnet's finances.

There were challenges in maintaining quality local news coverage with limited financial resources, several untrained or partially trained volunteers, and little access, at first, to the corridors of power and very few contacts. These last two issues gradually changed over time, as public bodies and politicians began to engage with the news service and provide press releases and tip-offs, respond to the Magnet's questions and give statements when requested. Through their reporting, the news service gained the trust of many local residents and activists who got in touch with their stories, issues and grievances.

The print edition went out free through the doors of 20,000 homes, and this penetration had the effect of raising the Magnet's profile and securing a large audience for advertisers, which in turn gave the Magnet greater authority to scrutinise those in power. Readers contacted the newspaper to say they were grateful to once again have a newspaper dedicated to their town, where their news was not slotted in between news stories about other places. There seemed to be an element of pride about the town having its own newspaper again. However, the remaining hurdle – financial sustainability – was elusive. The Magnet continued to pursue an advertising-based revenue model, but Howells lists many of the pressures in the evidence she gave to the National Assembly for Wales' Welsh Language, Culture and Communications Committee in the summer of 2017. Among these were the difficulty in recruiting advertising sales staff and the economic deprivation of the community. She said, "Many of our advertisers were not able to spend money regularly, or were not able to pay our rates, even reduced to cost prices" (Howells 2017). This economic deficit was further challenged when the 2016 steel crisis resulted in 750 job losses at Tata Steel and hit the confidence of local business owners.

However, the Magnet's team continued to work throughout 2016 for no pay in the hope of weathering the storm. In this time the Magnet broke an important story about the safety concerns of steelworkers following the reductions in manpower on shifts because of the redundancies. This story was not picked up in the mainstream press and caused some in the trade unions to try to uncover the identities of the whistle-blowers by underhand tactics. The team was also harassed by steelworkers for publishing the story, and the service closed within a few months. Howells said,

> We did not have the institutional muscle and legal advice we needed, and we felt exposed and stressed. This was certainly a contributory factor in our closure, but at the root of all our problems was the lack of a reliable income stream. We reluctantly concluded that there was insufficient wealth in the local economy in Port Talbot to support a news service.
>
> *(Howells 2017)*

There are examples of hyperlocals succeeding with print models that rely on advertising – notable among these are the *Caerphilly Observer* and the Filton Voice – and there seems to be growth in the sector. But it is important to acknowledge the difficulties inherent in attempting to run advertising-subsidised journalism businesses in deprived communities. In Port Talbot, there was no shortage of news and many of the stories were undoubtedly of public interest – a flooded opencast mine threatening to spill onto houses below, the facilities to be included in a new leisure centre funded by the council, the closure of the motorway junction leading to the town, air pollution from the steelworks, cuts to essential services – but the inability of local businesses to underwrite this essential journalism was also apparent. Alternatives to the advertising-led approach are still urgently required to address this need. In Wales, the National Assembly for Wales and the Welsh Government are both considering interventions in the sector, and the lessons of Port Talbot and the Magnet continue to feed into these discussions.

Conclusion

This chapter sets out the problems being faced by citizens living in a news black hole, which, as much of the evidence indicates, is a phenomenon marked by the withdrawal of journalists from a community, rather than the closure of newspapers. Similar research into newspaper closures in America suggests there are changes in citizens' civic and democratic behaviour in the years following the newspaper closure; however, the data for Port Talbot pointed to a turning point in both the news and the response of citizens happening much earlier than the 2009 closure of the *Port Talbot Guardian*, around the year 2000. This is when certain markers of quality in news stories appeared to worsen, when sources became less local and journalists began to rely more on PR and high-status sources and less on local

86 Inside a news black hole

contacts and personal attendance at meetings and events. It is also when Aberavon's election turnouts, which had almost exclusively been one or two percentage points above the national average since the 1970s, fell below average for the first time, where they have stayed.

Together, the data suggests that, in relation to the role of journalism, newspaper closures are not necessarily the crucial moment in any democratic deficit that may arise. Instead, it seems likely that the withdrawal of journalists from local communities is the marker of a democratic deficit. This withdrawal is far more widespread than simple newspaper closures. Redundancies of around 40 per cent since the 1990s and widespread district office closures point to a problem that is much bigger in scale that we might have realised. There is therefore likely to be a large network of news black holes caused by the withdrawal of local journalism and masked by the continuation of local newspapers that are now more like 'zombie newspapers' with scaled back staff numbers and a much smaller amount of locally relevant content.

It is worth underlining that a plurality of local journalists, working within, and accountable to, communities was found to be key. The advertising revenue model that allowed this kind of journalism to flourish in past years has proved that it is no longer able to support the required level of journalism in the midst of the structural changes and challenges of the digital age that have emerged in recent decades. Entrepreneurs have attempted to fill the gap in many places with small independent or hyperlocal offerings – the Port Talbot Magnet is an example – and though there have been many successes, only some have found sustainability and many continue to rely on advertising revenue for support. However, towns like Port Talbot, which has suffered from the decline and automation of its traditionally industrial economy, much of it centred on steelmaking, is a good example of a community that is in dire need of good-quality local journalism, but which is unable to sustain it in its currently weakened local economy.

In the next three chapters of this book we turn our gaze to the rise of hyperlocal publishing, discussing in detail the viability of this emerging sector and examining the motivations of practitioners. We begin by looking across the hyperlocal news landscape in the UK and its potential to make effective contributions to the public sphere based on its scale, scope and content, examining whether hyperlocal news services might – as has been argued by others (Metzgar *et al.* 2011) – be seen as elements within a reinvigorated public sphere.

Note

1 For example, The British Social Attitudes Survey, which has been carried out every year since 1983, contains some questions that relate to political efficacy (not knowledge); but these were not asked in every year of the survey, and when they were asked, the sample sizes for the Aberavon parliamentary constituency were too small to be statistically valid.

References

Anderson, Chris, Bell, Emily & Shirky, Clay (2014) *Post Industrial Journalism: Adapting to the Present.* Tow Centre for Digital Journalism White Papers. New York: Tow Centre for Digital Journalism.

Anderson, Peter J. (2007) Challenges for journalism. In: Anderson, P. J. & Ward, G. (eds) *The Future of Journalism in the Advanced Democracies.* Aldershot: Ashgate, pp. 53–69.

Baresch, Brian, Knight, Lewis, Harp, Dustin & Yaschur, Carolyn (2011) Friends who choose your news: An analysis of content links on Facebook. *ISOJ: The Official Research Journal of International Symposium on Online Journalism, Austin, TX,* Vol. 1, No. 2, pp. 1–24.

Brook, Stephen (2009, 16 June) Half UK local and regional papers could shut by 2014, MPs are told. *The Guardian.* Available at: www.guardian.co.uk/media/2009/jun/16/half-local-papers-could-shut-2014 [Accessed 8 July 2011].

Curran, James & Seaton, Jean (1991) *Power Without Responsibility: The Press and Broadcasting in Britain.* London: Routledge.

Davies, Geraint Talfan & Morris, Nick (2008) *Media in Wales: Serving Public Values.* Cardiff: Institute of Welsh Affairs.

Davies, Nick (2008) *Flat Earth News.* London: Vintage.

Frank, Mark, Walker, Johanna, Attard, Julie & Tygel, Alan (2016) Data literacy: What is it and how can we make it happen? *The Journal of Community Informatics,* Vol. 12, No. 3, pp. 4–8.

Frisby, Wendy & Millar, Sydney (2002) The actualities of doing community development to promote the inclusion of low income populations in local sport and recreation. *European Sport Management Quarterly,* Vol. 2, No. 3, pp. 209–233.

Gentzkow, Matthew, Shapiro, Jesse M. & Sinkinson, Michael (2009) *The Effect of Newspaper Entry and Exit on Electoral Politics.* NBER Working Paper No. 15544. Cambridge, MA: National Bureau of Economic Research.

Gillmor, Dan (2008) *We the Media: Grassroots Journalism by the People, for the People.* Sebastopol, CA: O'Reilly Media.

Howells, Rachel (2015) *Journey to the Centre of a News Black Hole: Examining the Democratic Deficit in a Town with No Newspaper.* PhD Thesis, Cardiff University.

Howells, Rachel (2017) News journalism in Wales. Evidence submitted to National Assembly for Wales' Culture, Welsh Language, and Communications Committee Inquiry into News Journalism in Wales [Online]. Available at: http://senedd.assembly.wales/ieListDocuments.aspx?CId=445&MID=4201 [Accessed 24 March 2018].

Jarvie, Grant (2003) Communitarianism, sport and social capital: Neighbourly insights into Scottish sport. *International Review for the Sociology of Sport,* Vol. 38, No. 2, pp. 139–153.

Kimber, Richard (2012) Turnout in General Elections [Online]. *Political Science Resources.* Available at: www.politicsresources.net/area/uk/turnout.htm [Accessed 18 May 2015].

Lewis, Justin (2001) *Constructing Public Opinion: How Political Elites Do what they Like and Why We Seem to Go Along with It.* New York: Columbia University Press.

Martin, Shannon E. (1988) Proximity of event as a factor in selection of news sources. *Journalism Quarterly,* Vol. 65, No. 4, pp. 986–989.

McChesney, Robert W. & Nichols, John (2010) *The Death and Life of American Journalism.* Philadelphia, PA: Nation Books.

McNair, Brian (2009) Journalism and democracy. In: Wahl-Jorgensen, K. & Hanitsch, T. (eds) *The Handbook of Journalism Studies.* London: Routledge, pp. 237–249.

Metzgar, Emily T., Kurpius, David D. & Rowley, Karen M. (2011) Defining hyperlocal media: Proposing a framework for discussion. *New Media & Society,* Vol. 13, No. 5, pp. 772–787.

Moore, Martin (2010, 22 July) Waving and drowning – the news from Wales [Online]. Available at: http://martinjemoore.com/waving-and-drowning-%E2%80%93-the-news-from-wales/ [Accessed 1 December 2017].

Morgan, Bryn (1999) *Welsh Assembly Elections: 6 May 1999*. Research Paper 99/51. London: House of Commons Library.

O'Neill, Deirdre & O'Connor, Catherine (2008) The passive journalist: How sources dominate local news. *Journalism Practice*, Vol. 2, No. 3, pp. 487–500.

Page, Benjamin I. & Shapiro, Robert Y. (1983) Effects of public opinion on policy. *American Political Science Review*, Vol. 77, No. 1, pp. 175–190.

Page, Benjamin I. & Shapiro, Robert Y. (1992) *The Rational Public: Fifty Years of Trends in Americans' Policy Preferences*. American Politics and Political Economy. Chicago, IL: The University of Chicago Press.

Phillips, Angela & Witschge, Tamara (2012) The changing business of news: Sustainability of news journalism. In: Lee-Wright, P., Phillips, A. & Witschge, T. (eds) *Changing Journalism*. Abingdon: Routledge, pp. 3–20.

Rallings, C. S., Thrasher, M. A. M. & Ware, L. (2006) British local election database, 1889–2003 [Online]. *UK Data Service*. Available at: http://dx.doi.org/10.5255/UKDA-SN-5319-1 [Accessed 12 May 2015].

Roberts, Gill (2014, 29 May) Neath Port Talbot Council hit back at pollution claims. *Neath Port Talbot Courier*. Available at: www.southwales-eveningpost.co.uk/Neath-Port-Talbot-Council-hit-pollution-claims/story-21159104-detail/story.html

Ross, Karen (2007) The journalist, the housewife, the citizen and the press: Women and men as sources in local news narratives. *Journalism*, Vol. 8, No. 4, pp. 449–473.

Schulhofer-Wohl, Sam & Garrido, Miguel (2009, March 13) *Do Newspapers Matter? Evidence from the Closure of the Cincinnati Post*. Discussion Papers in Economics No. 236. Princeton, NJ: Woodrow Wilson School of Public and International Affairs, Princeton University.

Shaker, Lee (2014) Dead newspapers and citizens' civic engagement. *Political Communication*, Vol. 31, No. 1, pp. 131–148.

Sheen, Michael (2017) Raymond Williams Memorial Lecture: Who speaks for Wales? Learning and Work Institute, Cardiff, 16 November.

Shirky, Clay (2008) *Here Comes Everybody: The Power of Organizing without Organisations*. London: Allen Lane.

Skinner, James, Zakus, Dwight H. & Cowell, Jacqui (2008) Development through sport: Building social capital in disadvantaged communities. *Sport Management Review*, Vol. 11, No. 3, pp. 253–275.

Thomas, James (2006) *The Regional and Local Media in Wales*. Cardiff: Culture, Welsh Language and Sport Committee.

Turner, Robin (2013, 20 June) Welsh Government launches action plan to improve Port Talbot air quality [Online]. *Wales Online*. [Accessed 24 March 2018].

Williams, Andrew & Franklin, Bob (2007) *Turning Around the Tanker: Implementing Trinity Mirror's Online Strategy* [Online]. Cardiff: Cardiff School of Journalism, Media and Cultural Studies. Available at: http://image.guardian.co.uk/sys-files/Media/documents/2007/03/13/Cardiff.Trinity.pdf [Accessed 2 December 2015].

Williams, Kevin (1998) *Get Me a Murder a Day! A History of Mass Communication in Britain*. London: Arnold.

4

FROM LOST PETS TO LOCAL CORRUPTION

What gets covered in hyperlocal news

In this chapter, we present an analysis of the UK hyperlocal news sector, largely covering the period 2012–2015. The chapter looks at extent, variety and content of hyperlocal news and information operations and asks how they contribute to local public spheres of information, bringing together empirical data from a range of research methods including a content analysis, a survey[1] and interviews. We also draw on research that Ofcom directly commissioned from the authors, as it attempted to make sense of both the challenges facing producers of news and the changes in news consumption practices that were creating those challenges. We begin by outlining the problem of the lack of robust data for the hyperlocal sector in comparison to the mainstream press and also discuss Ofcom's interest in hyperlocal as an element of local news ecologies which formed the initial rationale for this research. We then look at the range of topics covered by hyperlocal publishers in order to test empirically whether, in what ways and to what extent this online local community news can plug the gaps left by the retreat of local news from many UK communities.

Our starting point for this research was the lack of data on the sector as a whole, which had not seemed to prevent it from being championed by those keen to persuade policymakers of its value. It is worth noting the regulatory and wider economic context of the time as a way of understanding why policymakers and regulators began to take such an interest in hyperlocal news. In the late 2000s, commercial broadcaster ITV was keen to pare down its licence obligation to provide regional television news, potentially leaving regional BBC output as the only non-national television news provider. Further, as the economy slowed, the UK communications regulator Ofcom was worried about how the already-depleted local newspaper industry would emerge on the other side of the recession: "Some property and display advertising may return, and newspaper owners may be able to make further savings; however operating margins are likely to be much reduced, and some currently unprofitable titles could continue to lose money for some time" (2009a: 5).

This 'perfect storm' was further exacerbated when the plan to license a series of regional Independently Funded News Consortia (IFNC) (Ofcom 2009b) as a way to fill the local news gap was scrapped early in the life of the 2010 Conservative-Liberal Democrat coalition government. Ofcom's interest in hyperlocal media lay, therefore, in its potential to provide public service news content online in a cost-effective way. After all, it was Ofcom's 2009 public service broadcasting review that had made it clear that the Internet was now a space that was as legitimate a distributor of news as broadcast platforms: "We introduced the concept of public service content as a broader category that included public service broadcasting, but also captured the contribution made to public purposes by content distributed over other platforms, principally the internet" (2009b: 16).

Ofcom's remit to take account of the "wider media ecology ... such as local journalism, local and regional newspapers, and the internet" (2009a: 139) resulted in it welcoming some research that would shed light on hyperlocal publishing. Thus, the research presented here is a response to that request.

Hyperlocal news consumption

As of late 2017, despite the hyperlocal sector finally starting to coalesce around a representative body (the Independent Community News Network set up by the Centre for Community Journalism at Cardiff University in 2017), there is no formal collation of data about itself or its audiences. Although there are no audited readership figures, some data has emerged from individual hyperlocals and from recent research. For example, hyperlocals that publish as newspapers often list circulation figures, although they are not audited in the same way mainstream newspapers are. Brixton Bugle says it distributes 9,000 copies of its monthly free newspaper (2017), Kentishtowner claims it has 20,000 monthly print edition readers (2012), and South Leeds Life distributes 5,000 copies (2017). In a similar vein, the London SE1 website says that "7,300+ locals" read the weekly email newsletter it sends out (n.d.). Our 2014 survey of hyperlocal publishers (Williams *et al.* 2014) gave some indication of numbers of visitors to hyperlocal websites, but the data was self-reported rather than collated independently. We found that "the median number of monthly unique visitors is 5,039" (2014: 4) and that "the great majority of sites have relatively small audiences" (2014: 20). Of further concern is the 31 per cent of publishers "who do not know, who wish not to know, or don't know how to find out, about the kind of website analytics that are necessary for generating income" (2014: 20).

The same survey found that social media was a particular area of audience growth. In 2015 Talk About Local (Perrin 2015) listed the number of Facebook Page 'likes' and Twitter followers of 37 hyperlocals, set against population estimates. This seems to show that some hyperlocals had significant reach locally, with the hyperlocal site for Stone in Staffordshire having a Facebook Page and Twitter account which had likes and followers, respectively, in the region of 50 per cent of the local population figure. However, social media followers can come from outside a locality and may be interested more in the news project itself than in news and events in the area. Whilst the figures cited may provide a rough snapshot of hyperlocal audience reach, the problem remains that properly audited data for hyperlocals does not exist. By contrast, the Audit Bureau of Circulation (ABC) gives rich data on the print and online readership of the mainstream press, whilst The Joint Industry Committee for Regional Media Research (JICREG) offers a detailed socio-economic breakdown of local readerships to ensure advertisers can target spend appropriately.

Some data for the hyperlocal sector on 'who reads what' comes in the form of the Nesta and Kantar Media report (2013) based on a survey of 2,248 people. The research set out to ascertain how people engage with online hyperlocal information and found that 45 per cent of adults had accessed hyperlocal media of some form, with two-thirds of those doing so at least weekly (Nesta and Kantar Media 2013: 6). The report also found that mainstream media was the key source that most people (65 per cent) cited they turn to in order to find out what was happening in their local areas. Online 'native' hyperlocal media – "The website or app of volunteers or people with an interest in the local area / from the local area" (Nesta and Kantar Media 2013: 30) – was cited a source of news by 24 per cent of respondents. The research shows the growing number of native hyperlocals entering the news and information space, yet the findings suggest "that audiences tend towards using traditional media brands for their hyperlocal consumption" (Nesta and Kantar Media 2013: 4). The authors recognise that their findings are limited by the potential confusion over which platforms native hyperlocals use (newspapers, social media), with some possible mis-categorisation as a result.

However, the research did return some demographic data, noting: "it appears those who are more affluent and in the 35–54 age group are more likely to consume hyperlocal media" (Nesta and Kantar Media 2013: 8). Other data emerges from Ofcom's 2012 research, that found 7 per cent of people had looked at "local community websites, e.g. news website run by volunteers" at least once a week (2012a: 104). However, only 1 per cent said that such websites were their most important local media source (Ofcom 2012a: 106). Ofcom's ongoing research into news media use has, since 2013, been tracking whether people have looked "at websites / apps for news about or events in the local area/ the local community" (Ofcom 2015a: 11). Sixty-nine per cent said they had in 2015, up from 56 per cent in 2013. Whilst data on the consumption of hyperlocal media is subject to wide margins of error – as a result of being pulled from different surveys, at different times, with differing use of terminology – the research to date does seem to suggest that hyperlocal's audience share is modest at best. However, there is at least a published and recognised record of UK hyperlocals, and it is this – the Openly Local database – that we base our research in this chapter.

Mapping UK hyperlocal news

The Openly Local database was a regularly updated list of hyperlocal operations in the UK and Ireland. It was started in 2010 and existed until 2015, when it was superseded by another database. One might regard the database as comparable with the series of bibliographic guides to the alternative and underground press covering 1972–1996 (of which Spiers 1974 is the first) published by Harvester Press (later Primary Source Media and Research Publications International). Such guides sought to capture the ephemeral nature of much of the alternative press, and even one-off publications were included:

> All across Britain in the past 10 years underground papers have been erupting, ending, and beginning. ... [M]any papers have been short-lived, amorphous, fluid, constantly ebbing and flowing, individually impermanent, part of a new press deeply embroiled in a search for self-definition.
>
> *(Spiers 1974: 19)*

Spiers argued that the need to archive these publications was vital as they captured the prevailing countercultural mood of Britain at the time. Although he recognised that such publications were "virtually uncollectable" in their totality (Spiers 1974: 19), the collection, represented in microfiche files, was essential to "understanding the situation of the left today" (20). While the Openly Local database made a less politically charged rationale for its existence, it did recognise that the precariousness of the local press makes an alternative listing of emerging non-mainstream media very difficult but also very important.

The database's initiator, Chris Taggart, argues that hyperlocal publications form "a crucial part of the media future as the traditional local media dies or is cut back to a shadow of its former self" (2010). Taggart, a former journalist and web developer, initially developed the resource as a complement to his comprehensive Web listing of council services. He created the database to be compliant with Open Data standards, therefore its data could be reused freely "for mashups or anything else" (Taggart 2010). Although Taggart started the Openly Local resource, he notes that it was largely populated by others: "I actually started out with a very small number (probably a dozen or so, certainly less than 20), and then let the community do the rest" (personal communication with the authors). 'The community' in this instance included hyperlocal publishers themselves as well as others with an interest in the area. Taggart intended the database to be as inclusive as possible, but did indicate loose criteria on the submissions page. It is worth noting these did not set out to replicate the tensions between civic and commercial value that other advocates of hyperlocal had done, but did seek to exclude some forms of local information provision:

> The directory is for both non-commercial and commercial hyperlocal news and community sites – the news can be in the form of traditional news stories,

blogs, or (if they're very good) forums with news content. Local shopping, housing or other pure listings sites won't be approved.

(Taggart n.d.)

Whilst Openly Local was not the only database that has been developed for hyperlocal media, it was the only one regularly cited by proponents of hyperlocal (it is linked from a series of blog posts by the BBC which start in October 2010) and within policy documents (its first citation coming in Ofcom's *Communications Market Report* in 2010). In 2014, the Media Standards Trust published a report about the role of enterprise and innovation in local journalism and cited Openly Local as an authoritative source when discussing hyperlocal sites (Moore 2014: 11). Nesta have made several references to it in their work in this area (Nesta and Kantar Media 2013: 65; Radcliffe 2012: 9, 43). Prior to 2010, there were other attempts to make sense of this emerging area of news[2] in the UK, and since 2013 the Centre for Community Journalism at Cardiff University has been populating its own map (www.communityjournalism.co.uk/find-a-hyperlocal/), with an initial focus on Wales but gradually extending out to the rest of the UK. This latter map also seems to be largely community generated, although moderated by Centre staff, with an open invitation for those running websites to register. When Chris Taggart decided to shut the Openly Local resource in 2015, a new attempt to produce an updated map was initiated by Carnegie UK Trust with the help of Talk About Local, and this was published at http://localweblist.net.

Hyperlocal's place in UK local media ecologies

In noting the emergence of 'ultra-'local news websites in their 2009 review of local media, Ofcom expresses concerns about their sustainability, citing the need for more robust impact data as an issue affecting all aspects of community media: "it is difficult for community media to quantify their impact in order to make a case for funding" (2009a: 129). They draw on the thoughts of US media commentator Steven Johnson (2009), who argues for an ecological model to understand the place of emergent news media forms:

> Johnson sets out an eco-system. Local content would be delivered with far fewer fixed costs, relying on networks of volunteers and interested groups. But there would still be room for professional journalists, a smaller cadre of whom would be sustained by the reduced revenue streams available through this type of distribution model.
>
> *(Ofcom 2009a: 129)*

Johnson's position veers towards the utopian in seeing an exponential growth in the number of local bloggers and commentators who will eventually ensure localities are awash with information on all aspects of everyday life, leaving nothing more than a curation problem for citizens as they pick their way through the dense

94 From lost pets to local corruption

'forest' of information. The future of newspapers, he argues, may be as curators of the online, therefore freeing them up for original accountability reporting on more serious topics:

> If they [newspapers] embrace this role as an authoritative guide to the entire ecosystem of news, if they stop paying for content that the web is already generating on its own, I suspect in the long run they will be as sustainable and as vital as they have ever been.
>
> *(Johnson 2009)*

Also for the 2009 *Local and Regional Media* report, Ofcom commissioned Steven Barnett to offer an overview of the democratic role of local media. He made the case that although the emergence of "exciting, innovative, open and non-hierarchical" hyperlocal news websites may play a useful bonding role within communities, their contribution to plugging the 'democratic deficit' was limited:

> they are also precarious, shoestring operations, often sustained by a few dogged enthusiasts and unable to conduct investigative journalism, generate specialist knowledge across a range of local issues or have sufficient authority or deter- mination to scrutinise the various conduits of local power. They cannot interrogate, they cannot report in any depth, nor can they properly represent given the generally small number of people participating in such sites.
>
> *(Barnett 2009: 12)*

Yet Ofcom's interest in hyperlocal's role in local media ecologies persisted. As Ofcom make clear, they have a duty to examine the wider media landscape beyond their statutory remit: "we have to consider local and regional media in the context of a wider media ecology which touches upon areas that are outside Ofcom's remit, such as local journalism, local and regional newspapers, and the internet" (2009a: 139). In 2010, Ofcom commissioned a consultancy to set out the framework by which they would assess whether consumers would benefit or otherwise from any merger: "These include the size of the paper, the frequency of delivery, the extent of distribution, the price of the title, the quality of the jour- nalism, the extent of local presence, the variety of content, and the number of online services" (2011: 23). The framework developed by DotEcon Ltd (2010) argues that labour input into the creation of journalism should be measured along with output (size and frequency of publication). It lists frequency of online news updates as one of the output measures, although it is dismissive of online offerings that are not part of newspaper groups: "Online offerings in a local or regional set- ting are in most cases provided by companion sites of traditional media outlets, and we have therefore dealt with online as an adjunct medium" (DotEcon Ltd 2010: 11). To date, Ofcom have only carried out two Local Media Assessments (2011, 2013), with much of the data related to input/output measures heavily redacted. However, in their assessment (Ofcom 2013) on whether to refer the joint venture

Local World Limited to the Competition Commission, it does discuss online hyperlocal news publishers as part of the "market context". It cites the rise of independent hyperlocals, digital news sites and "social networks" as part of the "key trends in local media" that have seen citizens turn away from traditional newspapers: "we note audience fragmentation due to the large number of new media services" (Ofcom 2013: 5).

Media plurality

In 2013 the government, following a recommendation from the Leveson Inquiry, undertook a consultation to collect views on the scope of a measurement framework for media plurality (Department for Culture, Media and Sport 2013). The consultation document expressed interest in views about the viability of a measurement tool for local media plurality and noted that whilst hyperlocal publishers were beginning to have impact "where there may be gaps in provision of news or information from other sources", there was much variation: the "amount, quality and type of information that people are able to and actively do access in regions and local areas can differ enormously" (Department for Culture, Media and Sport 2013: 25). The government's response to the consultation (published in combination with its response to the 2014 House of Lords Select Committee on Communications report and recommendations on media plurality) quotes a respondent who sees value in assessing the role of hyperlocal when considering plurality:

> it seems obvious that in some cases the impact of hyperlocal web media and their audience size should feature in plurality considerations if the local paper, radio station, TV station are to be taken over or fall under same ownership.
>
> *(Department for Culture, Media and Sport 2014: 16)*

The report concludes that a measurement framework for media plurality should consider local and regional markets, "but this need not include a forensic examination of every locality" (Department for Culture, Media and Sport 2014: 17). This conclusion is practical, but works against the idea of taking account of hyperlocal media operations given there is largely no consistency between localities: two cities of similar size may have completely different hyperlocal media ecologies. The report tasks Ofcom with developing indicators "that can show how far the UK has an 'ideal' market in terms of plurality" (Department for Culture, Media and Sport 2014: 18). After consultation, Ofcom responded to the government by arguing that its previous 2012 advice was still relevant; that is, a focus "on three categories of quantitative metrics measuring the availability, consumption and impact of news content and a consideration of relevant qualitative contextual factors" (2015b: 11).

These metrics and factors for measuring plurality raise issues for the hyperlocal sector and make its lack of drawing together of relevant data a significant issue in fulfilling its potential to be seen as making a valuable, measurable contribution to

96 From lost pets to local corruption

the UK media ecology. In one example of a public interest test, data about hyperlocal publishing was discussed more widely. In June 2012, Global Radio Ltd acquired the outstanding share capital in Guardian Media Group's radio stations. The then Secretary of State for Culture, Media and Sport asked for a public interest test to be undertaken by Ofcom in relation to the acquisition in order to assess the degree to which such a merger was a threat to media plurality. Ofcom looked at the consequences for specific geographies (since the licences for each group's radio stations crossed over in some areas) and across media: "We believe that in assessing the sufficiency of plurality of owners of media enterprises, we must take account of all platforms through which consumers source news content" (2012b: 6). Alongside other radio stations, television stations and local print media, "online sites providing local content" were considered as part of the "availability" metric (Ofcom 2012b: 16). The report draws on the data outlined below to account for the number of active hyperlocal sites in 2012. It notes the issues with patchy geographic coverage and includes Ofcom's own statistic that such sites are regarded as an "important" local news source to just 1 per cent of people (Ofcom 2012b: 41–46).

Whilst hyperlocal publishing was part of the consideration of plurality in Ofcom's assessment, the area-by-area analysis in the annex of the report tells a different story of Ofcom's view on hyperlocal's importance. In assessing north Wales' media ecology, Ofcom declares that they "have seen no evidence to suggest that they [hyperlocal websites] have the capacity to influence the democratic debate in Wales" (2012c: 9). The same sentence is repeated in relation to Scotland (Ofcom 2012c: 27), the North East (46), Yorkshire (52), the North West (59) and the Greater Manchester area (65). So whilst hyperlocal might have secured a role as "one of the genres of interest in our public interest test" (Ofcom 2012b: 41) as a result of its "availability", its potential importance gets passed over in any analysis of plurality at nation or regional level. In the consumption data available to Ofcom, hyperlocal publishing is seen to play an insubstantial role in local media landscapes.

Had a more forensic examination of the data been drawn upon, then perhaps there might have been potential for the assessors to see hyperlocal's potential to "influence the democratic debate" (Ofcom 2012c: 9). Indeed, a 2014 by Ofcom report entitled *Internet Citizens*, drawing on outputs from the Creative Citizens and Media Plurality (mediaplurality.com) research projects, notes that

> not only are these sites providing their communities with information about local events, they are also playing an important role in upholding democratic accountability by initiating and conducting investigations into subjects as diverse as a waste incinerator breaching emissions guidelines, plans to develop land poisoned by previous industrial owners, and secret or illegal payments by local councils.
>
> *(2014: 52)*

Furthermore, whilst noting that research to date suggests that hyperlocal websites currently have only small audiences, "most are seeing audience growth on both their sites and social media, and some are branching out into offline publishing as a way of increasing their reach into their local communities and generating more advertising revenue" (Ofcom 2014: 53).

The 'availability' of hyperlocal media in the UK

In order to understand the potential reach of hyperlocal publishing across the UK and to give a sense of the fluidity of the sector, we carried out research between 2012 and 2014, in part commissioned by Ofcom, into the scale and scope of the sector.

The Openly Local database listed 572 sites in May 2012, rising to 632 a year later. In 2014 the database had 702 sites listed. However, many hyperlocal sites publish highly infrequently or fall into periods of non-use between editorships, so a broad definition of what an 'active' hyperlocal site consists of needed to be applied. In 2012 and 2013 the database was examined over two 11-day periods (8–18 May 2012 and 18–28 June 2013). Any site publishing a story in the five-month period before these sample periods was considered 'active'. Therefore, in 2012 there were 432 active sites, rising to 496 in 2013. In October 2014, we undertook another count of active sites, which showed a drop to 408. The disparity between the numbers listed on the database and the number of sites that were active marked a weakness in how the data was maintained (i.e. it was being added to but not systematically 'cleaned').

Most of the sites, with the exception of a small number of forum-only sites, produced identifiable news stories of varying length. We can take a broad view of what a news item would be – Harcup and O'Neill's (2001) reworked definition of what constitutes news serves is a point of reference – but most sites produce a mix of hard and soft news, event notices, reviews of local amenities or arts events, opinion pieces; to a degree, a not dissimilar mix to that in existing mainstream local media.

Number and frequency of hyperlocal stories

A count of the total number of stories produced by all sites was carried out in 2012 and 2013. This research found that during the period of 8–18 May 2012 (11 days), hyperlocal websites produced 3,819 stories. Of the 432 sites that were identified as 'active', 313 produced at least one news story in the sample period. The average number of posts per site over the 11 days was 12.2 and the median number was 7. Thirty-nine sites produced just one story and 133 sites produced five stories or fewer. In 2013, between 18 and 28 June (also 11 days), there were 3,482 stories published but this time from just 224 sites, meaning only 46 per cent of active sites produced a story as opposed to 72 per cent in 2012. The average number of posts per site was up (15.5), but the median was down (6 rather than 7). This suggests that a small number of sites were producing lots of stories, even more so than in 2012. Figure 4.1 shows the distribution of stories in 2012 across the sites, with 58 per cent of stories being produced by 20 per cent of the sites. It is clear that a small

98 From lost pets to local corruption

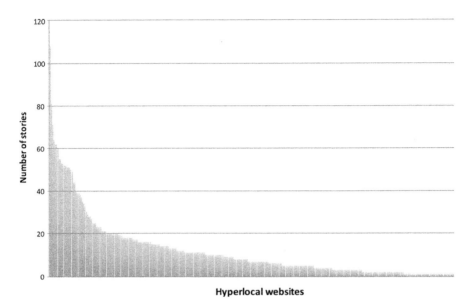

FIGURE 4.1 Hyperlocal's 'long tail' – distribution of stories across sites, 2012

number of sites were very active, but by far the majority, 259 sites, produced fewer than 20 stories during the sample period. The result when looked at across the hyperlocal sector as a whole produces a kind of 'long tail' effect.

Overall, an average of 15 items per hour were produced by hyperlocal websites in 2012. Hyperlocals were most active during the hours between 7 am and 7 pm. Indeed, it was during this period on the weekdays of the sample period that the average number of stories published rose to 24 items per hour, close to one story every two minutes. The peak day for stories was 14 May 2012, with 483 stories published, and a story every minute between 12 pm and 2 pm. The volume of stories published dropped by about a third at weekends. In 2013, an average of 13 items per hour were produced by hyperlocal websites and during the 7 am to 7 pm period on weekdays this average rose to 22 items per hour. The differences between 2012 and 2013 are marked in some areas. Although more sites were active, over half didn't produce a story during the sample period. This is partly explained by the decline in activity from sites linked to the Local People network, a series of citizen-led local news websites owned by the (now defunct) mainstream news publisher Local World. That is to say, they had produced some content, but it was sporadic and reflected the shift from these sites having paid-for editors to being run by volunteers or, in many cases, by no one at all. The data was beginning to show that those hyperlocal operations that were being sustained were run outside of this commercial network. The 2014 analysis further revealed the decline of the Local People network.

The analysis of hyperlocal websites in 2014 did not track the volume of stories published; rather, it was a simple interrogation of the Openly Local database to identify currently active sites. Although the number of sites listed had gone up to 702, only 408 were active, indicating a significant fall from the 2013 figure of 496. A total of 288 were recorded as no longer active, over twice the number for 2013. This figure is a mix of websites that had closed or that had not published in the five months prior to the sample period. Many of these websites (n = 86) were part of the Local People franchise. Although some (n = 37) still showed evidence of activity from local residents (such as events being published or reviews of businesses), the vast majority comprised nothing but spam postings and, although online, were therefore declared inactive. At this point the Local People network was no longer receiving financial support and had no paid editors in post (Lambourne 2013). The 2014 analysis was directly requested by Ofcom and the data included in their *Internet Citizens* report (2014).

Geographic distribution of hyperlocals

Of the 432 sites that were designated as active in 2012, 400 were located in England, 15 in Wales, 13 in Scotland and 3 in Northern Ireland. The Greater London area had 77 sites in total (85 by 2014), which collectively published 483 news items in the sample period. Overall Birmingham had 28 active sites in 2012 (although this had dropped to 20 by 2014) – the most for any local authority area – producing 92 news items. Not all clustering of sites was around urban areas; rural south Gloucestershire had 11 sites in 2012, largely aimed at small towns and villages, and Wiltshire had 10 (see Figure 4.2).

Hyperlocal news – what gets covered?

Drawing on the data produced during the sample period in 2012, we selected a sample of posts with which to carry out a content analysis. During this period, 3,819 posts were published on 313 active websites, and we coded every other story (odd numbers) on each site, a total of 1,941 posts. Our content analysis paid particular attention to: sources (who gets to define hyperlocal news?); topics (what news is covered?); the 'localness' of this news; and the civic value of the news (principally, here, in relation to coverage of politics). In order to better understand aspects of hyperlocal news coverage, we draw on a survey and semi-structured interviews with hyperlocal news publishers. These interviews, 42 in total, are drawn on throughout this book. In broad terms their hyperlocal operations could be said to fit within definitions put forward by Radcliffe (2012) and Metzgar *et al.* (2011), and in all cases they were active and publishing regularly at the time of interview. They represent a wide range of organisational set-ups. That is to say, some were operating not-for-profit, some were developing a business, and some were more in the guise of personal bloggers than journalists. In this chapter we hear from these practitioners about sourcing strategies, opinions of and relations with local mainstream media outlets, and examples of campaigning, critical and investigative hyperlocal journalism.

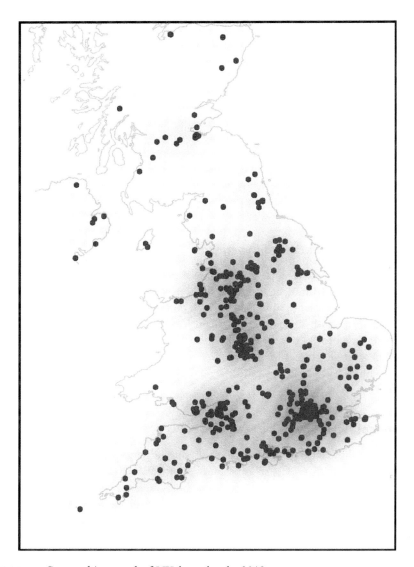

FIGURE 4.2 Geographic spread of UK hyperlocals, 2012

In terms of the topics covered by hyperlocal publishers (see Figure 4.3), we found that the largest category of news in the sample related to local community activities (13 per cent). This is, on the whole, a very geographically focused, community-oriented journalistic form. This category includes stories about local non-political civil society groups (e.g. the Women's Institute, community groups, local clubs and societies) as well as stories about community events like local festivals.

We also found many stories about local councils and the services they provide (11.7 per cent), so we know that hyperlocal audiences are getting a lot of

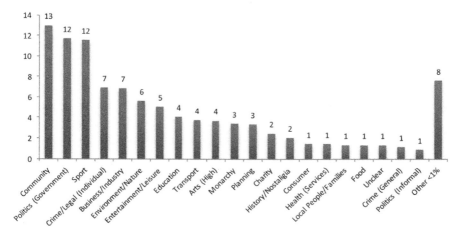

FIGURE 4.3 What gets covered? Percentage of topics covered by hyperlocal blog posts, 2012 (n = 1,941)

information that in principle could be of civic value. Indeed, this would have been our largest category if we had not separated out stories about local planning (3.3 per cent) which falls under the remit of local government in the UK. This kind of coverage of local politics contrasts somewhat with the UK's mainstream local and regional news media, which has scaled back such coverage in recent years. Other notably large categories included crime, business news, entertainment, and the arts.

Putting the 'local' back in local news

We have seen clearly from the data on story topics that readers of hyperlocal news are getting a large amount of information about politics, particularly the politics of local government, which relates to the ability of news to foster informed citizenship. To investigate this further, as part of our content analysis we looked for stories that made any reference to politics and determined whether or not they had an angle that was explicitly locally relevant. Here we generated further indications of the strength of this kind of news when it comes to reporting about local mainstream political spheres. More than a third of stories in our sample made reference to politics (39.1 per cent), and most referenced local politics (26.9 per cent). This is encouraging, especially because many of these sites exist in places where depleted local newspapers are operating on skeleton staffs, where they have already been closed down, or where there was never much local news coverage to speak of in the first place.

One of the complaints made about the decline of local and regional mainstream news in the UK is that it is becoming increasingly less local in its orientation, at least in part because of the continuing cuts to newsroom resources and the increasingly desk-bound nature of local and regional journalism work. This is not a charge which can be levelled at hyperlocal news. We aimed to assess the 'localness' of public discourse on these websites. First, we coded each source utterance[3] for whether it was talking about the local area, finding that almost all (87.2 per cent) of these citations had a local angle. Likewise, most posts (96.8 per cent) were published because of something that happened at a local level. There were some stories of national or international significance, but almost exclusively they were covered with a local angle that would make the story more relevant to local audiences. This may be encouraging in terms of the role of hyperlocal news in representing communities back to themselves, potentially fostering community cohesion.

Who gets to speak?

News sources are important indicators of social power. Who gets to define news events can affect public opinion, bolster authority and assign cultural meaning, and as such sources are a key indicator of civic and political value (Franklin and Carlson 2011). We coded for all directly quoted sources, but also all examples of indirectly reported speech. We deemed this important in order to test whether hyperlocal sourcing practice differed substantially from mainstream news journalism (which places a high value on quotations as an indicator of transparency in sourcing and as a way of enacting professional norms such as impartiality and objectivity). We found that this was also important for hyperlocals, with 93.8 per cent of citations employing direct quotation.

When we compare our broad findings on sources (see Figure 4.4) with studies of mainstream local news, there are some continuities but also important differences. As in the commercial local news, official sources in government, business and the

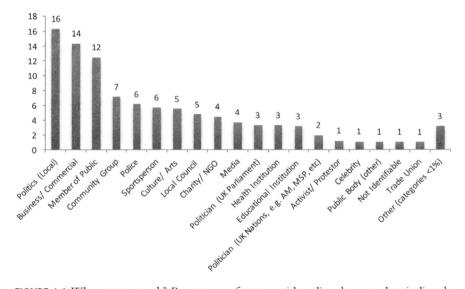

FIGURE 4.4 Who gets to speak? Percentage of sources either directly quoted or indirectly cited in UK hyperlocal news (n = 1,873)

police are very important: politics at various levels accounts for around a quarter of all sources cited (27 per cent), with business (14 per cent) and the police (6 per cent) also being very influential. But a key difference is the expanded role afforded to members of the general public and to representatives of local civil society groups in this emergent sector (12 per cent and 7 per cent, respectively). We expected to find more influence for members of the public actively organised in political struggles or campaigns, but explicitly political activists were thin on the ground in this sample (fewer political activists were quoted than recorded in a number of studies of UK mainstream local news). Informal political activists (those engaged in oppositional politics away from the mainstream) and trade unionists each made up just 1 per cent of the sources cited in our sample.

A plurality of voices?

The overall number of sources for news stories found in the sample was quite low given the number of stories in the sample, and this seems to signal a difference in practice between these emergent community news sites and more established providers of local news. Just over half the posts (56.3 per cent) cited news sources, meaning that many did not contain source input at all. Just as important, only around a fifth (21.7 per cent) cited more than one source. Studies of traditional news have been very critical of such under-sourcing, worrying that it leads to a lack of transparency, a lack of plurality in the sources of information to which audiences are exposed, and a lack of opportunity for audiences to learn about conflicting perspectives on particular issues.

We also set out to track the different functions of secondary source intervention. We asked whether each utterance from such sources was: corroboratory (in broad agreement with the primary source); contextual (adding further information to that provided by the first-quoted source); and/or oppositional (expressing disagreement with the first source).

Overall the sourcing of UK hyperlocal news in this sample seems to display a high level of consensus views. In terms of the level of debate and the amounts of alternative viewpoints presented on any given story, this journalism, on the evidence of this content sample, seems quite uncritical. Most of the interventions of secondary sources added context and further information to that provided by the first source. Many were in broad agreement with primary sources, giving

TABLE 4.1 Functions of secondary source intervention in UK hyperlocal blog posts (n = 421)

	Number of utterances	Percentage of utterances
Contextualization	358	18.4
Corroboration	304	15.7
Opposition	60	3.1

104 From lost pets to local corruption

corroboratory information. However only 3 per cent of all stories in our sample included disagreement between social actors. This further suggests that when it comes to sourcing, audiences are not being exposed to a wide range of alternative viewpoints in relation to the news they read. But the seemingly uncritical nature of the news in this sample needs to be understood in the context of our interviews.

Balancing sources is, of course, one of the principal ways in which mainstream professional journalists have practised their commitment to airing a plural range of perspectives on issues of public importance. However, hyperlocal news outlets take a variety of different positions on the issue of providing journalistic balance. Many hyperlocal news producers have a certain amount of journalistic training and experience, and these are more likely than others to both include quotes and balance news sources. But we were also told on numerous occasions that not all local news demands the use of multiple, or even single, sources. A key role that many (perhaps even most) hyperlocal sites play is the provision of often quite uncontroversial information about everyday life and activity in their communities. For instance, we found many posts consisted of promotional trails for, or post facto accounts of, events organised by broadly non-political community groups. We also found some evidence that this seeming under-sourcing of individual posts represents a (sometimes unconscious) rejection, or a critique in praxis, of some elements of mainstream journalistic sourcing strategies (Forde 2011: 118–140). For example, the editor of the Lincolnite told us in an interview of an example of a contentious story where he felt his team achieved fair coverage of key differing perspectives by covering competing local points of view in different stories on different days. His team wrote posts about a large street protest organised by librarians against County Council plans to close 30 out of 44 libraries in the area as part of their ongoing coverage of the campaign, but they put their commitment to providing fair coverage into practice by providing space for the local authority to have its say in a follow-up story the next day. It is unclear how widespread this practice is, but our content analysis coding frame was not designed to pick up such an approach to balancing.

Others, especially those who produce critical investigative hyperlocal news, take a much less conciliatory stance when it comes to providing space for the perspectives of those they critique. For instance, the retired journalist running Leeds Citizen describes himself as someone who produces critical news the mainstream local media "haven't got either the resources or, in some cases, the interest to cover". He is clear in his rejection of the need to offer an automatic right to reply in his coverage of local government:

> I'm scrupulous that everything I write is always accurate, nobody has ever challenged me about the accuracy of a story I've written. I'm choosing stories that are nearly always about the way interest groups, or political power, works. [But], for example, if I have a story about council stuff, I don't immediately slap off an email to them to the press office for them to give me a quote because they've got plenty of outlets for all of their stuff.

This unwillingness to balance sources in critical reporting is rooted, in part, in a pragmatic expectation that the PR office in question will not take any questions or allegations seriously, but also in a certain amount of contempt for the uncritical way in which local newspapers already routinely provide a mouthpiece for the output of local government communications officers. The campaigning London blog Love Wapping rejected the need to balance critical coverage of the council with quotes from relevant officers:

> I don't see why I should, as a resident, ring the town hall up or anybody else … . Because I know all they're going to give me is the usual bullshit. So what's the point? And they've got a huge media machine. … I don't see, to be quite honest, why any hyperlocal should. Because if you look at it in the broader context of media and communications in our society: if Tower Hamlets wants to get on TV, they can get on TV. They can send a press release to the *East London Advertiser* [the local weekly newspaper] … and they literally print the press release.

Another hyperlocal, Inside Croydon, elaborated on this, suggesting that the journalistic norm of providing balance through a right to reply sometimes offers council PR offices a way to "close down" critical reporting by simply refusing to comment. In such cases these hyperlocals have borrowed from the approaches of professional investigative reporting by relying on the quality of their documentary evidence as a way of guaranteeing accuracy and fairness. Referring to balance, and in common with others, Inside Croydon said: "I've adopted a different attitude. … In the end, it comes down to editorial judgement in terms of how you assess a source and the documentation … documents are the thing. If you get the document, you're away."

Hyperlocal campaigning

The dearth of non-party political activists and campaigners cited in our content analysis sample initially led us to suspect that campaigns may be under-represented in hyperlocal news. However, the interviews suggested there are two broad ways that hyperlocal news outlets cover campaigns: they actively campaign for change themselves and/or they cover existing local campaigns. Campaigning journalism, where a news outlet takes an overt stand in public debate with a view to changing things, is very common in the history of the commercial local and regional press in the UK. Even so, it is not something that many commercial local or regional publications enter into on a very regular basis. Based on our 11-day sample, the same seems to be true for hyperlocals, as we did not uncover much of this kind of coverage.

In order to glean a fuller picture of hyperlocal news practice in this area, we asked our survey respondents whether they had either started campaigns or covered the campaigns of others in the last two years. We found that most UK hyperlocals have joined in, supported or publicised the campaigns (73.3 per cent) of others, and a substantial minority (40 per cent) have themselves instigated campaigning journalism. We also asked them how often they undertook such journalism. The average number of campaigns instigated by hyperlocals themselves in the last two years was three, and the average number of campaigns they have "joined in or supported" was five. The raw figures only tell us part of the story. It is clear from the interviews, as well as the answers to more open-ended survey questions, that the subjects of these campaigns varied greatly in size, range and impact. Some issues were very local with the focus on issues likely to affect a small number of people, often in quite minor ways, and other issues were more wide-ranging in their effects and more explicitly political in focus.

We also asked survey participants to give us a qualitative insight into the campaigns they have run on their community news sites. We asked how many campaigns they have initiated themselves, and how many campaigns they have joined in with or supported that were initiated by others. The figures in Table 4.2 represent a breakdown of the focus of their most recent campaigns, and the focus of those they felt were most important, both initiated and supported.

Campaigns around planning and licensing were most likely to have been both supported and initiated by community news producers, and these mainly consisted of planning issues around contentious local developments. Many included an

TABLE 4.2 The focus of campaigns initiated and supported by UK community news producers

Focus of campaign	Most recent initiated (n = 64)	Most important initiated (n = 54)	Most recent supported (n = 93)	Most important supported (n = 74)
Planning/licensing	13	14	30	19
Local public services	11	11	23	18
Improvements to infrastructure	8	7	18	6
Local business issues	6	5	13	9
Local charity	2	1	9	2
Environmental issues	7	3	4	7
Community action	4	2	4	4
Improvements to amenities	10	12	3	5
Council (other)	3	2	2	5
Council accountability	11	4	1	1
Council malpractice	0	2	1	2
National political issues	3	0	1	1
Other	8	6	9	4

Note: some campaigns have more than one focus area.

environmental aspect to do with the protection of local green spaces or were related to local businesses (e.g. local opposition to the proposed opening of chain supermarket outlets), but a few were about minor local issues such as the granting of alcohol or take-away food licences. Campaigns around local public services (largely in opposition to cuts to such services) were also common in both categories. For instance, there were many campaigns against library closures, and a significant number around perceived threats to the provision of health care and education services. Campaigning for improvements to local infrastructure – calling on authorities to make, or lobbying against, substantial changes to local roads, train lines or provision for cyclists – was more commonly supported than initiated. Local business campaigns normally involved calls to promote local independent shops and restaurants, and included numerous 'shop local' campaigns. Community action campaigns were either in favour of or against local neighbourhood plans, or linked to the activities of neighbourhood forums, entities enabled under the 2011 Localism Act which are designed to enable more democratic control of planning issues. The numerous campaigns against these bodies, however, suggest concern in some communities about how democratic they actually are in practice. Community news producers were quite likely to initiate campaigns which called for improvements to local amenities such as signage, local parks, car parking, play areas, or the cleanliness of a local area (e.g. in relation to those favourite UK hyperlocal preoccupations: litter and dog poo). A number of campaigns dealt specifically with local council responsibilities. Several called for greater transparency and accountability from local government institutions, calling on councils to allow the filming, recording or live coverage of meetings. It is perhaps unsurprising that these were among the most likely to be initiated by community journalists, as restrictions on reporting directly affect their ability to cover the affairs of local political institutions. There were also a few instances of campaigning against much more serious council-related malpractice, such as campaigns around the misuse of public funds or illegal payments made to local businesses.

Hyperlocal coverage of many of these issues, it is claimed, was instrumental in numerous full or partial victories by the campaigners. But even when _campaigns were unsuccessful, much of this coverage is likely to have led to an enriched local public sphere in the affected communities. There is also evidence to suggest that coverage of campaigns, tapping in to existing networks of active citizens with an interest in local public life and covering issues which are of common concern to many, can help hyperlocal producers gain wider audiences, generate social standing, trust and respect, and become more visible in their communities. Hedon Blog told us their audience grew and became more engaged after a successful campaign against a pollution-based stench from the local sewage works. The coverage also prompted those in local political power to take the news outlet more seriously: "The blog has actually got some influence ... so people, now, in authority, I think, are not wary but respectful."

Hyperlocal accountability reporting: investigations

Our findings relating to the lack of conflicting perspectives among sources as well as those indicating low numbers of non-party grassroots or alternative campaigners raise the possibility that UK hyperlocal news, on aggregate, may be unlikely to undertake very much critical, accountability journalism. The content analysis findings are suggestive in this respect, but, again, the limitations of the sampling strategy necessitate further investigation. A more nuanced and differentiated picture can be obtained when triangulating these research findings with those from the survey and interviews, which allowed us to investigate two broad areas of hyperlocal practice in this regard: investigative hyperlocal news and non-investigative news which is nonetheless critical of local institutions.

In order to address the issue of investigative hyperlocal news and to interrogate hyperlocal producers' willingness or ability to carry out this form of watchdog reporting, we asked survey respondents whether they had carried out investigations in order to uncover controversial information of local concern in the last two years. It seems that a substantial proportion (42 per cent) of hyperlocal news producers were carrying out investigations (see Table 4.3). The average number of investigations respondents said they had undertaken in this period was 6.04 (n = 47), around three in four of which went on to be published; the average number of investigations which did not result in the publication of news stories was 1.48 (n = 42)

TABLE 4.3 The focus of investigations carried out by UK community news producers

Focus of investigation	Most recent investigation (n = 56)	Most important investigation (n = 44)
Planning/licensing	10	9
Local health/social care services	6	3
Council malpractice	6	7
Council cuts	6	6
Local infrastructure	6	6
Council accountability	5	5
Local amenities	4	2
Local business issues	4	2
Local education services	3	2
Local police	3	1
Environmental issues	3	3
Council waste	2	0
Other	4	2

Note: some investigations have more than one focus area.

(Barnett and Townend 2015). As before, respondents were asked for brief details of their most recent and their most important investigations.

Examples of investigations cited by survey respondents included: environment stories such as a waste incinerator breaching emissions guidelines and plans to develop land poisoned by previous industrial owners; council stories about lack of transparency or involving (documented) secret or illegal payments; planning issues around supermarket developments, the proposed High Speed 2 railway line, and greenfield sites being reallocated as brownfield in order to allow developments; as well a range of data-led stories about issues as diverse as parking fines, environmental enforcement activities, numbers and rates of crimes solved by local police, use of local libraries in order to argue against cuts to services, and lift failures in council-owned flats.

It is difficult to say with certainty with reference to our data whether certain kinds of hyperlocal outlet, or producers with particular skill sets or professional backgrounds, are more likely than others to produce investigative local accountability news. We found numerous examples of sites with quite a broad remit for general news provision which occasionally undertake investigations. In one high-profile example, the King's Cross Environment blog investigated the serious issue of Transport for London's culpability for a large number of cycling deaths on its patch (Perrin 2012). The investigation was long, multifaceted, employed numerous investigative tools and led to a Metropolitan Police investigation of Transport for London for corporate manslaughter. An example of a far less serious story, which nonetheless employed investigative tools, can be found on North Wales' Deeside.com (Sheppard 2013). For a story entitled "Has Shotton got the dirtiest street in Wales? 21 'loads' of dog dirt in a 4-minute walk", the author walked down the street, measured it and then photographed, catalogued and digitally mapped every dog poo they encountered. They then dug out contextual data specific to the county, Flintshire, from the Local Authority Cleanliness Index and the Welsh Index of Multiple Deprivation, as well as gathering and publishing critical comment from Carnegie UK Trust and a defence from the local council member responsible for Public Protection, Waste, and Recycling. The story led to the road being cleaned of the offending excrement within hours of publication.

As well as there being generalist hyperlocals who occasionally carry out investigations, a small but influential group of community news sites has developed in the UK that devote themselves almost exclusively to the production of critical and investigative news. Examples include Inside Croydon and Broken Barnett in London, the Leeds Citizen in the North of England, Carmarthenshire Planning Problems and More from rural West Wales, and Real Whitby in this seaside town in North Yorkshire. All of these sites have investigated and broken stories of local and national significance, chiefly about political corruption and transparency issues. One might expect, given the demanding, risky and resource-intensive nature of the research needed to take on local elites, that all of these hyperlocal producers would be trained journalists – this is not the case. The most commonly cited methods used in hyperlocal investigations during our interviews were: the careful

110 From lost pets to local corruption

analysis of public institutional documents and data; Freedom of Information Requests to public bodies (mostly councils) to obtain unpublished documents, data and correspondence; and leaks and tip-offs (mainly from within local councils, occasionally from private bodies). More risky methods such as undercover work were not encountered.

In order to explore the production of non-investigative news which nonetheless still includes source input critical of local institutions, or which may take an explicitly critical editorial stance, we asked a series of open questions in the interviews about producers' day-to-day practice and how their work relates to the output of other local news producers. Many were unequivocal about the need for local news producers to ask awkward questions, to air difficult issues and to hold elites to account. Yet when prompted, many defined themselves, their working practices and the news they produce as explicitly against the working routines and news output of mainstream professional local news companies. This is expressed in (sometimes quite vehement) critiques of: local press intrusion; exploitative treatment of community members at the centre of human interest stories; distant coverage which is not reflective enough of community life, is too reliant on press releases and is too deferential to authority; and coverage which is sensationalist and overly negative. One interviewee expanded on the last point: "The only time you ever read anything in the local mainstream press was when some things had been vandalised, or some kids had been nabbed for doing something. It was always doom and gloom" (The Ambler). This desire amongst hyperlocal practitioners to redress the reputational geography of a locality is something we explore in more depth in the next chapter.

Conclusion

In this chapter we presented findings on the scale, scope and content of the hyperlocal news sector in the UK. We found that the volume of stories collectively produced by these websites was impressive, with a high volume of stories being produced per day. The decline in the number of active sites by 2014 is largely attributable to the failure of a commercial network of hyperlocal websites, and some localities are either not served at all or very poorly served by hyperlocal news. The degree to which a hyperlocal website that publishes only one or two stories a week is making an effective contribution to the public sphere is debatable. Yet as Barnett and Townend argue, there is potential for hyperlocal to play a "major role in compensating for the decline of traditional local media and making a genuine contribution to local plurality" (2015: 344). Irrespective of their organisational set-up or the degree of professionalism of their journalists, Barnett and Townend argue that hyperlocals generally fulfil journalistic norms: they "contribute to local knowledge, to the accountability of local elites and to the ability of local people to lobby for change" (2015: 344). Our findings in this chapter would suggest that whilst this might be the case, it is only in those locations where sufficient numbers of hyperlocals are publishing regularly that their impact will be felt. To some extent, this research can be seen as an attempt to set a benchmark against which the future growth or otherwise of the hyperlocal sector can be mapped. What is clear is that this area of news publishing is highly dynamic, with many sites having relatively short but active lives. The findings outlined here should be viewed against the backdrop we outlined in chapter 2, in which local and regional newspapers have suffered from declining advertising revenues and circulations and have cut the number of journalists they employ.

Whilst the findings of our content analysis seem to suggest a lack of critical, investigative and campaigning journalism, the interviews and survey yielded clear data to the contrary. Many hyperlocal news producers cover the campaigns of others, and a significant minority have initiated their own campaigns. Critical investigations are also carried out by a (perhaps surprisingly) large number of UK community journalists on a wide variety of issues of public concern, and a small but effective group of hyperlocal sites devote themselves almost entirely to this kind of public interest news production. We found no evidence that any particular kind, or model, of hyperlocal outlet is more likely to produce campaigning, or critical, local news (e.g. sites run by former journalists are no more likely than those run by hobbyists to carry out such 'watchdog' journalism). We found a strong tendency among many community sites to want to produce news that paints their local areas in a positive light – something we explore later in this book – but this does not generally mean they shy away from writing critical stories where necessary. Many hyperlocals are, on the contrary, committed to producing news which fulfils the watchdog function of holding local elites to account. There remain doubts around whether online community news can actually play these roles in a balanced and meaningful way because of a range of potential problems, principally around economic sustainability and audience reach. In the next three chapters we shift our focus from examining what hyperlocals cover in order to further explore what motivates practitioners and how they sustain their operations.

Notes

1 Survey research was by Williams and Harte in partnership with Judith Townend and Steven Barnett. The sample was 183 publishers of hyperlocal sites and services in the UK, surveyed online from 5 December 2013 to −24 February 2014.
2 These attempts are archived at: https://web.archive.org/web/20100124213901/ http://map.hyperlocal.co.uk/ and https://web.archive.org/web/20110825045023/ http://www.nutshell.org.uk/about/
3 A source being the person or organisation who is quoted within an individual news story.

References

Barnett, Steven (2009) *Journalism, Democracy and the Public Interest: Rethinking Media Pluralism for the Digital Age*. Working Paper. Oxford: Reuters Institute for the Study of Journalism.
Barnett, Steven & Townend, Judith (2015) Plurality, policy and the local. *Journalism Practice*, Vol. 9, No. 3, pp. 332–349.

112 From lost pets to local corruption

Brixton Bugle (2017) Brixton Bugle [Online]. *Brixton Blog*. Available at: www.brixtonblog.com/bugle [Accessed 17 December 2017].

Department for Culture, Media and Sport (2013) *Media, Ownership and Plurality Consultation*. London: The Stationery Office.

Department for Culture, Media and Sport (2014) *Media Ownership & Plurality Consultation Report. Government Response to the House of Lords Select Committee on Communications Report into Media Plurality*. London: The Stationary Office.

DotEcon Ltd (2010) *A Framework to Approach Benefits to Consumers in Local Media Assessments*. London: DotEcon Ltd.

Forde, Susan (2011) *Challenging the News: The Journalism of Alternative and Community Media*. Basingstoke: Palgrave Macmillan.

Franklin, Bob & Carlson, Matt (2011) Introduction. In: Franklin, B. & Carlson, M. (eds) *Journalists, Sources, and Credibility*. London: Routledge, pp. 1–15.

Harcup, Tony & O'Neill, Deirdre (2001) What is news? Galtung and Ruge revisited. *Journalism Studies*, Vol. 2, No. 2, pp. 261–280.

Johnson, Steven (2009) Old growth media and the future of news [Online]. Available at: www.stevenberlinjohnson.com/2009/03/the-following-is-a-speech-i-gave-yesterday-at-the-south-by-southwest-interactive-festival-in-austiniif-you-happened-to-being.html [Accessed 24 February 2016].

Kentishtowner (2012) Advertise [Online]. Available at: https://www.kentishtowner.co.uk/advertise/ [Accessed 17 December 2017].

Lambourne, Helen (2013, 11 June) Freelance publishers axed from Local World sites [Online]. *Holdthefrontpage.co.uk*. Available at: www.holdthefrontpage.co.uk/2013/news/freelance-publishers-axed-from-local-world-sites/ [Accessed 12 May 2016].

London SE1 (n.d.) Spread the word about the SE1 website [Online]. Available at: www.london-se1.co.uk/spreadtheword [Accessed 17 December 2017].

Metzgar, Emily T., Kurpius, David D. & Rowley, Karen M. (2011) Defining hyperlocal media: Proposing a framework for discussion. *New Media & Society*, Vol. 13, No. 5, pp. 772–787.

Moore, Martin (2014) *Addressing the Democratic Deficit in Local News through Positive Plurality. Or, Why We Need a UK Alternative of the Knight News Challenge*. London: Media Standards Trust.

Nesta and Kantar Media (2013, April) *UK Demand for Hyperlocal Media: Research Report*. London: Nesta.

Ofcom (2009a) *Local and Regional Media in the UK*. London: Ofcom.

Ofcom (2009b) *Ofcom's Second Public Service Broadcasting Review*. London: Ofcom.

Ofcom (2010) *Communications Market Report*. London: Ofcom.

Ofcom (2011) *Proposed Acquisition by Kent Messenger Group of Seven Newspaper Titles from Northcliffe Media*. London: Ofcom.

Ofcom (2012a) *Communications Market Report 2012*. London: Ofcom.

Ofcom (2012b) *Report on Public Interest Test on the Acquisition of Guardian Media Group's Radio Stations (Real and Smooth) by Global Radio*. London: Ofcom.

Ofcom (2012c) *Report on Public Interest Test on the Acquisition of Guardian Media Group's Radio Stations (Real and Smooth) by Global Radio. Annex 4*. London: Ofcom.

Ofcom (2013) *Local World: Local Media Assessment*. London: Ofcom.

Ofcom (2014) *Internet Citizens*. London: Ofcom.

Ofcom (2015a) *Adults Media Use and Attitudes*. London: Ofcom.

Ofcom (2015b) *Measurement Framework for Media Plurality: Ofcom's Advice to the Secretary of State for Culture, Media and Sport*. London: Ofcom.

Perrin, William (2012) TfL and corporate manslaughter of London cyclists [Online]. *King's Cross Environment*. Available at: http://kingscrossenvironment.com/2012/01/16/tflcorp oratemanslaughter/ [Accessed 2 December 2015].

Perrin, William (2015) How big is my hyperlocal twitter audience? [Online]. *Talk About Local*. Available at: https://talkaboutlocal.org.uk/how-big-is-my-hyperlocal-twitter-audience/ [Accessed 17 December 2017].

Radcliffe, Damian (2012) *Here and Now: UK Hyperlocal Media Today*. London: Nesta.

Sheppard, Jonathan (2013) Has Shotton got the dirtiest street in Wales? [Online]. *Deeside.com*. Available at: www.deeside.com/front-page/has-shotton-got-the-dirtiest-street-in-wa les-21-loads-of-dog-dirt-in-a-4-minute-walk/ [Accessed 2 December 2015].

South Leeds Life (2017) Newspaper [Online]. Available at: www.southleedslife.com/news paper/ [Accessed 17 December 2017].

Spiers, J. (1974) *The Underground and Alternative Press in Britain: A Bibliographical Guide with Historical Notes*. Brighton: Harvester Press.

Taggart, Chris (2010, 13 January) Yet another UK Hyperlocal Directory … but this time it's open data [Online]. *countculture*. Available at: http://countculture.wordpress.com/2010/01/13/yet-another-uk-hyperlocal-directory-but-this-time-its-open-data/ [Accessed 12 February 2013].

Taggart, Chris (n.d.) New hyperlocal site [Online]. *Openly Local*. Available at: http://op enlylocal.com/hyperlocal_sites/new [Accessed 12 February 2013].

Williams, Andy, Barnett, Steven, Harte, Dave & Townend, Judith (2014) *The State of Hyperlocal Community News in the UK: Findings from a Survey of Practitioners* [Online]. Available at: https://hyperlocalsurvey.files.wordpress.com/2014/07/hyperlocal-community-news-in-the-uk-2014.pdf [Accessed 12 May 2015].

5

PRACTISING HYPERLOCAL JOURNALISM – AUTHENTICITY AND RECIPROCITY

In this chapter, we set out the motivations and practices of hyperlocal journalists. We describe how hyperlocal journalists draw heavily on a civic values discourse in order to contextualise their practice and how that in turn motivates them to be an authentic voice for citizens. The intention in this analysis is to reveal the discourses that are drawn upon by hyperlocal practitioners when discussing what they do. We set our findings against two interpretative repertoires – authenticity and reciprocity – that emerged in the analysis of our interviews. Wetherell and Potter make the point that "language is put together, constructed, for purposes and to achieve particular consequences" (1988: 171). Because language use varies amongst those who may be talking about the same subject, we need to look to the repertoires that are being drawn upon (Wetherell and Potter 1988: 172). The repertoires limit the possible ways that the speaker can talk about a subject but allow for variance: "repertoires can be seen as the building blocks speakers use for constructing versions of actions, cognitive processes and other phenomena" (Wetherell and Potter 1988: 172). Sally Reardon draws on Wetherell and Potter's work to analyse accreditation and training materials for journalists in order to reveal the "competing discursive constructions of what it takes to be a journalist" (Reardon 2016: 942). Reardon finds that the materials construct a set of repertoires related to the notion of what it takes to be a journalist. Ultimately, these repertoires narrow the framing of what the journalist does "either as a natural activity born of natural talent or learnt from those with experience and natural talent" (Reardon 2016: 946). Platon and Deuze also draw on Wetherell and Potter's work in order to examine how Indymedia activists "talk about, and give meaning to, their everyday experiences" (Platon and Deuze 2003: 344). They found that workers legitimise their voluntary labour by drawing on a set of "consensual ideals" (Platon and Deuze 2003: 345) that distinguish how Indymedia sites work from the operation of mainstream media sites. Yet Platon and

Deuze also found that when discussing journalistic practices, these same workers would draw on a normative journalistic discourse.

Our interviews were thus designed to gain a producer perspective on the practices of hyperlocal news and also to identify the repertoires they draw on in order to legitimise their work. It's worth nothing that the degree of formal journalistic experience varied enormously amongst our interviewees; the many gradations ranged from experienced, formally trained journalists to those with no experience at all. Some had worked as journalists in the mainstream press yet had never received formal training. Others had a public relations background with first degrees that involved elements of journalism theory and practice. Clearly, some could be regarded as 'amateur', but Denis McQuail sums up the increasing problem of trying to label journalists as either 'professional' or 'amateur', especially in the Internet age, which is "encouraging new forms of journalism ... rejecting formal organisation and with it any claim to professional status" (2013: 92). It's evident, argues McQuail, that journalism in mainstream organisations has become increasingly professionalised, requiring higher-level qualifications, whilst in the alternative realm such requirements do not apply. Yet the "traditional norms and practices" (McQuail 2013: 94) might be as evident in the latter as in the former. Tony Harcup's (2005) research into the motivations of journalists working across both mainstream and alternative journalism found that most had started with no formal training but had worked on alternative publications through a desire to "change the world" (Harcup 2005: 370). Formal training tended to come later or even, in some cases, not at all, the alternative 'journalist' being readily accepted into the mainstream through the richness of their experience.

First, we discuss 'authenticity' as key motivating factor and, second, how 'reciprocity' underpins almost every aspect of newsgathering practices. These discursive repertoires can be seen as part of a legitimising strategy by hyperlocal publishers. Nick Couldry's (2004) work provides a useful framing for this analysis. He argues that there has been a collapse in citizens' trust of the "large actors" of politics and economics in society. Trust is vital for successful democracies (and, for that matter, for successful economies), so where do we look to find trust being rebuilt? To citizens themselves: "the production practices of consumers aimed at generating or sustaining, through participation, new spaces of public connection, new spaces of mutuality" (Couldry 2004: 24). Couldry cites some specific examples of community media sites using open publishing platforms (such as Indymedia) that seem able to make highly effective contributions to the public sphere (2004: 26). Such examples are, claims Mark Deuze (2006), part of a move towards participatory media that began in the latter half of the 20th century as an inevitable reflection of the shift towards monitorial citizenships in Western democracies. Deuze even makes the claim that the default mode for media-making is local and participatory rather than commercial and closed:

> it becomes possible to argue that people using and making their own individual, local and communal media is the structural condition of media, culture

116 Practising hyperlocal journalism

and society relationships, whereas the notion of national mass media telling an invisible audience what they "need to know" is an anomalous trend particular to the forming of modern nation-states.

(2006: 267)

But such claims require empirical research, Couldry argues. Central to a questioning of media operations at the heart of this participatory shift is a need to examine "the stability of the new forms of trust on which they rely" (Couldry 2004: 27). For hyperlocal publishing, this requires a focus on the relationship between journalists and citizens as much as it does an examination of the sustainability of these operations. Thus, in the discussion of interview data here, we look at reciprocity practices as mechanisms for building trust. Are hyperlocal publishers "trusted agents" (Couldry 2004: 24) that can rebuild social capital in communities and thereby "refashion belief in larger forms of connection" (23)?

Authenticity as a motivating factor

In this section, we discuss what motivates hyperlocal publishers. Our interviewees were asked directly about why they started their publications or, where they had taken over another hyperlocal (which was only the case for three of them), why they had decided to become involved. Initial analysis suggested that those without any prior journalism experience had slightly different motivations than those who did have experience. Two key origin stories were cited by the former that were different to the group that had some form of journalism experience: first, the desire to redress existing media coverage of their localities and, second, the development of a single-issue campaign into a full-blown hyperlocal news operation. In both cases, issues of authenticity were to the fore.

Redressing reputational geography

Those without a formal journalistic background were more likely to outline origin stories that had a more reputational/civic emphasis. It was often cited that starting a hyperlocal media operation was a way to redress how mainstream media covered (or did not cover) their area:

> Another motivation was that the local newspaper, which … has a very kind of negative slant on life as we see it, and we felt there were a lot of positive things going on that basically didn't even get on the radar of the local paper because either they were very small local things which perhaps a citywide newspaper wasn't really interested in or, as we felt, they just didn't bother covering a lot of the good stuff that went on. So those were two of our motivations.
>
> *(Wrexham.com)*

The feeling that newspapers veered towards negative coverage was a repeated concern:

> they were cherry picking the news and they were verging towards more negative news. ... It was more 80 per cent negative with the rest of it being a mixture of mediocre beige and positive news, and I didn't like that. I didn't like that at all.
>
> *(Knutsford Times)*

Expressing a strong local identity was something that a hyperlocal might do where the mainstream press, covering a larger area, would not have the chance to:

> I'm very passionate about what's happening in Digbeth and how unique it is in terms of an area within a city. We have no chain outlets, all our shops are independently owned, all our restaurants and pubs are all independently owned, which makes for a really vibrant area.
>
> *(Digbeth is Good)*

The interviewees (with a single exception) lived in the places they operated from, so exploring the role of media in placemaking was an oft-cited motivating factor: "Something like that could bring people together to some degree, and it could create some sort of sense of place I suppose" (Bitterne Park). Righting a perceived wrong in terms of reputational geography was a gap that could be filled: "If the newspapers are not going to print what we know is right about the town, then why don't we start our own newspaper? And so, we thought, yes, that's a good idea" (Wayland News). This particular interviewee felt they were representing a wider community view about the way in which the press handles bad news:

> If there's a bad news story, it goes on the front page; if there's a good news story, it doesn't go in; and that is the perception. And people don't like that, certainly here people do still feel a connection with their community, and when people attack their community, there's a kind of collective backlash to that.
>
> *(Wayland News)*

One interviewee with a professional background in public relations saw the chance to bring their expertise in using media in a persuasive way to redress negative media representations:

> My background's in PR and I spent many years telling people that they needed stuff that they couldn't afford and they wanted stuff that they couldn't afford and they didn't need. So I know how you can shape people's feelings about things, and I find that the local press, if you tell someone something's shit long enough, they'll start believing it, and that's how the local press is

118 Practising hyperlocal journalism

about the town. My motivation was to reverse that trend and get people feeling positive about the place.

(Bedford Clanger)

The presentation of 'good news' about their localities was seen by these interviewees as a way to give a more authentic impression of place. But there was also recognition that this brought its own issues:

I think if we do get criticised, it's for being a bit too rose-tinted. I have heard us described as "an organ of puffery", which actually I took as a huge insult and sulked for quite a while and then decided it was probably fair actually. We're here to promote the town. We do acknowledge that there's the bad side of stuff, but I think we tend to let the mainstream press deal with that.

(The Ambler)

This tendency to let other news outlets deal with 'bad news' was widely cited. It was often a case of the hyperlocal feeling they were too personally tied to an area to be able to report on such issues: "I'm sometimes reluctant to cover crime because I know so many people in the community, or a sudden death in the community because it's kind of a bit in your face if you see it on a local site" (Gurn Nurn). The proximity to audience can result in uncomfortable encounters for those who do cover crime: "There's a couple of crime stories we've published where we've had people in the street shout at us and call us grasses" (Wrexham. com). Yet it is clear that crime stories generate traffic to the websites ("we clocked onto the fact that crime was quite a popular thing" – Balsall Common), which creates a tension for many hyperlocal publishers. They want the traffic to their websites, but feel that reporting too much crime results in an inauthentic impression of their area. One hyperlocal discussed this issue at length, at first realising that coverage of these stories was popular but then receiving backlash from locals directly named in the story. Their solution to deal with this was to stop doing their own coverage and instead simply point to mainstream local press coverage, creating a critical distance for themselves:

So what we try and do is, if there is a proper source … and they're covering some incident, we might make a reference to it and the article. So we still get all the traffic but we don't name names. We let the other side do that, and we don't show pictures of the people either. So we like doing crime but we have to have a distance with crime because of the local issue of you've got to walk down the same street as some of these people.

(Balsall Common)

The use of "proper source" in this response might suggest that the hyperlocal publisher has doubts about their own legitimacy. Yet in shifting responsibility to the newspaper they potentially retain legitimacy locally by remaining on the community's 'side' and purporting to be an advocate for the 'authentic' image of the area. Other interviewees also revealed how they tailor their news coverage to manage their area's reputation: "I do have concerns about reporting on crime, and my concerns are [about] creating the impression that the area is ... well, it could easily give the impression that it's a crime-riddled area" (Bitterne Park). Justin Lewis (2006) argues that coverage of crime can be problematic in creating an informed citizenship. The decision by a hyperlocal publisher to cover or not cover crime stories can be seen as part of a wider placemaking strategy that many of these publishers consciously enact in order to construct what they imagine to be a more authentic sense of place.

Other origin stories that were connected to a placemaking theme tended to be based around a personal desire to discover what was happening locally.

> After being made redundant, it was about setting up something for my home town so I could literally, after living away for a number of years, rediscover my own town.
>
> *(Hedon Blog)*

> I'd moved up ... from the south and I thought it was a good idea to join in, make friends and get involved, so that's how it started. Then I realised it might be exactly the sort of thing that I wanted to do; it was brilliant.
>
> *(The Ambler)*

Whatever the initial motivation, the desire to write against the grain of the approach taken by mainstream media and to gain legitimacy in the eyes of their audiences was most often enacted by telling 'everyday' stories. This approach acted to resist the dominant narratives of the mainstream press and also provided no end of content, even when the areas covered were very small.

> The amount of material a community [produces] is infinite because everybody has a story and everybody has a point of view, and if they're willing to talk to you, you can have this information.
>
> *(Gurn Nurn)*

> We also at the beginning, as probably most hyperlocal publishers do, thought we might actually run out of ideas when we're just dealing with a small geographic area, but that's been anything but the case. In fact there's a massive backlog of things we want to cover and simply haven't got round to doing.
>
> *(Kentishtowner)*

Starting with a campaign

Another theme to emerge in origin stories from non-journalists, but rarely from journalists, was the way in which single-issue campaigns had snowballed into broader-based operations:

120 Practising hyperlocal journalism

> I was never interested in anything to do with community; it just didn't interest me and then I think moving into an area and becoming settled, I got interested in how fast cars were going in front of our house. I got sick of it and I started, in the most minor way possible, a campaign to try and get traffic calming outside our house. … It was just one of those things that took over. It wasn't planned in any way, but then people in the local area started campaigns about things they did and didn't want to happen.
>
> *(Southwark Living Streets)*

> Another one came about due to our son's school being closed and at the time, this was 2007, there wasn't really much in the way of online activism or anywhere online people could get behind a cause and ask questions. So we felt we'd kind of been victims of the school closing and how that was done by the local council. We felt that we'd like to provide somewhere should issues as this occur again, and if it did occur again, people had somewhere they could voice their concerns and talk with other people online.
>
> *(Wrexham.com)*

One interviewee told a long story about the ways in which he was "messed around with the council" when dealing with a local road issue. He took to the Internet as a space in which to put his side of the argument: "I thought this was a big enough fib [by the council] to put on the website so I put up the documents with comments, and that's what gradually snowballed from other people with similar experiences" (Bexley Is Bonkers).

Direct involvement in politics was rarely cited as a reason for starting a hyperlocal operation, but in one case a desire to become a local whistle-blower after being involved in local party politics resulted in an operation solely focused on holding the local council to account (Star and Crescent). For another, it was the inability of the local newspaper to adequately deal with a campaign issue that turned into a catalyst for the beginnings of their own enterprise: "Personally speaking, it's come from the experience of local media covering an important issue to me personally, which was the plight of the local football club" (Wrexham.com).

Where those with some journalistic experience discussed campaigns that helped them begin their hyperlocal experience, these tended to be expressed in terms of the campaign's usefulness in helping them set out the terms under which they would operate, or as a useful boost to visitor numbers:

> So that [the campaign issue] came to the fore and there was a little bit of community activity around opposing that, and I thought that this was a way that the site could be used to put an alternative view really.
>
> *(Bitterne Park)*

In another case, concerns over a local regeneration scheme enabled the hyperlocal to situate itself as the voice of the community:

> The stories come from that community itself, and then what we do is we try and give them a voice as much as possible, backed up by investigative research, which is where I come in because, obviously, I've got the background to do that. You can't expect community people to go and research 100-page reports from the council or wherever.
>
> *(Salford Star)*

Filling the gap and learning new skills

Those with a professional journalism background had, broadly, two reasons for starting a hyperlocal news operation. One set of responses was around skills and the desire to learn new digital skills or different aspects of journalism:

> The motivation, really to train me up more as a journalist and get a feel for what it's like reporting more local news as opposed to the national things I was used to doing.
>
> *(Salford Star)*

> I kind of wanted to keep a hand in doing journalism-related stuff, and my job now isn't as directly related as it might be, so there's a personal motivation to actually keep my skills up in that area.
>
> *(Crosspool News)*

But like the group of non-journalists, this group also saw opportunities in addressing what mainstream journalism was failing to cover. In their view, the gap was not so much in terms of creating positive stories to address perceived misrepresentation; rather, it was a concern about what was being lost given the decline of the local press. "Local news is dying on its feet" (Wayland News), as one interviewee put it. Another noted, "You've got issues with crime and it's almost a shame because none of the traditional newspapers distribute to that area by large, so there's a big gap" (North Solihull). Other articulations of the problem offered a more detailed analysis:

> I always felt that, as regional papers lost more and more staff … they simply weren't able to get out into the communities as much as they used to, and I always felt that one of the USPs of a regional or local paper was that you felt it represented the communities. What I've noticed with the newspapers is they're having to kind of fall back on more centralised-type news – councils, courts and things like that – and they simply don't get out into the communities any more, and it seemed to me like there was a gap in the market.
>
> *(Filton Voice)*

> I was aware at the time that the [local mainstream newspaper] had limited coverage of council business, and what business it was running was largely based on press releases and contacts within the council. There wasn't very much that was there that was actually questioning how decisions were made, so I sort of rolled into it. I mean mostly because I enjoy it. I'm interested in finding stories.
>
> *(Leeds Citizen)*

In contrast to the non-journalists, this group were more likely to talk about the detail of how they could create stories for their area:

> I would see lots of things that weren't being covered. I don't mean big crime, just lots of things. There are characters from the area, there are people that have done unusual stuff, and it's almost the sort of thing you would make a 350-word page lead with a picture. It was just different, it was either really small or it just wouldn't fit in with what a newspaper would normally do.
>
> *(Cwmbran Life)*

This particular interviewee was one of very few who expressed that you might be able to do something a little different with the form of journalism produced, contrasting with the expectations of local newspapers: "Yes, the hyperlocal, the blogging side, allows you to do stuff that doesn't fit into that classic newspaper style" (Cwmbran Life).

On the whole, amongst both groups of hyperlocalists, 'filling the gap' was a common theme. Sometimes the motivation came about as a result of a seeming lack of innovation in the local press: "It was the fact that no one was doing it. The local paper were way behind on technology, I mean way behind" (Knutsford Times). In another case the interviewee had worked on a commercial hyperlocal operation that had ceased and wasn't keen to return to mainstream media: "I kind of got a taste for it" (West Leeds Dispatch). But the overriding rationale was articulated as a civic duty, rather than a gap in the market from which a clear, scalable entrepreneurial opportunity existed.

Shifting motivations

Some interviewees still felt a 'buzz' from their work when asked if their motivations had changed over time. In only one case was this feeling expressed in the context of the professional norms of journalism: "In a way, and I think most journalists will understand this, it's just the curiosity of wanting to know more" (Inside Croydon). The more frequent response was more emotive: "I still love doing it, I've no intentions of stopping it. But my motivation? The reasons why? Exactly the same" (Cwmbran Life). "I still get pretty much the same buzz" (Leeds Citizen). In one case, the hyperlocal practice had gone from a rather secretive affair (due to concerns about being unemployed and publishing at the same time) to a proudly public-facing one where being seen as the local 'blogger' was a point of personal pride:

> Something that gives me a real buzz is when I hear people say, or I'll see on Facebook, if you like, people are saying, "Oh we're going to get covered by the Hedon Blog", "They're coming down to take photos", and stuff like that. I get a real buzz out of that because it's like people get excited now by being on the blog, so that's good, so I get quite chuffed about that.
>
> *(Hedon Blog)*

Some felt that, over time, they had become more aware of the impact they were having in the community:

> As the site has gone on, three and a half years later, it's suddenly become a lot bigger for a start than I thought it ever would. So I feel that an audience has been built and now the site is trying to do something positive for the town with that audience in a way.
>
> *(A Little Bit of Stone)*

Most felt sure their endeavours were impactful and purposeful: "I really want to make a difference to the community, always wanted to make a difference to the community. That, I think at the moment, is what keeps me going" (Wayland News). For one trained journalist, the setting up and running of his hyperlocal site had deepened his commitment to the local area: "I love where I live, I love this town, and doing this site has actually increased and cemented that even more" (A Little Bit of Stone).

The journey for many has been one of discovery, both of themselves and of their community. Another interviewee came to realise that their personal blogging might have a wider benefit:

> I think I discovered a local community in my town which I was quite surprised existed, that actually there was lots going on. I started not just recording our own experiences of doing things, but it was very much about what I'd found out and what else was going on. So it started plugging notices about events and activities that were going on, and lo and behold, people actually started to read it. … So the whole focus of it changed from being one of something personal to one of actually this is providing something useful as well.
>
> *(Hedon Blog)*

In this case, the interviewee described how his operation went from being "useful" by listing events and publishing notices to being "useful" through participation in campaigning. Similar to those who described how they became involved with

124 Practising hyperlocal journalism

hyperlocals through a single-issue campaign, it was a campaign that proved transformative here:

> Since then, the audience for the blog has just kind of grown and grown. We've become not just something that comments on but also something that potentially people know that we – I always use this word "we", I think of us as we…
>
> *(Hedon Blog)*

It is clear that many working in this space have a real sense of pride in their work. When prompted about the stories they had published that they were most proud of, almost all the examples were of single-issue campaigns that they had ownership of from the outset and which played a key role in holding power to account and creating impact. These moments emerged as a key motivating factor for many to continue.

Authenticity as an interpretative repertoire

In looking across the range of motivations that hyperlocal practitioners had in starting, and continuing, their operations, central to all is a desire to be authentic. This was expressed by some as dissatisfaction with existing media representations of their locality, their frustration most often being with the lack of coverage or the wrong kind of coverage. A lack of coverage resulted in a 'gap' that could be filled, and thus the authenticity repertoire becomes about being authentic to the perceived role of journalism. Indeed, those from a professional journalism background noticed that the thinning out of editorial staff in the mainstream press meant that the opportunity for them to carry out investigative, accountability or campaigning journalism presented itself. Likewise, the wrong kind of coverage also created a gap of sorts; that is, a gap in positive news, a deficit in everyday stories, to counter the bad news. This issue was also framed around issues of authenticity in terms of how mainstream local press failed to reflect the authentic experience of living in the areas; what was at stake was the reputation of the area, and the hyperlocalists were there to 'save' it. In this way, they are active placemakers and perhaps more than a little conflicted by the position of power they hold. Hyperlocal publishers are very conscious that what they choose to talk about can affect their area's reputational geography. Those without journalism training felt most strongly that they wanted to say something positive and thought that existing press coverage simply was not giving the whole picture. For them, being positive was about being authentic.

As they continued their operations, hyperlocal publishers from both backgrounds were often motivated by a feeling that their role as the authentic voice of community was legitimised, and overall we can see that the "civil society purpose" (Flouch and Harris 2010: 2) is a dominant motivating factor for hyperlocal journalists. Indeed, as we observe in the next part of this chapter, this civic discourse looms large. They seek to strengthen their personal connection to their community by creating a resource that they consider useful: "A chance for me living in the actual community myself to give something back" (Crosspool News). In almost all cases, they began without a plan of any sort, but often with a sense of a 'wrong' that needed to be righted. They then began a journey in which they drew on journalistic practices that they considered to offer an authentic voice for the communities they represented. The reciprocal nature of these practices is discussed in the next part of this chapter.

Reciprocity in newsgathering practices

Hyperlocal producers are very much embedded in their neighbourhoods. The same might once have been true of the local press, as the case study in chapter 3 of local newspapers in Port Talbot suggests. Hyperlocal journalists offered up many examples of working both the digital 'beat' and the real-world 'beat'. Both are key elements of how they gather news, and in discussing these practices, interviewees further revealed their strategies to legitimise their operations in the eyes of their audience. Here we outline the range of practices that hyperlocals utilise in order to generate content for their services and sustain them. We note the emphasis is on developing authentic relationships with citizens and explore how these contribute to sustaining and legitimising their operations. The news-making practices outlined here, of gathering and publishing news, draw on but also sometimes reject existing professional journalistic norms and values. We utilise the notion of 'reciprocity journalism' in order to frame our discussion (Borger *et al.* 2016; Holton *et al.* 2015; Lewis 2015; Lewis *et al.* 2014). The concept approaches reciprocity as a social good underpinning strong communities, specifically in relation to the development of "trust, connectedness, and social capital", what Lewis *et al.* call "the bundle of normative expectations and networked resources that are critical for the formation and maintenance of community ties" (2014: 229). Reciprocity has, they explain, been central to the functioning of both geographical communities and virtual online communities, but theirs was the first application of the concept in the sphere of journalism. Such an application is important because journalists can no longer be seen simply as content creators, but increasingly must also be seen as community builders who can enable and catalyse reciprocal exchange in social media spaces in numerous ways: *directly* for their readers, *indirectly* among the broader community, and repeatedly over time in a *sustained* way (Lewis *et al.* 2014).

The communicative architecture of social media commonly invites direct reciprocal exchanges; for example, in acts of liking, sharing and commenting on the communications of others. We often give in ways that do not guarantee us immediately getting something back in return, in the expectation of being at the receiving end of equivalent acts of goodwill in the future. Indeed, as Lewis *et al.* point out, the success of most social media networks, and other Web 2.0 communications, rests on this kind of direct reciprocity (they cite the examples of bloggers hyperlinking to each other's posts, Reddit users upvoting each other's contributions, or journalists retweeting each other's stories). Direct reciprocity takes place at the level of the individual, and it helps cement relationships between individuals. But the Internet has also enabled more diffuse forms of reciprocal exchange. Indirect reciprocity happens "when the beneficiary of an act returns the favour not to the giver, but to another member of the social network" (Lewis *et al.* 2014: 234). This kind of collective act of paying it forward is seen as more effective than direct reciprocity when "producing social solidarity, social unity, and trust, as participants begin to see themselves as more of a collective" (Lewis *et al.* 2014: 234). Local social cohesion is potentially well served by this kind of community-building activity. Examples given include: using a network to relay information quickly and accurately; connecting people with useful sources of information; and matching resources with those in need of them (Lewis *et al.* 2014).

It is sustained reciprocity, though, that marks the apotheosis of reciprocal communicative exchange in communities. Direct and indirect reciprocal acts can often be immediate and fleeting, but sustained reciprocity can only be achieved when relationships of exchange can be sustained over time and in ways that ensure a steady stream of continued acts of mutual goodwill. This kind of reciprocity is desirable because it involves "lasting forms of exchange that deepen collective trust, social capital, and overall connectedness – essential components for the vitality of communities of all kinds" (Lewis *et al.* 2014: 230). This, it is suggested, will help with the development of normatively positive effects on communities; namely, that they will become more trusting, more connected and engaged with each other, and richer in terms of the social capital of their members.

The novelty of this theory in journalism studies means that it has not often been applied in discussions of news media of any kind, but some empirical studies have recently put the concept to use. Holton *et al.* (2015) aimed to analyse public perceptions of reciprocity and people's reciprocal practices on social media as a way of understanding potential participation in acts of news production and co-production. They found key indicators of the relevance of reciprocity in theorising "the news interaction process" as well as social media and society more broadly (Holton *et al.* 2015: 2526). Borger *et al.*'s (2016) application of the reciprocal journalism framework focused on a commercial hyperlocal news project in the Netherlands. They examined the specific mechanisms that allow for reciprocal exchange (such as those on a website) and found that sustained reciprocity (of which social capital is a vital part) was not achieved simply because the reciprocal mechanism existed. Rather, it had to be worked at, be committed to by the journalists, or else failure was inevitable (Borger *et al.* 2016: 722).

At its root, reciprocity, or "returning one favourable action for another" is seen as a social good which encourages participation, discourse and dynamism among online and offline communities (Lewis *et al.* 2014: 230). Community journalism is seen as a sphere where this form of exchange might be explored because of the "distinct closeness" between producers and audiences at this level (Lewis *et al.* 2014: 230), in contrast with the more or less distant, exploitative or dysfunctional exchange relations that seem common among established legacy media participatory practices explored above. We are drawn to this theory to help understand the value of UK hyperlocal news, at least in part, because of its levelling approach to understanding the value of participatory reciprocal acts both on- and offline. Lewis *et al.*'s (2014) examples relate overwhelmingly to the online journalistic social media practices of community news workers. We are acutely aware, however, that many in the UK hyperlocal sector encourage, foster and enable participation both in journalistic and non-journalistic ways and both in virtual communities on the Internet and in real-world community settings. In the section that follows, we demonstrate some of the ways in which online and offline reciprocal relationships can inform hyperlocal news and improve connectedness between people in local areas to the advantage of community cohesion.

Reciprocal practices on- and offline

Direct reciprocity refers to a mutual exchange between individuals. Lewis *et al.* (2014: 233) make the distinction between unilateral, informal reciprocal exchange (where nothing is expected in return but something is often given) and bilateral, negotiated exchange (where there is an agreement or contract in place, or perhaps just a clearer sense that information gathered would be used). The benefit of the unilateral exchange is that whilst there is a risk of not getting anything back, there is greater potential to "demonstrate and develop trust and social bonding" (Lewis *et al.* 2014: 233). We can see much evidence of unilateral exchange in newsgathering practices of hyperlocals.

Social media (particularly Twitter and Facebook; other platforms were very rarely mentioned in our interviews) is at the heart of newsgathering practices for hyperlocals. Facebook in particular has clearly become a key tool for newsgathering. Many hyperlocals talked about getting "tip-offs" through this platform, and it was repeatedly cited as a key resource for interaction with citizens. In fact, it was often the case that Facebook Pages for hyperlocals developed a life of their own with relatively little intervention from the publisher. As well as a place to enact the everyday digital beat, Facebook was also utilised to gather eyewitness accounts of breaking news incidents: "The first question would be to put something out on the Facebook group and ask anybody if anyone's seen what's going on in this particular area?" (Salford Online). Twitter was also cited as a place to gather news: "I might do a word search or a place name search on Twitter and see if there's anything going on there" (The Kirkbymoorside Town Blog). There was certainly a tendency to manage Twitter more carefully (usually by not following too many people) and to use it largely to seek out stories rather than as a distribution platform: "I use Twitter as a means of gathering information really; the people I follow are people who I think will provide me with leads for stories, just keep me informed" (Broughton Spurtle). However, in one case the interviewee felt there was a lack of willingness of citizens to participate in this way due to cynicism about the reputation of the mainstream press and the media in general: "I think some of that residual distrust sort of bleeds through a bit" (North Solihull).

128 Practising hyperlocal journalism

Social media's value as providing participatory news platforms was also seen in more serious hard news examples. During the UK's 2011 summer riots, one hyperlocal publisher used Twitter as a way to counter emerging myths about the extent of rioting in their locality. They identified tweets that were based on rumours and retweeted them with additional fact-checked input to counter the circulation of myths and untruths. Ironically, in this example it was the mainstream media that initially tweeted that the rioting had spread to this producer's area:

> Because the *Guardian* tweeted this, it got a huge amount of reaction and, frankly, panic and nervousness, and people getting very anxious about this. So I ended up, not really deliberately, sitting at my desk all evening and well into the night just kind of keeping a track of what was actually happening, what people were saying was happening, and trying to dispel the myths.
>
> *(West Hampstead Life)*

Unable to rely on mainstream media for a true picture of what was happening, the hyperlocal publisher drew on local volunteers, as well as trusted local eyewitnesses on social media, to provide their own verification: "A friend of mine ... basically got on his bike and cycled up and down the high road and reported back to me what was going on so I could keep people up to date; I trusted his reports" (West Hampstead Life). Another London-based hyperlocal publisher, with previous experience as a professional reporter, gave a similar account of using people he knew in order to provide eyewitness accounts:

> I sat at my desk that night and my older boy, who hadn't yet gone off to university, and his mate were sent out. I told them, under strict instructions, to observe and not engage and to text me and phone me with updates, send me pictures back and to be back here by 9.30.
>
> *(Inside Croydon)*

In each of these cases the online practices of the hyperlocal have been centred around using indirect reciprocity as a strategy to counter rumours; that is, using their own networks to identify trusted sources and combining those with the eyewitness accounts of their volunteers in order to create new and more accurate and reliable content that is then circulated within the network and beyond.

Beyond newsgathering and managing, the ability to like, share or retweet content on social media platforms is cited frequently as a way for hyperlocals to reciprocate the contributions from their audience. Using the direct reciprocal functions of social media was seen as a way to play a community role such as promoting local interests:

> I've got a list of local businesses who are on Twitter, and I go through that list of local businesses and see what they're tweeting about on a Saturday morning

and I retweet as many of them as I can if they are of any interest, just so local
businesses get a little bit of a boost on a weekend morning.

(Broughton Spurtle)

The other way I use social media … if someone says we could do with a tweet
about this, that and the other, I thought well, I know that they won't be able
to write the article. I certainly haven't got time to structure anything. There's
no photograph with it, so what I will do is I will retweet something or tweet
it or even copy it in on Facebook if I can to help someone get some exposure.

(Knutsford Times)

Social media thus makes reciprocation simple and swift. Likewise, the ability to
easily embed content from Twitter results in a simple way to create content on the
hyperlocal site and offers the reader a clear indication that their content may be
used: "So just embed that straight in – that's your story, that's the picture" (Gurn
Nurn). This is a direct reciprocal exchange process; which is to say, if someone
tweets about something in their locality, there is a chance that this will be utilised
by the hyperlocal. Many hyperlocals also make direct calls for participation from
their audience through their website or via social media:

Every article online has a begging letter attached to it saying, "What do you
think about this?", "Send us your views"; and we'll give people a range of
ways they can do it with links to our email, to our Twitter feed, to Facebook,
whatever they're more comfortable with.

(Broughton Spurtle)

In gathering news via this method and asking for contributions, the hyperlocal
publisher relies on a degree of trust built up between themselves and the audience;
that is, the audience trust that their content will be considered for use.

There is no doubt that social media content provides a set of 'assets' that
hyperlocal producers can create value from. It is increasingly as central to hyperlocal
practice as it is in mainstream practice. One publisher saw it as a valid emergent
form of journalism: "I came across someone who was doing something local-ish,
just retweeting stuff, and I thought, I wonder if we can do more with that. So that
was one angle, was Twitter a way of doing local news?" (West Hampstead Life).
For time-poor hyperlocal publishers, this practice of "gatewatching" (Bruns 2003)
was very common, with publishers acting as "internet 'librarians'" very much in
the mode that Bruns articulated for the role: "personally involved, 'of the people'
and partisan" (34). The use of networked strategies such as hashtags on social media
platforms could be seen as a more developed example of indirect reciprocity (Lewis
et al. 2014: 235). Hashtags allow anyone to contribute to conversations or infor-
mation-gathering and are not reliant on a direct exchange with the hyperlocal
publisher. Borger *et al.* (2016), applying the reciprocal journalism framework to a

commercial hyperlocal news project in the Netherlands, argue that they did not find examples of indirect reciprocity in either of the two projects they examined. There was plenty of direct exchange between individual reporter and reader, but concerns about quality prevented a more developed, networked participation (Borger *et al.* 2016: 721). In our research, practitioners rarely outlined strategies that were focused on developed inter-citizen, and therefore indirect, information exchange.

But some publishers did see value in the more ordinary, everyday use of social media: "[It's] just banal chat half the time, but that's a big community-building aspect" (West Hampstead Life). Others were beginning to recognise the value of the network that extended out from their own: "[I] send that out [via Facebook] and you know straight away that's gone out to 5,000 people, and then they'll share that to other people" (Saddleworth News). This shows the possibility of a more indirect approach, recognising the value in the more generalised connections that are created by a kind of 'pay it forward' approach: "Person A gives to Person B, who gives to Person C, and so on. Such gestures benefit members of the network and indicate to other potential members the bond shared within that group" (Lewis *et al.* 2014: 234). Lewis' suggestion is that the route to sustained reciprocity is through a recognition of the potential in this kind of network, therefore the development of a community-building strategy is vital: "community-builders … catalyze reciprocal exchange – directly with audiences/users, indirectly among community members, and repeatedly over time, altogether encouraging the kind of social norms associated with reciprocity writ large" (2015: 2).

For many hyperlocal producers, the key barrier to more sophisticated use of social media was time. In their eyes, it was too much of a distraction. Better to avoid reciprocation than to have too much information to deal with:

> We don't retweet anybody because, again, if you retweet one lost cat story or charitable jumble sale story, then why not do them all? So we've had to have a policy of not retweeting anybody and we don't interact.
>
> *(Kentishtowner)*

Others discussed their management of social media as part of a gatekeeping process in order to apply traditional news values to the information received from readers:

> It's just someone extending their garage and the neighbour has a problem with it; it's not the sort of story we would be looking at. We try to look at the stories which have impact on a larger amount of people.
>
> *(The Lincolnite)*

It was recognised that discourse on Facebook can also be problematic: "You know the way, how things in small communities can kick off on Facebook and they can become quite ugly and sometimes vile" (Gurn Nurn). Yet more than any other social media network, it was seen as a platform that people were willing to contribute to: "I suppose Facebook really is great because people are comfortable on Facebook, they're comfortable with responding" (The Ambler). However, in one case it was clear that the interviewee saw the potential of Facebook as a place to generate stories from contentious commenting, and they were not afraid to manipulate debate in order to generate lively interactions: "It's really quite easy and interesting to tweak that group and have a little firestorm of opinion and just watch it unfold" (Broughton Spurtle).

Reciprocation on the real-world 'beat'

Overall, social media was very much a space about which hyperlocal publishers spoke with a degree of tension, even when practitioners highly valued its reciprocal nature. In contrast, offline engagement was largely discussed in wholly positive terms. The interviewees offered up many examples of offline engagement with news sources in which direct, reciprocated, unilateral exchange took place. Some producers had a very deliberate real-world newsgathering routine which involved walking a self-described 'beat', taking in local high streets and making themselves visible within communities:

> I do the blog beat, I always try and do it at least once a day if I can … I know loads of people now as well, people are always coming up to me with snippets of stuff and all the rest of it, so just being out and about I think is great.
>
> *(Hedon Blog)*

Sometimes, the encountering of stories happened not in a deliberate way but from the hyperlocal producer going about their everyday activities:

> I could be walking along a street and just see somebody's put up a sign for an event and I could literally just take an iPhone photo of it and then write about it and that's it. I mean that's hardly a big deal.
>
> *(Love Wapping)*

> So just on a normal day walking to work, I would see a few things. I might see a new business park up or a sign or a group of people gathering some-where, and that would help me create content in terms of just what I was seeing and things that were happening.
>
> *(Digbeth is Good)*

Face-to-face encounters with local citizens were fruitful sources of news, with such encounters often taking place in shops or pubs ("I go to pubs, that's my kind of thing" – Cwmbran Life). This was discussed as something closer to gossiping, a more everyday, accidental form of newsgathering: "Once you sensitise yourself to picking up news … you go and you just talk to people on street corners, you go

132 Practising hyperlocal journalism

into shops, you keep your eyes open, you see things" (Broughton Spurtle). In one case a volunteer on the hyperlocal site was identified as having a particular expertise in this area:

> He's tottering off to the local shops every day and chatting to the shopkeepers. I work full-time so he does a lot of the finding out about stuff, so he's a good source and he's drinking in the local pub every night as well, which is a good place to find out stuff.
>
> *(Crosspool News)*

Others had stories thrust their way as they became better known in their local area: "Literally it's as I'm wandering around and someone says 'Oh, have you heard that such and such is happening?'" (Love Wapping). Local shops and pubs are both places where producers can demonstrate their social embeddedness in communities and places instrumental to newsgathering:

> It's not a question of the "beat", it's a question of going down to the local shops and saying hello to the traders really. There's a sort of fascination with the local string of shops, which is one of the things that people seem to be quite interested in locally. ... People like to read about what shops are coming and going and who's doing well, and there's issues about local traders versus supermarkets and things.
>
> *(Bitterne Park)*

Melissa Wall argues that scholars should note the importance of the "contingent places" (2015: 807) in which citizen journalism takes place. The pubs and shops that seem to be a site of reciprocal exchange for the hyperlocal journalist are such places. Indeed, they are seen as an important symbol of independence, something to be protected against more corporate encroachment: "We're about the community, we're about supporting the small businesses ... yes, that's exactly what we're about, buy local" (Wayland News). This kind of embedded social practice stands in marked contrast to the ways in which interviewees talked of professional local newspaper journalists as distant and removed from communities. It also stands as a reminder of what has been lost from the routine practice of professional local news journalists.

Reciprocity as an interpretative repertoire

The engagement that hyperlocal publishers have with their audience is, in general, a reciprocal one. The language used to describe their encounters is, in the main, positive, with the emphasis on exchange and participation. Reciprocity is both sought out and casually happened upon as a result of the everyday movements of hyperlocalists. The language of (an at times disappeared, anachronistic) journalism practice is repurposed within a broader technology-enhanced civic discourse ("I do the blog beat" – Hedon Blog). This practice of walking the beat, literally or digitally, is discussed by practitioners as key to developing relationships with audiences. Murray Dick (2012) charts the history of analysis of the beat journalist. Although this role has been critiqued as inefficient by managers and overly cosy by academics, Murray comes to the view that emerging digital practices in journalism have a chance to reinvigorate the beat journalist. Whilst the economics of modern journalism might leave journalists tied to their desks, social networking tools have the potential for them to replicate the way local networks were once nurtured on a face-to-face basis:

> The rise of the network, evidenced in everything from user-engagement via Twitter, to the processing of user-generated content, offers a means of … re-invigorating the "beat". It permits the re-constitution of journalism's traditional power-base, re-connecting journalists with their audience online within a wider social network.
>
> *(Dick 2012: 757)*

It comes as no surprise, then, that for hyperlocal publishers the beat is a space in which they seek to make visible an authentic connection to community. In directly reciprocating tweets or in receiving word-of-mouth updates in the pub, the process of newsgathering also becomes one of legitimisation. Making themselves visible in the real world demonstrates their embeddedness, whilst selectively sharing or retweeting updates from locals is a form of "gatewatching" (Bruns 2003) that makes clear they share the same values as their audience. This is not unproblematic, and one can be too embedded: "I am so deeply embedded in the community; that actually is a problem to me and I don't know how to deal with that" (Wayland News). Here too the language of professional journalistic practice is brought to bear with the hyperlocal publisher in this instance feeling that they were simply too close to the community to write from an impartial perspective. This surfaces a key tension that many hyperlocal publishers feel: how to write for the community but still write within the conventional journalistic mode of objectivity.

Borger *et al.*'s research into the extent of use of reciprocal practices amongst commercial hyperlocals found that "participatory journalism as a functioning social system, based on stable and reciprocal expectations of what all actors involved would deliver and receive, did not materialize" (2016: 722). In the research we carried out, we certainly came across practices that might involve direct reciprocal exchange, but our findings concur with Borger's in that there was relatively little in the way of developed participatory journalism on display. Yet there were examples of tangible offline action that helped build local social capital and strengthen communities in concrete ways. In one case, for example, we found that a hyperlocal publisher had created a range of social-media-facilitated, offline community enterprises to supplement their news coverage, such as: a school uniform exchange service using Facebook to connect families wishing to swap clothes their children had grown out of, thus avoiding expensive

134 Practising hyperlocal journalism

purchases; social media calls to audiences to (successfully) help local victims of a house fire replace belongings and find temporary accommodation; and smaller instances of matching individuals with common community resources such as wheelchairs. Other relatively common examples included hyperlocals setting up, or participating in, social media surgeries to help community groups, businesses and individuals learn new online skills, or working directly with community groups to improve Internet literacy and digital communication (e.g. by teaching them to set up websites). These kinds of actions would not be possible without deep and lasting relationships of direct and indirect mutual exchange repeated over time, and in the next chapter we will look at a case study where the possibility of "sustained reciprocity" (Lewis *et al.* 2014: 235–236) is potentially achievable.

Conclusion

In this chapter, we examined how hyperlocal publishers talk about their news operations. Overall, we can see that these hyperlocal publishers seek to situate themselves in a civic value discourse, and we found that publishers utilise a range of interpretative repertoires in order to frame their practice thus. They utilise narrow interpretations of 'authenticity' in order to situate themselves as playing a pivotal role in either 'saving' journalism (by returning it to its 'authentic' origins) or 'saving' communities (by offering alternative representations of what they perceive to be the 'real' experience of living in their communities), and sometimes both at once. Of course, it could be argued that local mainstream journalism also draws on a repertoire of authenticity as it seeks to position itself as the 'voice' of local people. Yet here the difference is that issues of representation are very much to the fore with resistance shown by many to covering issues that might sully the reputation of the local area. The professional journalist, whether or not they personally want to avoid covering tricky subjects on their 'patch' (those that might still have a patch, that is), has editorial requirements to fulfil, and good and bad news alike must be covered. One of the ways in which authenticity is expressed for hyperlocals is through newsgathering practices that rely on reciprocal exchanges with audiences. This reciprocation directly acknowledges contributions and, to a modest extent, was seen by hyperlocals to have potential as a way to develop more participatory approaches to their journalism. This desire for a deeper participation, through reciprocity, acts as an interpretive repertoire whereby such exchanges are couched as unproblematic and equal in terms of power relationships. In the next chapter, we look in greater detail at how hyperlocal journalism practices are put to use in three different community contexts.

References

Borger, Merel, van Hoof, Anita & Sanders, José (2016) Expecting reciprocity: Towards a model of the participants' perspective on participatory journalism. *New Media & Society*, Vol. 18, No. 5, pp. 708–725.

Bruns, Axel (2003) Gatewatching, not gatekeeping: Collaborative online news. *Media International Australia incorporating Culture and Policy*, Vol. 107, No. 1, pp. 31–44.

Couldry, Nick (2004) The productive "consumer" and the dispersed "citizen". *International Journal of Cultural Studies*, Vol. 7, No. 1, pp. 21–32.

Deuze, Mark (2006) Ethnic media, community media and participatory culture. *Journalism*, Vol. 7, No. 3, pp. 262–280.

Dick, Murray (2012) The re-birth of the "beat". *Journalism Practice*, Vol. 6, No. 5–6, pp. 754–765.

Flouch, Hugh & Harris, Kevin (2010) *London's Digital Neighbourhoods Study: Typology of Local Websites*. London: Connected London.

Harcup, Tony (2005) "I'm doing this to change the world": Journalism in alternative and mainstream media. *Journalism Studies*, Vol. 6, No. 3, pp. 361–374.

Holton, Avery E., Coddington, Mark, Lewis, Seth C. & Gil de Zúñiga, Homero (2015) Reciprocity and the news: The role of personal and social media reciprocity in news creation and consumption. *International Journal of Communication*, Vol. 9, pp. 2526–2547.

Lewis, Justin (2006) News and the empowerment of citizens. *European Journal of Cultural Studies*, Vol. 9, No. 3, pp. 303–319.

Lewis, Seth C. (2015) Reciprocity as a key concept for social media and society. *Social Media + Society*, Vol. 1, No. 1. doi:10.1177/2056305115580339

Lewis, Seth C., Holton, Avery E. & Coddington, Mark (2014) Reciprocal journalism: A concept of mutual exchange between journalists and audiences. *Journalism Practice*, Vol. 8, No. 2, pp. 229–241.

McQuail, Denis (2013) *Journalism and Society*. London: Sage.

Platon, Sara & Deuze, Mark (2003) Indymedia journalism. *Journalism*, Vol. 4, No. 3, pp. 336–355.

Reardon, Sally (2016) Mixed messages. *Journalism Practice*, Vol. 10, No. 7, pp. 939–949.

Wall, Melissa (2015) Citizen journalism: A retrospective on what we know, an agenda for what we don't. *Digital Journalism*, Vol. 3, No. 6, pp. 797–813.

Wetherell, Margaret & Potter, Jonathan (1988) Discourse analysis and the identification of interpretative repertoires. In: Antaki, C. (ed.) *Analysing Everday Explanation: A Casebook of Methods*. London: Sage, pp. 168–183.

6

INSIDE THE HYPERLOCAL NEWSROOM

Having examined the motivations and practices of hyperlocal publishers, we now in look in detail at how hyperlocal publishing is operationalised, what distinct practices emerge and how producers attempt to connect to their audiences. The insights here offer a degree of triangulation with those in the previous chapter, and similar issues emerge here also; that is, issues of representation and community, but also sustainability. However, in these case studies we can also see at first hand the nature of hyperlocal publishing's working practices and the way relationships with citizens are managed. The voice of the citizen is present in two of these case studies in addition to the voice of the practitioner. Collectively the case studies examine the "communicative ecology" that Nick Couldry (2004: 27) points to as emerging in the digital landscape and so further contribute to producing a holistic picture of the role of hyperlocal publishing as an aspect of local media ecologies.

These case study hyperlocals have similar characteristics: they are news-focused operations; they are run from within the communities they serve; and they are operated by very small numbers of people. Yet their operational characteristics are different, with varying approaches and attitudes to technology, sustainability and levels of citizen participation. The first case study, of B31 Voices in Birmingham, involves in part an analysis of audience engagement online. This operation is run from a family home by a husband-and-wife team who utilise social media to allow for high levels of citizen participation. Here we draw attention to the process by which citizens are facilitated to "become producers themselves" (Couldry 2004: 27) through their engagement on social media. The next case study, on Castle Vale in Birmingham, examines the challenges faced by a community news operation that has variously been run as a business, a charity and a non-profit element of a local housing trust. It offers a critical examination of how citizens can become sensitive to externally imposed "negative reputational geographies" (Parker and Karner 2011: 309). In Castle Vale, we look at how assumptions about the 'voice of the people' role of community media belies the reality of how the norms of journalism practice come up against the expectations of audiences. Like B31 Voices, our final case study also involves a husband-and-wife team, also based in their own home. Yet unlike B31 Voices, On the Wight are focused on building a financially sustainable enterprise built on a more open approach to newsgathering and dissemination with innovation at the core of their offer. Whilst they began their operation in order to celebrate the cultural life of a very local community where they live, they then expanded to a broader area already covered by (an albeit depleted) mainstream local media, and they see themselves very much in competition with them. Here the value created by their operation can be seen in the context of discussions about media plurality. As we will see, their practices situate them very much in the guise of the 'fictive' hyperlocal entrepreneur discussed in the policy literature and the focus of the next chapter.

B31 Voices: towards sustained reciprocity

In this first case study, we discuss the online and offline production cultures and networks of B31 Voices, a hyperlocal news operation covering a series of suburbs in south Birmingham and run by husband-and-wife team Sas and Marty Taylor from their home. Typical of many in the hyperlocal sector, the Taylors undertake their role voluntarily, have no journalistic training and receive no income at all for their work. Yet their media operation attracts significant audiences, particularly through social media, and they are seen as a significant media node in their area of south Birmingham. B31 Voices operates as a website (b31.org.uk), a Twitter account and a Facebook Page (although from time to time they have experimented with other social networking platforms). From the outset B31 Voices have made it clear that their inspiration to start the website came from others doing similar work. As the welcome page on their website says, "Inspired by other local bloggers and talkaboutlocal.org this is to be a hyperlocal blog" (Taylor 2010). They seek to operate very much within what we might call the "civic web" (Buckingham and Banaji 2013). The case study in this instance has the opportunity to examine the norms that underpin their work and offer insight into the role that social media technologies play in connecting audiences to each other and to hyperlocal publishers.

The area covered by B31 Voices has a population in the region of 100,000 with a higher than average (for Birmingham) White British population, varying from just above the 59 per cent Birmingham figure in Weoley ward to 90 per cent in Longbridge ward (2011 Census data). In general, the areas covered would be considered working class, and the locality is dominated by the former Longbridge motor works, a vast former factory space that employed 22,000 workers in its heyday and which, since its closure in 2005, has been the subject of extensive regeneration. Many former factory workers still live in the area. The Taylors moved to Longbridge in 2003 and started blogging in 2010 out of concern about the representation of their estate's reputation. This desire to redress negative press coverage is, as we saw in the previous chapter, a common concern amongst hyperlocal publishers. Not long after commencing, it was clear that their blogging became something of value to the wider public:

> The area has got quite a bad reputation and we wanted to learn more about it really. So we just started with a little blog that covered the estate that we live on, and it just snowballed from there really. I think as it grew and people started interacting with it more, peoples' expectations of it then changed, so we started to deliver more to them.
>
> *(Sas Taylor)*

In the intervening years, the website they created has developed to become a significant news node in their area of the city. It has circa 40,000 likes on its Facebook Page and circa 11,400 followers on Twitter (as of February 2018). The degree to which their operation has become popular with the public has taken them by surprise:

> We're always interested in what people want to know about, but I think now it's got to a point where it has snowballed out of control in a way and people actually rely on it now. So the motivation was a little hobby about the small area we live in, and it's kind of developed into a feeling that you have to deliver a service to people now.
>
> *(Sas Taylor)*

The 'newsroom' of B31 Voices is the Taylors' home. As part of our research approach we asked Sas Taylor to photograph the areas in the house where they undertook B31 Voices work. This revealed both the places of work within the home (which turned out to be just about everywhere) and the role of technology in the domestic setting, as Sas chose to take her mobile devices on a tour of the places in which they are put to use in the course of updating B31 Voices' various online outputs. The results were images of her smartphone and tablet computer in the bedroom, the bathroom, the car and the living room (see Figure 6.1). These, and other, domestic spaces become places to carry out their operations:

> When I'm out and about taking my kids to school or shopping, or whatever else I'm doing. Whenever I park up or get back into the car, I'll sit and just check all the social media sites and see if anything's happening.
>
> *(Sas Taylor)*

Keeping up with the social media output takes up most of the time. The photographs taken in the bedroom represent the tendency they had to check social media at any time: "We might have a missing person or a missing pet that's touched everyone, and I will check in the middle of the night to see if there's any news", said Sas. Marty Taylor added, "So when we're talking about a dog, it can

Inside the hyperlocal newsroom 139

FIGURE 6.1 Compilation of photographs in the Taylors' home, representing where B31 Voices is produced

be about 4 o'clock in the morning, we might wake up, has that dog been found? Yes, it's ridiculous, it really is, it's wrong."

Although in many ways, the work of B31 Voices is informed by the textual norms of journalism (seen in the standard journalistic construction of stories on its website), the production culture is certainly very different. It is difficult to describe the Taylors' working processes in traditional newsroom terms as there is no evidence that editorial decisions are made prior to publication and little consultation between them about what does or does not get covered. The vast majority of the material published on their website is their own, and keeping this operation afloat invades every aspect of their daily lives, as evidenced in the photographs which elicited Marty to admit that "it's constant, we talk about B31, it's like 24/7 pretty much". Hyperlocal news-making practices for B31 Voices are bound up in the domestic lives of the publishers rather than the professional norms of mainstream journalism, and the photographs reveal how the 'habitus' of hyperlocal, whilst free from the hierarchies of traditional newsrooms and their working practices, might instead be subject to other, domestic rules and social structures ("I won't tweet at the dinner table unless there's an emergency" – Sas Taylor).

The relatively unstructured nature of B31 Voices' domesticated newsgathering arrangements perhaps reflect Sas and Marty's lack of professional journalism experience. As we have noted, many other hyperlocal publishers from a similar background tend to draw heavily on a civic value discourse in order to frame their

140 Inside the hyperlocal newsroom

practice. The same is true here, and like others, Sas and Marty situate what they do as being more authentically community orientated than the local journalism produced by the mainstream press: "It's about bringing a community together and being a community. If you've got newspapers, they're just about money, that's all they're there for" (Marty Taylor). Instead of seeing their role as contributing to a mainstream local news culture, Sas and Marty cite Birmingham's thriving culture of place-based blogging as a key influence in getting them started. Other suburbs in the city have similar news blogs, and there are citywide blogs covering politics, arts, environment and sport – indeed any topic you might expect the local press to cover. This network has veered in and out of formal organisation, with occasional 'Birmingham blogger' meetings and many, including Sas and Marty, participating in regular 'Social Media Surgeries' to support charities and community groups wishing to increase their media impact. Such surgeries and the wider city blogging culture feel distinctly part of a more civic-orientated Internet culture than a news one. Citizens are seen as active contributors, which in some way has eased the pressure on hyperlocals of having to be constantly finding new material. Indeed, the particular domestic circumstances of Sas and Marty (on top of the routine of the school run, shopping, etc., Sas is a full-time carer for Marty, who is disabled with limited mobility) mean that some conventional newsgathering strategies are next to impossible to carry out.

Networked citizenship

In the previous chapter we noted how many hyperlocals have reported that their operations have grown in scale to a point where is can be a burden. Yet Sas and Marty have developed a more networked approach using active citizen contributors, who help ease the pressure on the Taylors of having to constantly find and publish new material themselves. The potential, as Spyridou *et al.* (2013) note, is for new audience-orientated, participatory approaches to journalism to emerge in contrast to established routines within the professionalised newsroom that can act as a barrier to innovation and lead to devaluing of the audience contribution: "the practice of considering the audience's opinion on the content produced is not widely incorporated into the journalists' working routine, connoting authoritative rituals based on one-to-many communication models" (Spyridou *et al.* 2013: 88). The domesticated B31 Voices newsroom is not burdened by these professional norms, and the approach to social media utilised by Sas and Marty is very different. An examination of the Facebook and Twitter feeds for Sas and Marty's hyperlocal news operation revealed that whilst the news blog they run might only post two or three stories daily, their Twitter and Facebook networks play host to a continuous, noisy conversation about everyday living, a flourishing of assets "designed to be networked" and creating a new local commons (Dovey *et al.* 2016: 98). Everything from the trivial to the more serious concerns of local governance and crime gets covered, acting to bring people together online through shared everyday concerns. Reports of car accidents and traffic delays often result in near-live updates from the scene as witnesses and participants come together to offer up their version of events. This makes Sas and Marty's role as administrators difficult as "the people formerly known as the audience" (Rosen 2006) take control of the online space and offer every possible angle to a story, contributing more than just opinions, offering also vivid detail and eyewitness accounts.

In March 2014, an analysis of the Facebook group showed that there were 2,399 comments on 233 posts. Whilst there is plenty of evidence on B31's Facebook Page of citizen engagement with issues such as politics and crime, any mention of pets – lost or found – received the bulk of likes, shares and comments (see Table 6.1). In our analysis, each post by the administrators was categorised according to its subject matter. An engagement with the story was counted whenever a story was liked, commented upon or shared. This may require the user to do no more than simply click or press an icon on-screen, but it does at least suggest the content has been read.

Information about local events (47) and lost or found pets (50) were the two largest story categories. Pet stories were the most likely to receive some form of engagement, with the average number of engagements per story being 90. The category with the next highest level of engagement was 'Celebrations'. In this

TABLE 6.1 Facebook engagement according to subject matter, March 2014

Subject	Stories	Comments	Likes	Shares	Total engagements	Average number of engagements per story
Pets	50	788	1,296	2,429	4,513	90
Celebrations	18	116	1,194		1,310	73
Other	13	94	814	23	931	72
Jobs	3	66	48	94	208	69
Education	2	45	65		110	55
Crime	31	408	489	281	1,178	38
Community updates	23	282	276	87	645	28
Traffic	12	195	80	32	307	26
Events	47	142	812	128	1,082	23
Arts	19	80	296	43	419	22
Calls for support	15	96	175	57	328	22
Crowdsourcing	6	76	8		84	14
Sport	2	4	3		7	4
Local government	7	7	11		18	3

category were acknowledgements of birthdays, special occasions or achievements (e.g. "10 year old ballroom dancer [name] from Northfield has been selected to represent Great Britain! Well done! :) #Positiveb31"). These updates were not shared at all, but users often tagged other Facebook users via the comments box to alert them to the content. This could be seen as a form of targeted sharing rather than the networked sharing that happened with pet stories, which was intended to bring the content to new audiences by ensuring it appeared in the users' news feeds. Overall, stories about pets received 76 per cent of the total shares for March 2014, with one lost dog story receiving 132 comments on its own. In contrast to this everyday, 'banal' content, with its high engagement rates, stories concerning local government, albeit only seven in number, were never shared. The networked effect of platforms such as Facebook results in a form of "secondary gatekeeping" (Singer 2014). Jane Singer's research notes the impact of social media and social bookmarking platforms on the gatekeeping process. What was once within the control of the news-producing organisation has become something "that is both more complex and more collaborative" (Singer 2014: 66). Indeed, the complexity of what happens to B31 Voices' material that is liked, commented upon or shared is bound up in the decisions Facebook makes about how its algorithm works and is also dependent on the security settings of the B31 Voices' Facebook Page users. Precise engagement statistics are only available to the administrators of pages, but what is clear is that pet-related stories receive an average of 50 shares per story (all other genres of stories were below 5 shares per story), thereby creating significant visibility for this kind of content. In some sense, the banal is a place where indirect reciprocity practices are most in evidence and perhaps works to build community more effectively than other story genres (see Turner 2015 for a detailed discussion of the value to local online networks of "banal pet stories"). Sas and Marty seem very aware of the value of this banal content: "It's just these silly little things, but it will get hundreds of likes on a post like that. People want to hear good stuff, don't they?" (Sas Taylor).

Hashtags as networked newsgathering

The volume of material contributed by citizens on social media has resulted in B31 Voices' increasing use of hashtags across its platforms in order to help organise elements of the conversation and create greater value from them. Hashtags act as a way to gather and collate news, to generate and maintain mutually supportive networks within their area, and to facilitate storytelling. By way of example: during snowfall, they use a single hashtag (#B31Snowwatch) across all platforms to tag their own content and to bring together that of citizen contributors. Such material is then accessible to all by clicking the hashtag on the various platforms, but it is also curated by B31 Voices using social media aggregation platforms (such as storify.com) to create a clearer narrative from the material. For Sas Taylor, #B31Snowwatch was evidence of the value of their service:

The B31 Snowwatch as well, I think was a big thing that sort of proved how much people relied on it and were interacting with it as well. So then you think, if B31 Voices hadn't done that, what would have happened. ... They really got a lot of benefit from it and so then you feel that you've got to keep that up, you've got to keep giving them that.

Outside of newsgathering, hashtags are used in a way that attempts to highlight positive news stories (#B31positivenews) and also to encourage citizens to support each other (#B31supportinglocal and #B31crowdsource). In one case even a lost dog had its own hashtag (#runningcollie). The extent to which the hashtag #runningcollie went viral provided a point of realisation for Sas and Marty of the real-world impact they were having:

So everybody knew this hashtag and I was like, wow, people really do read it and people do actually pay attention. ... That was a bit of a realisation because you know that you've got x amount of followers and they're talking to you and that's fine, but to know that actually out there in the community when something was happening, people were more aware because, yes, it's a silly example, but people are more aware about what's going on so it might be affecting them.

(Marty Taylor)

These are examples of indirect reciprocity as their use is amplified by the network, not just the producers of B31 Voices. The hashtag allows for Person A's social media update to be shared by Person B, which then results in Person C also sharing it. Person C may not be a member of Person A's network, and so on, which means that the reach of the original message extends beyond the habitual hyperlocal audience. Such use of social media has the potential to achieve sustained reciprocity (Lewis *et al.* 2014). In updating their research on news values, Harcup and O'Neill (2016) discuss how "shareability" has become a contemporary news value. In the case of B31 Voices, it is most likely to be stories or communications about the everyday that get most shares; it seems such content is most conducive to indirect reciprocity.

But it not just residents of the locality who contribute updates to local information. Local politicians, public sector workers, police and other official bodies use social media (particularly Twitter) either in an individual or organisational capacity. It is content from these sources that is most likely to be shared (retweeted) by B31 Voices on Twitter. Our analysis of social media activity for one month saw a fifth of retweets (n = 64) were of police accounts (individual officers and corporate accounts), with various other council and public services accounting for 10 per cent of retweets (n = 31). Overall, the majority of tweets retweeted were for accounts run on an organisational basis or individuals tweeting only in an organisational capacity (e.g. a journalist, police officer or politician whose account was work related). Retweets of individual citizens not affiliated to any organisation made up

144 Inside the hyperlocal newsroom

28 per cent (n = 90) of retweets, and the remainder were from 77 different accounts affiliated to organisations. Sas and Marty expressed wariness when it came to using updates from citizens:

> If it was a significant accident, if someone was saying a road was closed, we would tell people straight away but clarify that it had come from a reader, and then once we can get official information, we would add that as official information then.
>
> *(Sas Taylor)*

Although they did not talk specifically about formal verification processes, they did mention one example where once a Twitter user had taken photographs of an accident, they were more comfortable in publishing the information (in this case, ahead of official confirmation). The prominence given to official sources and organisations on Twitter is partly a consequence of the differences in the nature of users on Facebook compared to Twitter:

> If people are telling us things on Facebook, the first thing I'll tend to do is turn to Twitter through the contacts we have, the official contacts we have who use Twitter, because they're more reachable and they use it more in that way. For example, they wouldn't comment on our Facebook Page, councillors or police officers wouldn't.
>
> *(Sas Taylor)*

Summary

This case study explored the everyday nature of undertaking hyperlocal journalism and the everyday nature of engaging with hyperlocal news content. The personal circumstances of B31 Voices mean that their newsgathering is centred around a highly developed use of social media, with reciprocation at its heart. This allows the public to act as newsgatherers, effectively chronicling the everyday, and also as secondary gatekeepers, shaping B31 Voices' news agenda through sharing, commenting and liking specific kinds of content. To an extent, what we see here is the degree to which B31 Voices facilitate the creation of a local networked public sphere of information and debate. In contrast to what most other hyperlocals told us about their social media use, B31 Voices seem to undertake little in the way of gatekeeping and consciously retweet or share just about any content requested of them. The publishers of B31 Voices operate more in the civic domain than a journalistic one, and the editors draw on a community discourse to contextualise their work. As Marty Taylor makes clear, the intention is for B31 Voices to serve a civic purpose:

> I don't think it [the community] necessarily needs us. It needs something like B31, every area I think needs something like that to bring communities together, to bring people together, to share so you know what's about,

because otherwise you don't know what's actually going on in your area. So I think being able to do that is … well, it's all about being a community, isn't it, I guess.

(Marty Taylor)

Newsgathering is carried out as they traverse the domestic realm, using mobile technology in the bedroom, in the bath, in the car and at any time of day. It might be a stretch to infer from this that their content is partly shaped by this setting, but on Facebook at least there is certainly an emphasis on the everyday concerns of ordinary people. Sas and Marty's own perception of how they use social media is that they tend to firefight rather than plan, and social media becomes something of a flow that they react to whatever the time of the day. For this reason, they cannot quite imagine anyone taking over from them: "It's quite a hard thing to hand over, I think, what we do on social media; we'd have to find the right person to trust to do it to the same level as we're doing it now" (Sas Taylor). Yet their management of social media could be seen as a mirror of how their audience use it; that is, using it to keep up to date with what is happening within their community, always glancing at it no matter what else they are doing.

But their sometimes-casual attitude to social media masks a well-developed strategic use, with clear distinctions made between platforms. On Facebook, the individual citizens whose successes and losses (of pets, for instance) produce high levels of engagement, are a resource who turn to B31 Voices to tell them of breaking news of a more conventional nature (be it snowfall, local politics or car crashes). On Twitter, official sources are given prominence, but there is constant direct reciprocation in order to sustain the hyperlocal's networks. Reciprocation is at the heart of their social media practices across both Facebook and Twitter, with the use of hashtags enabling their network to participate in newsgathering or in promoting civic values. Such digital practices are aimed at "suggesting future interactions and benefits" (Lewis 2015: 2) and are necessary for the success of a news operation that prides itself on the participation of ordinary citizens. Research by Borger *et al.* (2016) into the (lack of) participatory practices within a commercial hyperlocal operation found that audiences assumed they would be addressed as newsgatherers as much as users: they "considered it the journalists' task to create the preconditions for a participatory environment and to encourage participants to become active in it and make the actual news" (Borger *et al.* 2016: 716). It is this culture that B31 Voices encourages; but it is a time-consuming process that, at the time of the research, had no clear model for sustainability. However, the issue was beginning to loom large as server costs rose due to increased traffic: "What I'm working on at the moment is funding, is how we can get funding, grants and just generate more money … well, money. Not more money, just any money" (Sas Taylor). There is recognition that routes to income generation beyond advertising are needed, with grant funding and crowdsourcing considered as options: "Looking at things like the server [costs], we were talking about crowdsourcing some funding for that. There's a lot of people who rely on us. Even our Facebook followers, if

146 Inside the hyperlocal newsroom

we got a pound or a small percentage of each, could cover that" (Sas Taylor). These issues are addressed in more detail in chapter 7, but in most regards, B31 Voices represents a well-developed example of a hyperlocal that successfully operates within a civic discourse and one that has nurtured reciprocal relationships with the people and organisations of South Birmingham despite, or perhaps partly because of, the focus on issues of seemingly little importance. In the suburbs of B31 in Birmingham, people are happy to come together around everyday, personal crises and, in so doing, to show their networked potential.

Tyburn Mail: community journalism in times of austerity

Having looked at a case study where the newsroom is largely informal (B31 Voices), this case study focuses on a hyperlocal news operation that although equally small in size (having just two people at its heart), is more formally situated as a professional news operation. But rather than focus solely on the news production process in this case study, we instead examine the ways in which assumptions about the democratising, empowering function of community media comes up against the tensions over representation that exist between readers and producers. The focus therefore is on both the hyperlocal media operation and its audience on the Castle Vale estate in north-east Birmingham. Our research here was based on workshops with residents, interviews with owners and employees of the estate's community media organisation, and reflections from the undertaking of a participatory journalism project. The case study offers a critical account of the 'banality' of everyday activism by citizens sensitive to what David Parker and Christian Karner have described as externally imposed "negative reputational geographies" (2011: 309).

Tyburn Mail was a monthly newspaper and regularly updated news blog (with associated social media accounts) that covered the largely working-class Tyburn council ward in north-east Birmingham. It operated from 2001 until the end of 2016. It covered an area that included the large Castle Vale housing estate, originally one of the largest such estates in Europe. Known locally as The Vale, the area is home to 25,297 people (Birmingham City Council 2016) and is in the top 10 per cent of the most deprived wards in the UK (Office for National Statistics 2017). Its white population is higher than the average across Birmingham (76 per cent compared to 59 per cent) (Birmingham City Council 2016). Adam Mornement's account of Castle Vale's post-1990s transformation – from troubled high-rise housing estate to a less imposing mix of suburban houses and low-rise flats – is entitled *No Longer Notorious*, reflecting the widely held belief among citizens of Birmingham that for much of the estate's history, it was considered something of a 'no-go' area: "the media didn't help. Castle Vale was constantly portrayed as a den of iniquity by local papers" (2005: 84). Ali Madanipour's description of Castle Vale shows how much it had in common with many other failed 1960s estates that were already looking tired within 20 years of being built: "the neighbourhood suffered from poor quality infrastructure and buildings, lack of services, fear of crime and vandalism, poor health, unemployment, low educational standards, and a poor image" (2005: 51). The building of the largely council-run estate was begun in the early 1960s following extensive slum clearances of inner-city properties in Birmingham. By the time it was completed in the late 1960s, it included 34 high-rise blocks. Mornement highlights how the estate's social issues were exacerbated by the poor condition of the housing stock.

> For years Birmingham City Council had been aware of the gravity of Castle Vale's problems. Final confirmation came in 1991 when a chunk of concrete fell from one of the tower blocks. There was nobody underneath, but Castle Vale was falling apart.
>
> *(2005: 9)*

It was clear something had to be done. By the early 1990s there was "an identified need to develop a long-term strategy for Castle Vale encompassing the key priorities of a regeneration initiative" (Coatham and Martinali 2010: 91). The solution was the development of a Housing Action Trust (HAT), of which there were only six in the UK (see Evans and Long 2000 for an overview of the HATs). These trusts were a policy of the 1980s Conservative government, designed to deal with problematic estates by providing investment but taking them out of local government control into the hands of a non-departmental public body. Tenants in estates where a HAT was proposed were given a vote on whether to leave the control of the council. As well as new funds, the HAT promised a more holistic approach that saw social problems as related and encouraged partnership working with police, education and other parties (Mornement 2005: 15). In 1993, Castle Vale residents voted overwhelmingly in favour of joining the HAT: "the residents of a 1960s experiment in social housing had voted to be part of a social engineering experiment in the 1990s. It was a leap of faith" (Mornement 2005: 14). The Castle Vale Housing Action Trust saw its role, as did the other HATs, as being the "redevelopment of the social infrastructure and combating social exclusion" (Evans and Long 2000: 309). The importance of emphasising citizen participation was central to how the HAT went about its subsequent regeneration of the area. The 1995 masterplan for the area makes clear that the future for the estate would mark a move away from central control and towards a more significant role for citizens:

> A revitalised Castle Vale ... must engender a greater pride of place and community spirit than at present. In turn this may lead to the residents assuming greater responsibility for setting standards and taking wider responsibility and authority for the future management and maintenance of the new Castle Vale.
>
> *(Castle Vale Housing Action Trust 1995: 2)*

The development of community media in Castle Vale

While improving local social capital was seen as a central part of the regeneration process, it was also clear that the external perception of the area needed addressing.

148 Inside the hyperlocal newsroom

Adam Mornement (2005: 82–93) describes the role that public relations and art played in helping shift the story of The Vale to something other than crime and depravation from the mid 1990s onwards. However, the area also developed community media outlets, tasked partly with playing a similar role. In the first instance, a community radio station, Vale FM, was set up in 1995. Its manager at the time, Neil Hollins (interviewed in 2013), describes its early development: "Vale FM was born out of an idea by local residents who were maybe involved in pirate radio or who were maybe mobile DJs and believed that a community radio station would be good for Castle Vale". Hollins became the station's first employee in 1996 and was employed directly by the HAT. The station broadcast on the basis of applying for restricted service licences, which confined its output to a 28-day period at any one time (this was the most common way for community radio stations to legally operate at this time). Castle Vale Community Radio (CVCR) Limited had been set up in 1999 as the vehicle through which to bid for grant funding that was not directly from the HAT. Hollins became adept at securing external funding ("a mix of funds, which would be regional and European, and then some which were more local") and at expressing the value of Castle Vale as a place where funders could see the potential for interventions to transform lives: "This is about putting out an image of Castle Vale as a vibrant creative place, where things are happening. It might not be the best place in the world, but things are happening" (Hollins). Different funders might have required different articulations of place, but the desired outcomes were always the same: "The primary benefits were very much about the personal outcomes for beneficiaries. The secondary ones … were about reputational aspects and challenging negative stigmas" (Hollins).

While the radio station might have initially been developed out of concerns to address wider public perceptions of the area and to give voice to residents, it also provided training and development for individuals who might then go on to fulfil educational or creative ambitions: "[From 1998] we began running training courses under franchise contract radio courses for unemployed people to use it as a way of developing skills, confidence, employability" (Hollins). By the time it was applying for one of the new community radio licences in 2004, its role in supporting Castle Vale's transformation was recognised by a local councillor in the licence application: "CVCR has been an important player in the regeneration of Castle Vale since the mid 1990s" (Castle Vale Community Radio 2004: 21). In 2001 a community newspaper was developed (with just four pages at that stage, and called *Vale Mail*) which, like the radio station, was directly linked to and funded by the HAT. Hollins argues that there was initial distrust of the impartiality of the newspaper: "It was still under the control of the HAT, so wasn't particularly trusted, it was seen [as] a bit of a propaganda sheet, and it was rather disorganised and didn't look very nice really" (Hollins). As the HAT was heading towards being dissolved, it supplied some funding for the newspaper to be further developed and to help secure its future editorial independence. The funding supported the employment of a trained journalist/editor, Clive Edwards. Edwards (interviewed in 2013) describes the role of the newspaper before he arrived: "No indication of any bad news or anything. Its function was to improve its [the HAT's] reputation." In the years that followed, as well as growing in editorial confidence, the newspaper expanded in size (to 24 pages eventually) and in area (to cover nearby council wards outside Castle Vale in order to develop an income stream from advertising). It has always been delivered door-to-door, free to residents.

The HAT was designed to have a limited lifespan, with residents allowed to choose to go back to local council control or to a housing association at the end of the HAT period. On the winding up of the Castle Vale HAT in 2005, almost all residents agreed for their properties to be managed by Castle Vale Community Housing Association. This also resulted in change for the community media operation. It was expected that the HAT's closure would result in the likely withdrawal of funding for community media in Castle Vale. However, the HAT had surplus funds to dispose of from the sale of its stock to the housing association, and these funds were to be distributed via a charity called the Castle Vale Endowment Trust Fund. Some funds from this source went towards maintaining the radio and newspaper in each year since 2005 until the newspaper's closure in 2016. A change to charity status (and a renaming to Headline Media) in 2008 was part of a strategy to target National Lottery funds, but two bids were unsuccessful. In 2010, with a crisis in funding looming, the charity came under the sole control of Castle Vale Community Housing Association: "We were subsumed into this large organisation. Huge change – for all sorts of reasons … that was a massively difficult period for the organisation but we survived, we came out the other end" (Hollins). During this time, which saw problems with trying to get the radio station permanently on air, the newspaper went "from strength to strength", argues Hollins. It became "the predominant form of communication in Castle Vale at the time" (Hollins). In doing so, it secured advertising income in the region of £33,000 in the financial year up to March 2012 (according to its published accounts, this is a similar amount to the grant received), compared to only £3,000 generated by the radio station. In 2013 another change would happen, this time separating out the radio and newspaper operations and severing the formal link with the housing association (although it remained one of the newspaper's biggest advertisers). Headline Media was wound up as a charity and Topcliffe Media was established (named after the tower block that housed its offices on the estate) to run just the news operation.

Tyburn Mail *as normative local media node*

In 2016, *Tyburn Mail* had just two employees: one journalist (Clive Edwards), and a manager (Frank Kennedy) who sold advertising space and ran the operation on a day-to-day basis as a limited company. Edwards is a trained journalist who also does sports reporting for a national radio station. He argued that the newspaper's role at the time was to provide critical commentary on the ongoing regeneration of the estate: "Our independence is crucial to providing a sensible and level-headed

150 Inside the hyperlocal newsroom

critique of the progress that is or isn't being made" (Edwards). The newspaper acted very much in the mode of traditional, local journalism: "We follow rather than innovate. Everything that we do mirrors the bigger players within our society. We just operate on a smaller level. The way that we report, we report in the same genre than they do" (Edwards).

As if to reinforce the point, Edwards articulated his pride about one of his stories having "a real *Sunday Mercury*[1] stance". However, the shift to a more formalised journalistic tone was not a comfortable change to make by any means:

> [We] took the view that we would include bad news as well as good news. We still hold true to that for all of the downside that that creates. It creates an uncomfortable relationship sometimes within what is a fairly small community. We can, and we have, alienated some organisations and some individuals as a result.
>
> *(Edwards)*

Coverage of crime was considered an essential element of *Tyburn Mail*'s remit by Edwards. He had pride in how it was covered and argued it offered value to citizens as a route to better understanding how society works:

> We tackle crime stories very well when we go to Court. When I say "we", I mean "I". So the reporting of a case that happens either at Magistrates' Court, or more particularly at Crown Court, a more serious case, has some kind of prurient or titillating interest for members of the public. It's also there as a narrative which offers some insight into human behaviour. Also, the way that society works or doesn't work, in the way that it deals with deviant behaviour, or disruptive behaviour.
>
> *(Edwards)*

Edwards saw the *Tyburn Mail* as playing a monitorial role alongside other media. He lamented that the size of his organisation limited this role:

> All of these journalistic jobs, their raison d'être is to make organisations and individuals accountable to each other and to the community or society in which they live. Our minuscule size means that we can do a job for Tyburn, but there are huge swathes of geographic areas and institutional areas that we just touch on the surface.
>
> *(Edwards)*

While there was a reliance on local residents as paid door-to-door distributors of the monthly newspaper, there were only occasional written contributions from citizens, who sometimes wrote column pieces on fashion, music, history and suchlike. Although *Tyburn Mail*'s digital outlets (website, Facebook Page, Twitter account) proved useful both for newsgathering and for gaining a sense of which content its audience was most interested in, it was the newspaper that remained the focus of its operation: "There are some stories that we leave out of the web, because we want the print version to have impact when it comes out ... I think the newspaper has got more status than the Web output" (Edwards). Mechanisms for engagement with the audience in any form are limited. Indeed, this was recognised by Edwards:

> We don't communicate with the average person who's happy to keep their head down and stay anonymous, except for within their own group of friends that they socialise with or live nearby. I don't think we have a mechanism for getting feedback from the silent majority.

Edwards pointed out that his local contacts were largely formal in nature (school, police, council, local politicians), although he recognised that digital media had a role to play in allowing citizens to express civic pride: "If you look at social media sites, such as people's Facebook Pages, they are always referencing the community ethos around Castle Vale". Although there were ample opportunities for feedback on matters of content, Edwards claimed that was not what concerned most people: "The most frequent feedback we get is about delivery of the newspaper. In terms of either it hasn't been delivered to them, or they've had three delivered."

Edwards' view on the value of participation via the Web was fairly entrenched. Although *Tyburn Mail* made use of social media platforms, Edwards never engaged in comment threads, shared user-contributed content or undertook any action that might be regarded as reciprocal. In our wider research, we found this approach to be the exception, but some hyperlocals that were developing a more business-orientated approach similarly failed to make use of the reciprocal functionality of social media, arguing that it was distracting and wasted time. At *Tyburn Mail*, Edwards saw potential in Facebook only as a route to reach an elusive younger audience: "When I've written an article and I want to reach the younger generation, I put a link to it on our Facebook Page and we then see, about half an hour later, a spike in our figures". But beyond such observations, there was little sense that reciprocal engagement via social media was a useful way to build relationships with this or any other group of readers.

The views of residents

While in our case study of B31 Voices we heard from the audience via their use of social media, in this case study we chose to directly engage with them through a series of research interventions. First, there were two exploratory workshops with citizens (that took place in early 2013) in order to help understand how *Tyburn Mail* was perceived. Residents were asked to map out how they engaged with a wide range of news media throughout the day and how *Tyburn Mail* fitted into that. Further, they were asked to imagine what kinds of stories they might write for *Tyburn Mail*, prompting them to mock up a newspaper front cover. Second, a

152 Inside the hyperlocal newsroom

'news café' was organised. Here Edwards, as the journalist from *Tyburn Mail*, would meet local residents and see what stories emerged from conversations with them. To further facilitate these interactions, a series of blank spaces were created on a page in the monthly newspaper into which citizens could write their own news stories. Chris Atton describes a similar project in a New York underground paper of the 1960s: "*Other Scenes* once offered an entirely blank set of pages for readers as a do-it-yourself publishing project" (2002: 24). Readers were then asked to bring this to the news café, which was organised in a local supermarket. The café was intended to bring readers into contact with journalist and enable them to discuss and co-create stories based on the sheets they had filled in. In consultation with Edwards, some direction was given on topics, but there was also an 'anything else' space (see Figure 6.2 for an example of a completed page). These interventions were designed to allow Edwards to see where in the cycle of story development the citizen can play a role; to see, as Luke Goode notes, "possibilities for citizen participation at various points along those chains of sense-making that shape news – not only new possibilities for citizens to 'break' news" (2009: 1291). The intention was also to see what potential there might be in Castle Vale citizens playing more of a "produser" (Bruns 2008) role in their local media.

Across the workshops and the news café there was a tension between the ways in which *Tyburn Mail* represented Castle Vale through the prism of normative news values and the expectations of citizens that it should play a more effective role in redressing the historic representation of Castle Vale as a no-go area. While one resident (in their written response on the newspaper blank page) argued that the *Tyburn Mail* should "tell it like it is" and worried about problems being "swept under the carpet", this largely proved an exception. Most citizens were concerned that there was "too much focus on individual crime" (newspaper blank page response). The issue of crime and how much of it was covered was a recurring theme. One resident argued that the coverage of crime on the estate was disproportionate: "The problem is it's no worse than others, but it gets reported more, so it makes it look worse. ... It's reporting more, giving it a worse opinion of Castle Vale" (workshop respondent). During the workshops, residents were asked to react to example stories from the *Tyburn Mail* news blog as points for discussion; the first story was about local crime: "It gives a bad name to Castle Vale ... . Someone from Castle Vale is always getting arrested for doing something, always." The people of Castle Vale were acutely aware of the mediatisation of their locality, something which Irene Costera Meijer (2012) found in similar research in Utrecht. Limited as it was by its one-off experimental nature, the blank space in the *Tyburn Mail* did at least offer readers a modest role in countering the "problem neighbourhood frame" (Costera Meijer 2012: 18). There was also a degree of suspicion and confusion about how *Tyburn Mail* was organised and who it represented. Some thought it was still linked to Castle Vale Community Housing Association: "Lots of people's negative articles or opinions are being filtered out, especially if it's against the housing and social", said one resident in the workshop. Likewise, there were concerns that coverage of the city council tended to shy away

Inside the hyperlocal newsroom 153

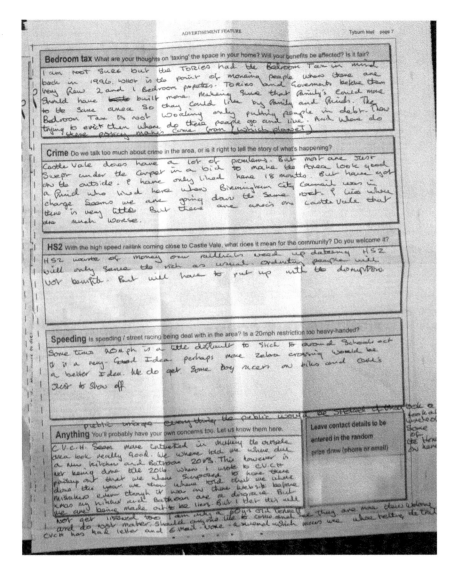

FIGURE 6.2 Completed 'blank' page in the *Tyburn Mail*

from controversy: "There's always something about what the council are doing. They print all the good things, of course. It's very, very rare you get failings, unless it comes from the locals."

Overall, the workshops concurred with the journalist's view that the majority of his audience was disengaged. But when asked about the use of social media by *Tyburn Mail*, residents by and large saw it being used in a way that was no different to the newspaper. Just as they tended to read the newspaper quickly and then discard it, there was a similar laissez-faire attitude to its presence on Facebook. One resident said, "I think I've got better things to look at when I'm on the Internet".

154 Inside the hyperlocal newsroom

However, a workshop exercise to create a citizens' version of the newspaper revealed examples of citizens as both active community members (one person talked about their attempt to tackle local traffic speeding) and potential chroniclers of the everyday (another talked about wanting to write about a local homeless person who had not been seen for a while), often mixing fact and fiction to create alternative narratives about life on the estate. One resident, in filling in the blank space we created, came up with a whole list of story and content ideas, some participatory in nature, that could be taken up:

> Maybe have a panel of moms review baby groups … . The children's centre is going through major cuts and changes, and this needs covering … . More coverage on what's on for under-fives … , advice on how to pick nurseries and schools.

To a degree, the news café helped to place the organisation more centrally in people's gaze, and Edwards continued to run it on a monthly basis for a short period after this intervention (a column called "News from the Café" was created). At least one news story from the completed blank pages was followed up, and in the subsequent interview with Edwards, he was clear that he understood not only that citizens can play a role in newsgathering, but also that the initiative had changed perceptions of the *Tyburn Mail*:

> Clearly the news café is a good idea. We feel that it has worked for us in terms of opening us out and saying we are after domestic stories. … It may well be that we are now being perceived as a voice of the people, as opposed to a voice of the council, or a voice of the councillor.

Yet the nature of the journalism at *Tyburn Mail* remained largely the same. As Michael Schudson's critique of the US public journalism movement points out, despite the strong desire and concrete initiatives to engage the 'public' in the co-production of news, "authority about what to write and whether to print stays with the professionals" (1999: 123).

Summary

As with our previous example, this case study draws attention to the working practices of a hyperlocal media operation. Although initially set up in part to play a role in addressing the negative reputation of a specific locality, *Tyburn Mail* prided itself on being an independent voice that played a monitorial role and had the potential to hold local power to account. In late 2016 its grant funding was removed entirely, and it produced its last issue in December 2016. During its lifetime, it was an operation that shifted from a not-for-profit arm of a non-departmental government body (the HAT), to a limited company scouring for grant funding, to a charity, and back to being a limited company. Its existence throughout had been precarious, and there was an inevitability of the drying up of its funding source (the Endowment Trust Fund). Unlike similar operations, it had not quite built up the level of trust where funding through citizen patronage or crowdfunding were likely options,[2] and it therefore closed without any succession plans or any other group or organisation coming forward to run it.

While *Tyburn Mail*, in some ways, did a good job of fulfilling a public interest role for its citizens, it came up against tensions in the area's troubled history. As Adam Mornement points out, "the tangled knot of notoriety cannot quickly be undone" (2005: 82). Residents are clearly conflicted about the extent to which 'bad' news should be talked about, and many of the research participants want to see their local media cast Castle Vale in a more positive light. While there is a shared desire to "tell it like it is", the residents of Castle Vale seem to contest the idea of what "it" is and, in that sense, engaged in a hegemonic struggle with *Tyburn Mail* to claim what they feel is a more authentic representation of The Vale. As much as anything, the lack of reciprocal exchange in *Tyburn Mail*'s news-making practices resulted in residents themselves taking an oppositional stance to their community news provider; it is *Tyburn Mail* that was seen as the incumbent mainstream news operation whose utilisation of normative news practices closed down the opportunities for a more participatory journalism to emerge. This is ironic given the history of citizen participation in local decision-making that has been a feature of Castle Vale's regeneration process to date. Ultimately, *Tyburn Mail* played a vital role in charting the effects of austerity on what remains of local public services. But its failure to refocus on the banal, everyday concerns of local residents meant it failed to articulate a citizen-led vision of what life in areas such as The Vale are really like.

On the Wight – 'mom-and-pop' journalism

In this final case study, we look at how Simon and Sally Perry operate On the Wight (onthewight.com). This case study offers insight into how a news operation seeks to gain legitimacy and sustainability within an existing local news ecology. It begins by setting out that wider media ecology before looking at the motivations of the publishers and examining their newsroom practices. While On the Wight represents, to an extent, the 'fictive' hyperlocal entrepreneur as discussed widely in policy-focused literature, the publishers draw on a much broader discourse to situate their practice, rather than simply an entrepreneurial one.

The Isle of Wight sits on the south coast of England in the county of Hampshire. It has a population of 139,105 (mid-2014 estimate), and 94.8 per cent of residents are of white British origin (Isle of Wight Council 2017). Over a quarter of residents are over 65. The island is a destination for retirees and is largely rural with several small to medium-sized towns. Five of its wards are in the 20 per cent most deprived in the UK, and the rate of managerial occupations is half that of the south-east as a whole (Department for Communities and Local Government 2015), indicative of its economy having a high level of service sector jobs to meet the

156 Inside the hyperlocal newsroom

needs of the large number of summer visitors who visit the area's seaside towns. It also hosts two large music festivals and other cultural and sports (largely sailing) festivals that attract visitors. The island has only a small range of media outlets dedicated to it, one of which is a weekly newspaper, the *County Press* (circulation 23,927; average for January to June 2017). The *County Press* is the only surviving newspaper title on the island, which, like many other areas in the UK, has had a rich history of local newspaper publication. There was much amalgamation of smaller titles in the late 19th and early 20th centuries. The British Library lists 64 newspaper titles for the island (the earliest in 1845), with some beginning their life covering small towns (e.g. *The Shanklin Gazette*, 1899–1937). The *County Press*, like other local newspapers, has seen a decline in income from advertising. In its 2015 financial report, it admits that the climate has become tougher due to "structural changes" (Isle of Wight County Press Limited 2015: 1), and this has seen its traditional advertisers switch away from printed classified ads to online. But online advertising is also a competitive space: "the market for online display advertising is very competitive with many choices available to potential local and national advertisers" (Isle of Wight County Press Limited 2015: 1). The *County Press* saw its income drop to £3.872 million in 2015 from £4.025 million in 2014, a 4 per cent decrease.

Isle of Wight Radio is an independent commercial station that has changed ownership many times since it began in 1990. It was briefly owned by Global Radio but is now part of a small media group (Media Sound Holdings) which also publishes a glossy magazine (*Beacon Magazine*) that has four editions for different areas of the island. The magazine includes advertising for local businesses along with some feature-style editorial. The island saw some experimentation with local television in the late 1990s, with television 12 becoming one of only a handful of local television stations in the UK to operate on an analogue Restricted Service Licence. It was followed by Solent TV, which had less locally focused content and relied on imported international programming to fill its schedule. This closed in 2007 (BBC 2013). The island has coverage from the BBC's local *South Today* programme, but the BBC does not have a dedicated journalist on the island and relies partly on On the Wight as a feeder for stories: "The relationship with the BBC is very good; they will come to us for stories or come to us for photos and credit and they'll link back" (Simon Perry). The nearest rival to On the Wight in online terms is the online Island Echo, which describes itself as "the Isle of Wight's only true 24hr news source" (2017). Begun in 2012, it has an emphasis on breaking news. The Isle of Wight News (isleofwightnewsdaily.com) is an aggregation service that draws together content based on hashtags related to the Isle of Wight. Typically, its content comes from On the Wight, Island Echo and the The *County Press* as well as official sources such as the local council.

On the Wight

On the Wight was was set up by Simon and Sally Perry in 2005, not long after they moved to the island from London, and it was originally called Ventnor Blog

(Ventnor – population circa 10,500 – being a small town at the southern end of the Isle of Wight). They publish "a minimum of ten" (Sally Perry) news stories a day, although that number is sometimes higher: "it can be between 10 and 15 sometimes" (Sally Perry). As well as the website, they also run a Twitter account (approximately 13,300 followers as of February 2018), a Facebook Page (approximately 22,750 likes, February 2018) and also a WhatsApp group (which sends news updates with links to stories on the website). The Facebook Page is used to link back to news stories on the website but also sometimes shares readers' photographs and tags the reader in questions as part of a direct reciprocal exchange. The Twitter account uses this kind of content much more rarely, largely acting to direct people back to the website. The different uses of the platforms are deliberate: "What's popular on Facebook is different to what's popular on [our] site. Twitter is always quite hard to get a handle on really. It's not very well used on the island" (Sally Perry). The Perrys admit that neither platform is used to directly engage with readers: "It's something we've lost. We have lost … the social part of our social media" (Simon Perry).

The Perrys' main motivation for starting Ventnor Blog is not dissimilar to that expressed by B31 Voices, in that they were attempting to redress negative perceptions about the area. However, in their case they were motivated less by countering stories about crime or deprivation, and more by letting their friends know that the Isle of Wight was not a cultural backwater. Its initial focus was therefore intended to be a cultural one:

> We started the site to talk about the local art scene when we moved to Ventnor. … We were just amazed by how active a scene there is … so we were writing about gigs that were coming up or exhibitions that we'd been to … . It was sort of almost to show our friends in London that actually there's a really vibrant art scene out here.
>
> *(Sally Perry)*

Like the Taylors in our first case study, the Perrys situated their origins within the blogging community. Simon Perry had run an online technology publication (with a global audience) in London. It was during this time he received training as a journalist on a course at the London College of Printing, but he describes himself as having come from the "world of blogging". For Simon, this comes with a particular sensibility:

> In the blogging world, transparency, openness and dependability were, you know, the absolute core. So when we were starting this, we thought well look there's no other way to do it because you've got to be open and transparent because why would it be anything else?

However, this intention to retain a focus solely on the cultural was never carried through, and Ventnor Blog started from the outset, almost unintentionally, to include news:

158 Inside the hyperlocal newsroom

> The very first post was actually about a bomb being detonated in the harbour in Ventnor; it was an old World War 2 bomb that had washed up and I guess we just thought ... we just decided if we're going to start it, we may as well start it today, because this is, you know, great content. And so I stood down there for about eight hours with a camcorder.
>
> *(Sally Perry)*

Again, much like with B31 Voices, there was a sense that the operation grew at a rate that surprised them. An example of this was the Ventnor Blog forum, which saw thousands of individual contributions: "It became a thing on the island where people, not just Ventnor people, people from all over would contribute" (Simon Perry). Its success helped the Perrys realise that they were providing a platform that was useful to citizens, and although the forum eventually stopped being used, the Perrys believe it situated their operation as one where the citizen's voice can be heard, anonymously if need be:

> It was anonymous on the forum, it was anonymous on the site; we've had tremendous pressure to ... the people who control the Island have exerted various forms of pressure to try to get us to make people use their own names.
>
> *(Simon Perry)*

The desire to offer a platform for debate is partly linked to the Perrys' status as 'incomers'. They are certainly sensitive to how their audience perceive them: "We would never be accepted in the same way as someone who has grown up here" (Sally Perry). Their tactic has been to "stick their neck out" (Simon Perry), but building trust has taken time and has involved getting past what they argue is quite a "closed mentality" (Sally Perry) on the island.

Managing Ventnor Blog and forums was soon becoming time-consuming ("Sally had the nightmare of admin-ing the forums" – Simon Perry), and it was clear that the operation as a whole would need to move from a hobby to a business: "We were putting too much time into it and not getting an income from anywhere else, so it had to become commercial" (Sally Perry). The operation now relies on a mix of income sources. Some of these relate directly to the website (display advertising, sponsored features), whereas others are separate activities such as creating websites for local businesses ("few and far between really" – Sally Perry) or offering consultancy. They have tried running events on the back of the On the Wight brand, but the time and organisation needed is not matched by the income generated. While there are clear signs of the enterprise maturing and stabilising after ten years in operation (by 2016), Sally Perry pointed out that "it's been a real struggle really". Attempts to use third parties to sell advertising for them were not successful, and they remained frustrated at their own failure to make more significant inroads into the near monopoly enjoyed by the *County Press*: "What people commonly say to me is that 'we advertise in the paper, but we don't know why'; and it doesn't stop them doing it" (Simon Perry). One other source of income for On the Wight has come from their participation in a funded programme aimed at developing the hyperlocal sector. In 2015 they bid successfully to be able to participate in a programme run by the innovation charity Nesta (Geels 2015) aimed at developing expertise in audience analytics. As well as advice on social media and search engine optimisation, the programme paid a grant ($£6,500$) in exchange for participants taking actions to adapt their content to attract more visitors to their websites.

The 'fictive' hyperlocal publisher

On the Wight's participation in the Nesta programme comes as little surprise given they have long been cited by Nesta and others as fulfilling an ideal about what hyperlocal publishing can achieve. Damian Radcliffe's 2012 report for Nesta, *Here and Now*, lists Ventnor Blog as one of a number of hyperlocals that are "excellent at identifying and meeting the requirements of a local community" (2012: 16). Earlier still, in 2009, they were cited in a BBC report as being "in the vanguard of the UK's hyperlocal news movement" (BBC 2009). Ofcom mention Ventnor Blog in their 2009 report on local and regional media as an example of the "ultra-local" community media that has "raised their profiles and generate tens of thousands of unique visitors a month" (2009: 45). The journalism industry website journalism.co.uk wrote favourably about On the Wight's coverage of a local trade dispute (Townend 2009) that attracted national coverage in 2009, contrasting its detailed reporting and live blogging with that of the *County Press* and *The Guardian*: "the Ventnor Blog has done an excellent job of providing the islanders (and outsiders) with raw and useful material, showing us how high-quality hyperlocal reporting is done" (Townend 2009). Talk About Local acknowledged this work with two awards in 2010, one for best overall site and one for best hyperlocal story (Hartley 2010). The Society of Information Technology Management described the site as "prolific", citing its coverage of severe weather in January 2010 as an example of how hyperlocal sites can keep local communities informed (SOCITM 2010: 163).

In 2015, On the Wight was one of five case studies featured in a publication by Carnegie UK Trust (Pennycook 2015: 15–16). Praise for the operation continues here, but its work is set in the context of its struggles to sustain itself. The case study pitches On the Wight as an innovator that is able to fulfil a fourth estate function despite only being able to pay "a modest salary" to Simon and Sally Perry, who work "over 10 hours a day" (Pennycook 2015: 16). The author argues that they have repurposed content around "audience demand for more civic news" and that it is an online operation which enlivens the local news media ecology, forcing incumbents to follow its innovations:

> in order to compete, the local news landscape on the Isle of Wight was forced to shift to a culture of more immediate and comprehensive local news provision, with outlets publishing more content online, at a faster rate;

highlighting exclusive content; and using social media to cover council meetings in real time.

(Pennycook 2015: 15)

In all of the five case studies detailed by Carnegie UK Trust there is a sense of precarity about sustainability. The case studies make clear that despite On the Wight and the others having a role in "help[ing] inspire those who are considering starting a hyperlocal news group" (Pennycook 2015: 7), relying on the market alone will not allow them to succeed: "for the sector to reach its full potential and meet this demand, further support for hyperlocals must be forthcoming" (3). The Carnegie UK Trust therefore emphasises the public service role played by On the Wight and the others rather than their role as journalism entrepreneurs. In a sense, the case studies are shaped to fit the Carnegie UK Trust's (reasonable, and in many ways justified) agenda that hyperlocal publishing should receive state subsidy.

The home office as hyperlocal newsroom

While the 'newsroom' for B31 Voices is similar to On the Wight in that it is a domesticated space, there is a sharp contrast in that the Perrys use a home office space and largely confined their hyperlocal operation within it. Their hyperlocal newsroom is a relatively formal one. It has two desks, with Sally and Simon sitting diagonally from each other (see Figure 6.3). The walls have some posters on them

FIGURE 6.3 On the Wight newsroom

related to running the business. One says, "We get paid to connect businesses with Islanders through our News and other information services", and another, "Quality first, last and forever". In the corner of the room is another desk which gives live updates on a computer screen of the number of visitors coming to the website (see Figure 6.4). Although during my observation Simon expressed a lot of pride in having set up this system (it shows the Google Analytics platform and is run from a microcomputer called an Arduino), during interview he argued that knowing which story resonated more with the readers was shaped by instinct as well as statistics: "Well we've got the live stats in the corner which gives us a pointer, but you know when you've found a story, you know; you just know, don't you?" (Simon Perry).

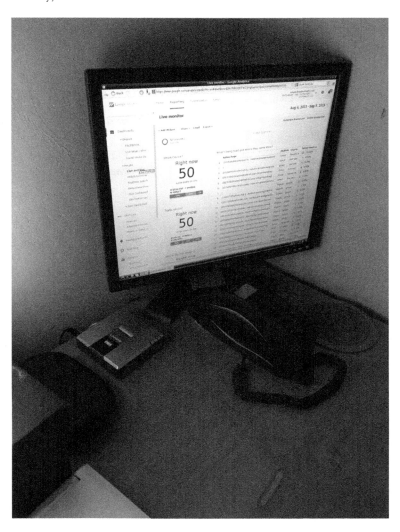

FIGURE 6.4 Live analytics screen for website visitors

162 Inside the hyperlocal newsroom

Although the Perrys can sometimes work long hours, it is not quite to the extent of spending late nights waiting for updates on lost pets, as B31 Voices acknowledged doing. The Perrys' day is partly built around family time, but they do admit to spending evenings working on stories: "We used to stop but now it's bled back into evenings again" (Sally Perry). Maintaining a separation between home and family can be difficult: "Because we are married and we live together and we work together, the conversations about work will continue elsewhere and pretty much all of the time. You know it is one of my bugbears actually" (Sally Perry). The presence of the newsroom in the family home means that the temptation to carry on working is always there: "Because the office is in the home, yeah, if something happens, then we will just come down and start working" (Sally Perry).

The working relationship around the Perrys is built on there being very little communication between the two of them in the newsroom, with short utterances ("yeah, that's fine") made seemingly in relation to nothing at all. However, they utilise instant messaging – in this case a popular digital messaging and collaboration tool called Slack – in place of a lot of direct verbal communication. This has a number of advantages:

> We just find it easier using instant messaging for passing over links, that sort of thing, but as we showed you with Slack, being able to categorise everything and go back and search, you know it might be you've forgotten and I've sent something and forgotten the details, you [can] go back and find it easily.
>
> *(Sally Perry)*

The mix of online messaging and non-verbal communication is part of a news production system that has a clear separation of roles in the newsroom:

> Yeah we have a sort of system; we know how we work. We've worked so closely for so long that it's almost telepathic. If Simon is publishing the article, I generally just look at them all. I'm the last person normally to do the publishing because I'd have to read over; he's [Simon] dyslexic. So I will do the final read over and then I'll publish, and then I rejig the front page and I do Twitter and I do Facebook and Simon will do WhatsApp, and so there's a sort of routine of how we do stuff.
>
> *(Sally Perry)*

As well as keeping a close eye on website visitors, the Perrys are also attentive to the output of other media on the island. There is a copy of the *County Press* newspaper with stories highlighted throughout. This is to identify stories that appear in the newspaper but that On the Wight may not have covered. Sometimes they follow up these stories and write their own versions of them. Discussion about this practice revealed that they have a tense relationship with the *County Press*:

We have this thing where we, as you saw when you looked through the paper, we looked up highlighted stories which we might then follow up on. But we will always source them, and we always credit them as a source and they take lots of stories from us and they never do. Back and forth with them about it. The editor says it's not their policy, their policy is to not credit any sources.

(Sally Perry)

This policy of crediting others is core to the practice of On the Wight. Indeed, Simon reacted to Sally's statement above by saying, "which coming from the blogging world is, is absolutely revolting". When press releases are used on the site, the practice is to give the author of the press release a named account in order to make it clear to readers that it has not been written by On the Wight.[3] Simon described this as an "open and honest way" to deal with press releases as opposed to the more common method in journalism of lightly adapting them and giving a byline for the journalist.

The gendered hyperlocal newsroom

By far the bulk of material published for On the Wight is written by Sally. On the majority of days[4] the output is a mix of original material, press releases (with bylines as indicated above) or pieces from guest contributors: "That'll be people who might send a weekly piece or might send a monthly piece or a one-off piece" (Sally Perry). Press releases might be from public sector sources or from activist groups (e.g. from the local council, or from anti-fracking campaigners). Our observation noted that Simon's contribution to the writing on the site is, as Sally had indicated, to write headlines for the WhatsApp service and field phone calls related to the commercial side of things ("I can't close a sale, Simon can", said Sally Perry). It became clear that Sally wrote much of the copy for the site and managed much of the day-to-day operations.

She is the engine of the site ... output is amazing. Absolutely amazing and without her the site would be nothing, we would be delivering hardly any content at all. She doesn't like hearing this because she is over-modest but that's the reality. And by her saying about doing the admin, what she means is that she is the organised one and she's the one who stays on top of everything.

(Simon Perry)

Sally has a system for "staying on top of everything". She uses a diary to list what needs to be done on each day and crosses it off when complete (see Figure 6.5). The list includes family commitments as well as On the Wight business. Where a story is listed, it also includes the time it went live:

The day starts for me writing a list of the stories that I'm going to do that day and that generally gets doubled as the day goes on, and then things will move

164 Inside the hyperlocal newsroom

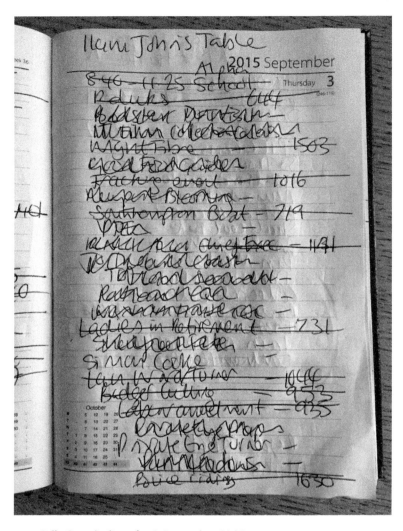

FIGURE 6.5 Sally Perry's diary for 3 September 2015

over to the next day. And then there's always stuff coming in and it can be, you know, really juicy stories or it can just be really quite simple things.

(Sally Perry)

Yet despite the amount she writes, Sally resists being labelled a journalist:

I would never call myself a journalist, I refer to myself as a reporter. I think there is a distinction between the two. When people call us journalists, … I say, "I'm not a journalist, I'm a reporter, I report what goes on".

(Sally Perry)

Sally makes a careful separation between the kinds of stories she writes and those that Simon takes a lead on: "Simon is more interested in investigative stuff because that is what he is better at" (Sally Perry). She argues that she is under-confident and, unlike Simon, has not had any training:

> Things to do with the MP perhaps and council stuff where; or things where's there a lot of research and knowing who's the right, knowing the right route to find that information, I think Simon is a lot better at that.
>
> *(Sally Perry)*

Yet despite this view, Sally cited an example of where she took on an investigation into the closure of a local road after a landslide. The story was a long-running one (from 2007 to 2016) and 55 of the 89 stories written on the subject were by her.[5] Yet she argued that she felt "less confident" doing such work:

> So I will do investigative stuff and I have done in the past, but I feel less confident doing it. I mean I guess there's things like Undercliff Drive as an example, which was done probably in the last year and a half, I don't know; if there's been a landslide in those landlocked properties and the council handled it really badly and I've kind of taken that as my thing. … That's been one thing that has been, it's holding people to account, and it's along those lines.
>
> *(Sally Perry)*

The distinction she made between her own investigative work and Simon's was that his might require a challenge to authority over the phone or face-to-face: "In terms of social skills and in terms of some sort of social engineering of being able to phone someone up and get the answer, I don't feel confident doing that" (Sally Perry).

Recent research has examined the extent to which female journalists in mainstream news organisations are allocated 'soft' news topics because of their gender: "women remain steadfastly pigeon-holed in soft news areas that are deemed less prestigious than hard news genres" (North 2016: 369). Whilst the analysis here has not looked in detail about whether the allocation of story topics is gendered, there is a degree to which the On the Wight newsroom is "hegemonically masculine" (North 2016: 369). Sally situated her own role as 'admin' despite the work she does on investigations and in live reporting local council meetings (a regular and distinctive feature of On the Wight's work). In contrast, Simon's role was described (by Sally) as more reflexive and focused on research. Her response to questions about the use of technology in the newsroom was telling: "Simon's thing is that he will look at stuff, where I would continue working in the same way in which I work, because Simon's background is in technology, and he's always looking to innovate" (Sally Perry). To an extent, the gendered newsroom of On the Wight is inevitably an extension of the gendered domestic space within which it is physically situated.

Summary

This case study looked at the practices and discourses that operate within what we might describe as a semi-professional hyperlocal newsroom. At the time of our research (2016), On the Wight seemed to be at a critical point in their development whereby they recognised the civic value they have as an independent news operation and the role they play in enlivening the Isle of Wight news ecology, yet they had not quite developed the business model that will enable them to sustain their operation at a level that provides a living for them. Much like the Taylors at B31 Voices, they situate themselves partly within a discourse of openness that comes from "the blogging world" (Simon Perry). They give space to other voices on their platforms but rarely in the developed reciprocal way through social media that B31 Voices do. Their main concern is to retain their authenticity, which they operationalise through choosing to publish press releases or statements from third parties in full and with a byline attributed to the organisation, and allowing anonymised comments and articles from citizens.

On the Wight presents an attractive case study for policy-lobbyists in that it is well organised, civically orientated and has a successful shared editorship in place. Yet it is clear that Sally has the responsibility for carrying out the day-to-day practices that sustain the operation and ensure enough content of any kind is published onto the site. All stories end up being checked by her before publication, and although Sally and Simon seem to work relatively autonomously (Sally's notebook is evidence of this), they consult constantly via instant messaging or the occasional verbal exchange. Karen Ross and Cynthia Carter make the point that professional newsrooms have taken-for-granted conventions and routines "which make them difficult to identify as gendered" (2011: 1149). The On the Wight newsroom is certainly highly routinised, and its tasks are, to a degree, divided on gendered lines (Simon can "close a sale", takes on technology projects, and is seen as sufficiently "confident" to undertake investigative work; in contrast, Sally sees her work as 'admin'). The implications of this divide may not, as other studies have focused on (North 2016), be seen in the output of On the Wight. Rather, the perceived success of the operation – that is, its partial fulfilment of the 'fictive' promise of hyperlocal as envisaged by policymakers and lobbyists – is built upon Sally soaking up the burden of its precarity.

Conclusion

This chapter has drawn together three examples of hyperlocal news operations. While *Tyburn Mail* may have operated on a semi-commercial basis (at least in its final iteration) along normative news production lines – paying its small staff, using a trained journalist/editor, operating out of a formal newsroom, securing widespread distribution (via door-to-door delivery) of its print publication – it ultimately failed to secure the trust of its audience, who might have helped offer alternative models of funding in austere times for the part-grant-funded project. As opposed to more radical participatory forms of community news production, *Tyburn Mail* maintained a more formal constitution throughout its lifetime, largely as a result of the need to attract grant funding and sometimes deliver outputs in return for funding. Its necessary flexibility – switching from non-profit to commercial business – often came as a result of having to meet specific funding requirements. While both B31 Voices and On the Wight displayed the potential to become "trusted agents" (Couldry 2004: 24) in their communities, our case study of *Tyburn Mail* shows how the "network of trust" (Couldry 2004: 26) proves a more problematic concept. Citizens in this instance are not invited to participate in co-producing journalism as a matter of course and are, instead, suspicious about the value of the output of the hyperlocal news operation.

In their examination of a suburb of East Birmingham, David Parker and Christian Karner reflect on the notion that "localities contain multiple 'subjugated knowledges' and previously largely private, rarely heard memories of social struggle, exclusion and self-assertion. Such subjugated knowledges need to be excavated, captured and articulated" (2011: 308). They claim that such an excavation needs to take place online via the social Web as much as offline through found local cultural expressions such as graffiti. The point is to counter the partial accounts of communities coming through mainstream media that position places such as Castle Vale within a very narrow representational frame in the public gaze. Instead, richer 'spatial biographies' might have a counter-hegemonic role in working against dominant external myths and instead "recognise the intertwined histories of places and people, roads and their residents" (Parker and Karner 2011: 309). Peter Matthews' account of research interventions in Wester Hailes in Edinburgh notes how working-class residents "resist the discourses of policy-makers that seek to denigrate their neighbourhood to justify intervention" (2014: 25). In Castle Vale, we witnessed similar resistance from residents to the ways that community journalism tells stories that denigrate rather than celebrate.

B31 Voices and On the Wight, on the other hand, might be seen as even smaller-scale, digitally mediated examples of what Charles Eisendrath (1979) calls the "mom-and-pop" press. Eisendrath's portrait of small-town USA community newspapers has many parallels with the operations of the Taylors and the Perrys. Eisendrath makes the point that these tiny operations work in ignorance of the travails of the market and with no desire to push alternative political agendas: "they avoid rigid politics, support the idea of small, workable communities, and pour everything they have into intensely local, rather than personal coverage" (1979: 72). In doing this, and in common with those hyperlocals in chapter 5 who advocate for the importance of fostering relationships on real-world or digital local news beats, they fill a gap that the diminished and retreating mainstream local press has let slip from its grasp. The same is true in our examples. The minutiae of lost pets and keys in South Birmingham certainly does not seem to interest the city-wide *Birmingham Mail*, while On the Wight work hard to distinguish themselves from what they feel is the *County Press'* over-commercialised offer. The gap that On the Wight saw was the lack of authenticity in incumbent media, which they

168 Inside the hyperlocal newsroom

promptly filled in order to go from outsiders to insiders: "We've stuck our necks out where other news, other media, didn't" (Simon Perry). In both the B31 Voices and On the Wight case studies, women are at the centres of the operations; but while Sas Taylor has developed reciprocal strategies that take the pressure off her and instead allow the audience to generate and sustain content, at On the Wight we can see how routines become (no doubt unconsciously) divided along gender lines as the process of generating news content becomes framed as 'admin'.

Each of these case studies offers insight into the stability of "the new forms of trust on which [community media] rely" (Couldry 2004: 27). Couldry was interested, on the one hand, in the extent to which such forms were participatory – and in B31 Voices we see a well-developed example of participation – but he was also interested in how such forms might rely on "hidden subsidies" (2004: 27). Our case studies relied on hidden subsidies in various ways. As sophisticated as it has been over the years in its securing of grants to make up the shortfall from advertising, *Tyburn Mail* found itself in the precarious position of relying on grant funding from a single source. Having lost that grant, it couldn't increase its revenue from advertising sufficiently to provide enough income for it to continue with its full-time journalist still in place. Its closure was inevitable. Unlike B31 Voices, it lacked recourse to the wider community to fill an impending content gap. It is the wider community that provides B31 Voices with its hidden subsidy. In tandem with the exploitation of their own labour, their use of indirect reciprocation enables them to exploit the text and images of the audience as they turn to social media to share their everyday experiences; an example perhaps of finding value in the collective "cognitive surplus" (Shirky 2010) of South Birmingham. The hidden subsidy within the 'fictive' newsroom of On the Wight is again, principally, the self-exploitation of labour. On the Wight attracts interest from philanthropic investors and policy-lobbyists because they manage to situate themselves as disruptive innovators in the local news ecology. They embrace new platforms (such as WhatsApp) and experiment with new journalistic forms (they have undertaken trials with data-generated news stories), yet their operation remains highly precarious. In the next chapter, we examine further how hyperlocals manage the economics of their endeavours.

Notes

1 The *Sunday Mercury* is a tabloid-format regional Sunday newspaper for the West Midlands published by Reach plc (formerly Trinity Mirror Newspapers).
2 Brixton Blog and A Little Bit of Stone are two examples of hyperlocal media operations that have run crowdfunding campaigns with some success.
3 For example, all stories by 'Claire Robertson' on the website are press releases from Island Roads who manage the highways on behalf of the local council. See: http://onthewight.com/author/clairerobertsoncontributes/
4 On the day we undertook our research (3 September 2015) 12 stories were published to the site. Of those, six were written by Sally and the rest were press releases or guest contributions. A regular contributor on sailing had an article published, as did a representative of a local theatre group who reviewed performances.

Inside the hyperlocal newsroom   169

5 The actual figures are: Sally, 55 stories; Simon, 11; joint, 2; official (press releases), 17; other, 4.

References

Atton, Chris (2002) *Alternative Media*. London: Sage.

BBC (2009, 20 October) The fight for a right to report [Online]. Available at: http://news.bbc.co.uk/1/hi/technology/8303381.stm [Accessed 3 May 2016].

BBC (2013, 3 September) The bizarre world of 1970s hyper-local TV [Online]. Available at: www.bbc.co.uk/news/magazine-23906703 [Accessed 6 June 2016].

Birmingham City Council (2016) Census 2011 profiles for Birmingham, wards and constituencies [Online]. Available at: https://www.birmingham.gov.uk/directory_record/75406/census_2011_profiles_for_birmingham_wards_and_constituencies [Accessed 17 December 2017].

Borger, Merel, van Hoof, Anita & Sanders, José (2016) Expecting reciprocity: Towards a model of the participants' perspective on participatory journalism. *New Media & Society*, Vol. 18, No. 5, pp. 708–725.

Bruns, Axel (2008) *Blogs, Wikipedia, Second Life, and Beyond: From Production to Produsage*. New York: Peter Lang.

Buckingham, David & Banaji, Shakuntala (2013) *The Civic Web: Young People, the Internet, and Civic Participation*. Cambridge, MA: MIT Press.

Castle Vale Community Radio (2004) *Community Radio Licence Application Form*. London: Ofcom.

Castle Vale Housing Action Trust (1995) *Castle Vale Master Plan*. Birmingham: Castle Vale Housing Action Trust.

Coatham, Veronica & Martinali, Lisa (2010) The role of community-based organisations in sustaining community regeneration: An evaluation of the development and contribution of Castle Vale Community Regeneration Services (CVCRS). *International Journal of Sociology and Social Policy*, Vol. 30, No. 1–2, pp. 84–101.

Costera Meijer, Irene (2012) When news hurts: The promise of participatory storytelling for urban problem neighbourhoods. *Journalism Studies*, Vol. 14, No. 1, pp. 13–28.

Couldry, Nick (2004) The productive "consumer" and the dispersed "citizen". *International Journal of Cultural Studies*, Vol. 7, No. 1, pp. 21–32.

Department for Communities and Local Government (2015) English indices of deprivation 2015 [Online]. Available at: https://www.gov.uk/government/statistics/english-indices-of-deprivation-2015 [Accessed 17 December 2017].

Dovey, Jon, Alevizou, Giota & Williams, Andy (2016) Citizenship, value and digital culture. In: Hargreaves, I. & Hartley, J. (eds) *The Creative Citizen Unbound: How Social Media Contribute to Civics, Democracy and Creative Communities*. Bristol: Policy Press, pp. 75–102.

Eisendrath, Charles R. (1979) Back to the people with the mom-and-pop press. *Columbia Journalism Review*, Vol. 18, No. 4, pp. 72–74.

Evans, Richard & Long, Derek (2000) Policy review. Estate-based regeneration in England: Lessons from Housing Action Trusts. *Housing Studies*, Vol. 15, No. 2, pp. 301–317.

Geels, Kathryn (2015, 18 September) Action research in audience analytics … our 10 projects announced [Online]. *Nesta* [blog]. Available at: www.nesta.org.uk/blog/action-research-audience-analyticsour-10-projects-announced [Accessed 15 May 2016].

Goode, Luke (2009) Social news, citizen journalism and democracy. *New Media & Society*, Vol. 11, No. 8, pp. 1287–1305.

Harcup, Tony & O'Neill, Deirdre (2016) What is news? News values revisited (again). *Journalism Studies*. doi:00A0;10.1080/1461670X.2016.1150193

Hartley, Sarah (2010, 19 April) Winners at the Talk About Local and Guardian Local awards. *The Guardian*. Available at: www.theguardian.com/local/2010/apr/19/talk-about-local-unconference-award-winners [Accessed 17 December 2017].

Island Echo (2017) About us – Island Echo [Online]. *Island Echo*. Available at: www.islandecho.co.uk/contact-us/island-echo/ [Accessed 17 December 2017].

Isle of Wight Council (2017) Isle of Wight facts and figures – Census 2011 [Online]. Available at: https://www.iwight.com/Council/OtherServices/Isle-of-Wight-Facts-and-Figures/Useful-Sources [Accessed 17 December 2017].

Isle of Wight County Press Limited (2015) Report and Financial Statements: Year Ended 30 June 2015.

Lewis, Seth C. (2015) Reciprocity as a key concept for social media and society. *Social Media and Society*, Vol. 1, No. 1. doi:10.1177/2056305115580339

Lewis, Seth C., Holton, Avery E. & Coddington, Mark (2014) Reciprocal journalism: A concept of mutual exchange between journalists and audiences. *Journalism Practice*, Vol. 8, No. 2, pp. 229–241.

Madanipour, Ali (2005) Value of place: Can physical capital be a driver for urban change? The experience of Castle Vale, Birmingham. In: Commission for Architecture & the Built Environment (ed.) *Physical Capital: How Great Places Boost Public Value*. London: CABE, pp. 48–70.

Matthews, Peter (2014) Neighbourhood belonging, social class and social media: Providing ladders to the cloud. *Housing Studies*, Vol. 30, No. 1, pp. 22–39.

Mornement, Adam (2005) *No Longer Notorius: The Revival of Castle Vale, 1993–2005*. Birmingham: Castle Vale Housing Action Trust.

North, Louise (2016) The gender of "soft" and "hard" news. *Journalism Studies*, Vol. 17, No. 3, pp. 356–373.

Ofcom (2009) *Local and Regional Media in the UK*. London: Ofcom.

Office for National Statistics (2017) Most deprived areas in the UK [Online]. Available at: https://www.ons.gov.uk/aboutus/transparencyandgovernance/freedomofinformationfoi/mostdeprivedareasintheuk [Accessed 17 December 2017].

Parker, David & Karner, Christian (2011) Remembering the Alum Rock Road: Reputational geographies and spatial biographies. *Midland History*, Vol. 36, No. 2, pp. 292–309.

Pennycook, Lauren (2015) *Click And Connect: Case Studies of Innovative Hyperlocal News Providers*. Dunfermline: Carnegie UK Trust.

Radcliffe, Damian (2012) *Here and Now: UK Hyperlocal Media Today*. London: Nesta.

Rosen, Jay (2006, 27 June) The people formerly known as the audience [Online]. *PressThink*. Available at: http://archive.pressthink.org/2006/06/27/ppl_frmr.html [Accessed 15 December 2014].

Ross, Karen & Carter, Cynthia (2011) Women and news: A long and winding road. *Media, Culture & Society*, Vol. 33, No. 8, pp. 1148–1165.

Schudson, Michael (1999) What public journalism knows about journalism but doesn't know about "public". In: Glasser, T. L. (ed.) *The Idea of Public Journalism*. London: Guilford Press, pp. 118–133.

Shirky, Clay (2010) *Cognitive Surplus: How Technology Makes Consumers into Collaborators*. New York: Penguin.

Singer, Jane B. (2014) User-generated visibility: Secondary gatekeeping in a shared media space. *New Media & Society*, Vol. 16, No. 1, pp. 55–73.

SOCITM (2010) *Better Connected 2010*. Northampton: Society of Information Technology Management.

Spyridou, Lia-Paschalia, Matsiola, Maria, Veglis, Andreas, Kalliris, George & Dimoulas, Charalambos (2013) Journalism in a state of flux: Journalists as agents of technology innovation and emerging news practices. *International Communication Gazette*, Vol. 75, No. 1, pp. 76–98.

Taylor, Sas (2010, 7 July) Welcome to B31 blog [Online]. *B31 Voices*. Available at: http://b31.org.uk/2010/07/welcome/ [Accessed 20 May 2017].

Townend, Judith (2009, 29 July) VentnorBlog shows us high-quality hyperlocal reporting with the Vestas story [Online]. *journalism.co.uk*. Available at: https://blogs.journalism.co.uk/2009/07/29/ventnorblog-shows-us-high-quality-hyperlocal-reporting-with-the-vestas-story/ [Accessed 20 June 2016].

Turner, Jerome (2015) Good dog, bad dog: Exploring audience uses and attitudes to hyperlocal community news media through the prism of banal pet stories. *Anthropological Notebooks*, Vol. 21, No. 3, pp. 39–50.

7

SUSTAINING HYPERLOCAL JOURNALISM

In this chapter, we look further at the extent to which hyperlocal publishing can be sustainable in economic terms, having begun to address these issues in our case studies. For the one- or two-person operations that largely comprise the UK hyperlocal sector, sustainability practices are as important as journalistic practices, occupying just as much time and often carried out by the same person. In the last two chapters, we have looked at how reciprocity is a key factor in ensuring the viability of what are, for the most part, lightly funded or unfunded hyperlocal operations, and our case studies noted the risks of relying on grant funding as well as the hidden labour costs of operations with a strong community focus. One might come to the conclusion that for a sector upon which much rests in order to 'fill the gap', it all seems rather precarious. Yet writing in 2012, Johanna Vehkoo and Clare Cook outlined the potential of hyperlocal publishing as a space of interest for journalism start-ups. Noting the interest taken by policymakers and a technological shift that makes start-up costs low and the potential to reach new audiences high – as a result of growing dominance of mobile devices "capable of accessing this local content" (Vehkoo and Cook 2012: 45) – their verdict was that the sector was "vibrant yet struggling" (44). That vibrancy came as a result of the ease with which hyperlocal can get off the ground and the fact there was seemingly no shortage of concerned citizens wishing to talk about their neighbourhoods. It seems that whilst doing hyperlocal journalism is seemingly straightforward, making money is an altogether trickier business.

Jones and Spicer (2009: 10) argue that the term 'entrepreneur' has moved beyond the narrow Schumpeterian notion of the 'self-made' person profiting from disrupting the market. It is now applied in a much broader sense to a range of individuals who might display entrepreneurial behaviours in different contexts. Entrepreneurs might be socially rather than economically focused, or they might perhaps operate in the public sector, identifying efficiencies or improving relationships with citizens. Jones and Spicer argue that this generalisation in the use of the term is symptomatic of the way in which an enterprise culture reached into many aspects of public life in the 1980s and 1990s. Irrespective of setting, there has emerged a clear, dominant discourse of entrepreneurship: "[It] is a relatively coherent discourse which emphasises risk taking, calculation and economising, and represents these points in unfailing positive ways" (Jones and Spicer 2009: 15). It's clear that the entrepreneurial "fictive" (Jones 2014) figure of the citizen as journalist permeates the wider commentary on hyperlocal, yet there's little reference to the precarious lived experience of doing hyperlocal that we discussed in the last chapter.

Some research has touched on issues related to precariousness in journalism careers. Mirjam Gollmitzer's (2014) study sought to highlight the potential for self-exploitation within the working lives of German freelance journalists. She found stress and satisfaction in equal measure within the independent context in which they carried out their profession (Gollmitzer 2014: 832–833). Yet there was a strong desire to do justice to the normative values of journalism, even if it required a degree of self-exploitation: "the complex narratives of freedom, independence, and public service ethos illustrate the will to journalistic professionalism, even as the acute awareness of economic insecurity and high stress levels relativizes those claims" (Gollmitzer 2014: 837). Gollmitzer's study contributes to the growing literature about the experiences of workers in the creative industries which have focused on the issue of precariousness (Hesmondhalgh and Baker 2008, 2011; Ross 2008). Gill and Pratt (2008) describe two ways in which we can understand the term. First, "precariousness (in relation to work) refers to all forms of insecure, contingent, flexible work – from illegalized, casualized and temporary employment, to homeworking, piecework and freelancing" (Gill and Pratt 2008: 3). However, they also note how the term "embodies a critique of contemporary capitalism in tandem with an optimistic sense of the potential for change" (Gill and Pratt 2008: 10). Those working in a "precarious" way have the potential to see "new subjectivities, new socialities and new kinds of politics" (Gill and Pratt 2008: 10). Hesmondhalgh and Baker's workplace ethnography of the television industry shows "the specific ways in which precariousness is registered and negotiated in the lives of young workers in one media industry" (2008: 104). Their findings identify the vulnerability of working in the creative sector, yet they also draw attention to the "symbolic nature of cultural products" (Hesmondhalgh and Baker 2008: 114) produced by workers. Like the television programmes they discuss, local journalism also has a "symbolic power" (Hesmondhalgh and Baker 2008) that comes with pressures and bears a certain weight of responsibility in terms of enacting inherent normative values.

In looking across research into the motivations of journalism students, Baines and Kennedy note that students are less motivated by the normative public service ideals of journalism than they are by the promise of a career that shares the attractive features perceived to be common to other jobs in the creative and cultural sector: "independence; risk-taking; non-routine; autonomy; creativity; control (and

174 Sustaining hyperlocal journalism

in some cases the prospects of high earnings)" (2010: 105). These features, they argue, are also ones that are dominant in discourses of entrepreneurship. They specifically cite the opportunity that running hyperlocal media operations offers for the enterprising journalism student: "the establishment of such an enterprise can offer the autonomy, independence and routine-free career sought by many would-be journalists and which is often no longer found in traditional hierarchical corporate media organisations" (Baines and Kennedy 2010: 98). Traditional approaches to enterprise education need rethinking; an emphasis on experimentation and creativity can better prepare the graduate to deal with reality of a career that might never experience secure, full-time employment in the mainstream news industry. Journalists should be trained "not only to work as journalists (employed or freelance), but to establish independent enterprises" (Baines and Kennedy 2010: 98). Thus hyperlocal is situated as an ideal that not only deals with issues of precarity and scarcity of employment opportunities, but is also a vehicle through which the socially conscious entrepreneur can "extend the plurality and diversity of journalism – and journalists – serving society" (Baines and Kennedy 2010: 109). Whilst running hyperlocal websites has now become a useful feature of undergraduate and postgraduate journalism training (in the UK at least), it is unclear how many emphasise the need for entrepreneurial skills alongside journalistic ones.

This chapter thus addresses hyperlocal publishers as entrepreneurial subjects as much as journalists. It draws on the responses from our survey and interviews related to the financial status of hyperlocal operations. We explore the underlying attitudes that hyperlocal publishers have towards the economics of hyperlocal within the context of volunteerism and working for a 'greater good'. Essentially, we ask the question: why do so many of these publishers seem content to make little or no money from their activities? We begin first, though, by drawing attention to the fact that mainstream media organisations do not have that much success themselves when operating in this space.

The failure of commercial hyperlocal media operations

It would be fair to say that corporate news organisations have a chequered track record in developing hyperlocal media operations. In the UK, "the *Guardian*'s toe dipped in the waters of hyperlocal journalism" (Thomas *et al.* 2013: no page) through the setting up of three city-based blogs in Edinburgh, Leeds and Cardiff. This Guardian Local experiment closed in 2011 after just over a year of operation, with the newspaper claiming that it was "not sustainable in its present form" (Pickard 2011). It had been set up with the hope of "connecting local citizens to information sources and resources" (Pickard 2011), and its approach was to work with local online activists to create genuine impact on issues of local governance and accountability. Their Leeds blogger described making the shift from following "the story in a very traditional journalistic way" (Thomas *et al.* 2013: no page) to one that worked through bringing together citizens with politicians and mainstream journalists via 'Tweetups' and other offline events. In many ways they acted as brokers rather than journalists; as William Perrin of Talk About Local argues: "Guardian Local showed that you can create a distinctive local voice online that adds to the local news ecology and engages the local blogosphere" (2011). It was sustained for its short life by "subsidy from their charitable parent" (Perrin 2011) without seemingly any plan to seek out local advertising for the blogs.

Perhaps the largest commercial experiment in hyperlocal publishing run in the UK was the Local People network operated at the time by Northcliffe Media, which did at least think through the financial aspects, operating as a franchise operation. A network of paid community publishers curated content and wrote stories in small towns across the UK. However, it gradually removed financial support with around 100 publisher roles reduced to 75 in a restructuring process in August 2012 and the remaining posts axed the following year (Lambourne 2013). Research by Thurman *et al.* examining this network found that it suffered in comparison to smaller-scale, more embedded hyperlocal sites with a more civic-minded approach:

> the reliance on community publishers from journalism backgrounds suggests that particular assumptions were made about the needs of such a community-driven project In particular, the idea of community management as a skill distinct from traditional publishing roles appears to be, if not completely absent, then not a priority.
>
> *(2011: 7)*

David Baines (2012) offers a similar story of a lack of authentic community voice in a case study of a major UK regional (unnamed) news publisher's hyperlocal project. This ultimately foundered as a result of meeting the "Media Company's corporate needs, not the community's" (Baines 2012: 163). Partly, the issue was in the desire of the media company to have a network of hyperlocal sites that were identical in nature and situated as spokes with a mainstream media title at the centre. Thus, there was "one-way traffic from centre to periphery" which "tended to reinforce this community's isolation" (Baines 2012: 163–164). Andy Price (2010) gives a detailed description of the development of a hyperlocal web strategy by another local newspaper, the *Evening Gazette* in Middlesbrough. This allowed a network of about 300 citizen bloggers to create content for the for the Trinity Mirror-owned newspaper. Price notes the venture's success for the newspaper, but argues that the exercise was limited in realising its "full democratic potential" (Price 2010: 147). In detailing the editorial and technical process, he reveals that those blogging in the service of the newspaper ultimately conform to its practices and its news agenda: "there doesn't tend to be anything too contentious", claimed the newspaper's assistant editor (in Price 2010: 147).

A similar critique of large-scale commercial interest in hyperlocal is made by St John *et al.*, whose analysis of Patch.com in the US suggests that it lacked a "community sensibility" (2014: 208). Patch's decline was a significant moment in what had been a much-heralded hyperlocal scene in the US. By 2011 the multinational media corporation AOL had invested significantly in Patch's widespread network of hyperlocal news providers, employing 800 journalists in 850 communities covering 22 states (Auletta 2011). AOL's CEO Tim Armstrong told the *New Yorker*: "Local is … an untapped market, for the most part, and one of the largest commercial opportunities online that have yet to be won" (in Auletta 2011). But a few years later AOL's resolve was faltering, and by 2012 the company had laid off up to 200 of its full-time editorial staff on the project, signalling "deep financial difficulties for the hyperlocal news marketplace" (Pavlik 2013: 9). The next year "up to 550" further layoffs were announced by the company (Wilhelm 2013), and in January 2014, after losing around $200 million, AOL sold its majority shareholding in what the *New York Times* called its "troubled hyperlocal news division" to the investment company Hale Global (Kaufman 2014).

Also in the US, Jeff Kaye and Stephen Quinn, writing in 2010, noted the failure of Backfence (active from 2005 to 2007), which "never really caught on" (2010: 45) despite investment of $3 million. After its collapse, its founder Mark Potts said that the missing ingredient, essential to success in the hyperlocal space, was community: "You have to get the community involved. There's no substitute for that" (Potts 2007). Without that, "Backfence's hyperlocal sites were drying up, short of news, advertisements and readers" (Kaye and Quinn 2010: 45). Mark Glaser (2010) argues that a key explanatory factor behind such trends lies in the differences in motivations between community members and commercial media in starting and maintaining hyperlocal operations. Commercial outlets "that have created hyperlocal sites are trying to engage their readers, while also creating a place for smaller, niche advertisers who want to reach a highly geographically targeted audience" (Glaser 2010: 585). In contrast, Glaser points out, the "motivation for starting independent hyper-locals is often to tell the untold stories of communities" (2010: 585). The independent sites "are run as a labor of love by their publishers and their communities" (Glaser 2010: 585). Jones and Salter's overview of commercial hyperlocal services (2012: 103–107) similarly notes the potentially compromising tensions between the need for hyperlocal sites to have an emphasis on community engagement whilst also ensuring they attract advertisers.

The economics of hyperlocal publishing in the UK

Drawing on the survey research carried out by Williams and Harte (with Judith Townend and Steven Barnett), we gained insights into the economics of hyperlocal news in the UK. The survey found a sector that was quite fluid in nature, with some sites starting up and then closing in quick succession, while others had been operating successfully for several years. Nearly three-quarters of survey respondents (73 per cent) had been publishing for more than three years and around a third for more than five years (32 per cent). Inclusive of all aspects of editorial, management and finance, most respondents (83 per cent) said they worked less than half a week on their hyperlocal publications and 17 per cent worked something close to a normal working week (more than 31 hours). When factoring in the work of other contributors, more than four in ten publishers (43 per cent) worked ten hours or less per week, but a quarter had a collective labour time of more than 50 hours of work each week.

As Pekkala and Cook (2012) note, the availability of easy-to-use and largely free blogging software has resulted in virtually zero start-up and ongoing costs in terms of technology. That's not to say all sites are operating in this way, and the survey found that the larger sites had significant financial costs to bear. While around eight out of ten (78 per cent) put the cost of running their site at less than £100 per month, at the other end of the scale, ten sites (or 6 per cent of respondents) spent over £1,000 per month. In between, around 10 per cent spent between £100 and £500, and around 5 per cent (nine sites) spent between £500 and £1,000. Many of those running at a very low cost base covered all costs themselves and retrieved none of their albeit modest outlay from income generation. Nearly two-thirds of respondents (63 per cent) said they do not generate revenues. Some do raise money from other sources, but for one in ten of these, the revenue raised does not cover their costs. Ten per cent raise just enough to pay their bills, but only one in six make enough to return a profit, which is paid to themselves or others or reinvested in the site. Thus, the UK hyperlocal sector is characterised by its reliance of financial subsidy from publishers themselves, not to mention the subsidy of labour in the form of volunteerism.

Where money was earned, it was in relatively small sums. Of the 62 who said they earned income, 23 were making less than £100 in an average month and 15 were earning between £100 and £500. A further 10 respondents generated between £501 and £1,000, and 14 earned the more significant sum of over £1,000 per month. The majority of these (n = 47) cited advertising (which included print in a few cases as well as online) as the most common funding source. A further 19 said they employed sponsored features, 15 secured donations, 4 generated income from subscriptions, and 15 received grants. Most attempted to use multiple sources of funding, but even then, 27 of this group of 61 still had to supplement their operations with their own money. Other methods of income generation cited included: selling merchandise through local businesses; selling editorial content to other news organisations; affiliate schemes (such as commissions on restaurant bookings); paid-for listings in a business directory; and sponsorship of the site by a third party. There were also some who had separate business endeavours which cross-subsidised the community news operation.

Despite their lack of income from hyperlocal sites, most publishers seemed confident they could sustain their endeavours, in the short term at least. Just over half (53 per cent) believed they could move beyond the current level of output and increase it, while over a third (36 per cent) were confident they would maintain current levels. Only one in ten thought that current levels were unsustainable or that – in the case of just four respondents – the site might have to close down completely. Reasons for a predicted decline or possible closure consisted mainly of changing personal circumstances or the challenges of making enough money to remunerate themselves adequately for their time. One respondent felt they were "spending far too much time" on their blog, while another cited "burnout" before stating that they do not have enough time and the revenue which would buy that time was not forthcoming. (The issue over lack of time and the feeling that they were exploiting their own labour also arose in further research, as we shall see later in this chapter.) Another respondent said they had set themselves a deadline of three months to find paying advertisers, otherwise they would close; and another said that they needed time to "create a critical mass of visitors to attract business sponsorship to sustain the project". Concerns also arose over having the right skills with which to find that funding: "I'm not a sales person, and would rather be developing the site editorially". There were also various personal reasons given that included: no longer having financial support from an employed spouse; moving out of the community; and having a new job which resulted in "less time and enthusiasm" for running a hyperlocal news site.

The conflicted hyperlocal entrepreneur

The survey responses offer a glimpse into the precarious financial underpinning of hyperlocal in the UK, offering similar findings to van Kerkhoven and Bakker's study of the "difficult circumstances" facing Dutch hyperlocals (2014: 307). Further interviews would reveal the lived experience of running news operations with such seemingly slim resources, and it is to these interviews that this chapter now turns in order to discover what range of attitudes to entrepreneurship emerge within a practice so often situated as primarily a civic endeavour but that is playing an increasingly important role in local media spheres. Specifically, we focus on the range of motivations of practitioners, look at the extent to which they draw on an entrepreneurial discourse in describing their practice, and explore the degree to which there is self-exploitation and precariousness within the sector. Again, while our focus is on the UK, the issues discussed here mirror the concerns of researchers in the US and Europe who are investigating similar networks of community news operations. We ask: what discourses – "institutionalised and taken-for-granted ways of thinking" (Jones 2014: 241) – of entrepreneurship do hyperlocal publishers draw upon? In what ways do they situate themselves as civic activists or digital business innovators, or indeed both, at the forefront of a journalism enterprise revolution?

In our research, hyperlocal publishers fell into two broadly distinct camps. Like the subjects in Gollmitzer's (2014) research, the majority of those interviewed tended to exploit their own labour while drawing on a discourse that emphasises the civic value of their work. The sacrifices they make were explained away in that context. A smaller group of interviewees were situated within "historically masculine-framed ideas of entrepreneurship" (Jones 2014: 241) whereby they discussed their work within "a relatively coherent discourse which emphasises risk-taking, calculation and economising, and represents these points in unfailing positive ways" (Jones and Spicer 2009: 15). As one interviewee made clear, "I've always been very sure about the fact that there's no point in setting up something that doesn't have a commercial footing, because to me that's just a hobby" (Filton Voice).

The schism between the two groups was often made evident when they came together at networking events, where there seemed to be a clash of discourses: "We've been to this conference … a couple of years ago, we were commercial and we kind of felt we had a bit of a devil's eye there, how dare you be commercial" (The Lincolnite). This is not a sector that one could call internally cohesive, and another interviewee also talked about feeling ill at ease in the company of others doing the same thing: "I went [to an event on hyperlocal] and I was the only person it seemed, it may not be true, who wasn't either a hard, right-on campaigning activist or an absolute über geek. I seemed like the only journalist there" (West Hampstead Life). However, members of both groups talked about the many roles they had to assume within their operations in a positive and unproblematic light. It is clear that upon starting a hyperlocal there was a need to then develop a wider spectrum of skills that had not always been anticipated:

> I do everything really. So, there's selling and then making up adverts, because I tend to do artwork for most of the people who advertise, and then invoicing and chasing money for that, so that's another side of it. Writing and editing, doing techy work really.
>
> *(Bitterne Park)*

The approach to picking up the required skills and knowledge was often a matter of just learning on the job: "I'm completely self-taught … I practised writing through blogging and basically picked up everything else on the way. I taught myself to video edit and shoot video" (Salford Online). Sometimes practices were gleaned from observing other hyperlocals:

> We've picked stuff up. I think some stuff we've learned from other hyperlocal sites. We always keep an eye on other sites across the country to see what people are doing, the ideas they have, the stuff they're covering, how they're covering it.
>
> *(WV11)*

Learning new skills was part of the pleasure of having to (usually) manage every aspect of the operation themselves:

> I do quite enjoy laying out adverts. It's another skill I'm developing, it's another string to my bow that I've learnt. I've always been a firm believer in that the more skills you have, the more adaptable you become.
>
> *(Caerphilly Observer)*

The gap between the discourses in the two groups was most evident when interviewees were asked directly about how they sustained their operations. The majority articulated a clear rejection of their hyperlocal operation needing to sustain itself on an economic basis:

180 Sustaining hyperlocal journalism

> I'm really wary of the linkage of community stuff and money … I just think when money gets involved, it can be really tricky. I don't care if there's money involved, it's more about what people feel they want to do.
>
> *(Southwark Living Streets)*

The resistance to generating income often involved a fear of losing independence and tainting the authentic relationship interviewees felt they had with their community; a fear of no longer being their 'voice': "It's always been seen as the independent and uncensored voice … and I think that's how I want it to continue" (Digbeth is Good). There may have been an element of bravado in some responses, with a sense that making money was entirely possible, just not desirable: "If I was interested in becoming a small business, I could do that, but it doesn't interest me in the slightest" (West Hampstead Life). One described the potential of their site to make "£50,000–£100,000 a year" but said they would rather operate it as a community venture: "I feel it's more of a community service than anything else … . I sometimes feel I'm just doing it for a labour of love. It's for the readers. So that's the part I like about it" (Saddleworth News).

(S)hyperlocals

But confidence was also a problem. Indeed, some of the same people taking ideological positions against making money also cited confidence issues. Some publishers recognised that they needed funding, usually very modest amounts, to avoid the situation of having to pay for running costs themselves, yet they simply did not feel able to approach businesses, or indeed anyone, for funds: "I'm terrible about going and asking people for money, just really don't enjoy it at all" (The Kirkbymoorside Town Blog). Some waited until businesses approached them rather than seeking them out: "If somebody wants to advertise and there's a couple of quid in it, then it happens" (Gurn Nurn). Those happy to accept advertising, and able to ask for it, did so within a discourse of community enterprise whereby it is fine to receive funds local traders but less so large corporate organisations:

> [We were asked] what would you do if Tesco came along and said they wanted to advertise in your paper, and we said we wouldn't do it. And actually, I hold the same view. We're about the community. We're about supporting the small businesses.
>
> *(Wayland News)*

Still, many reported that they found the balance between doing journalism and reaching out to the local business community too time-consuming and often a distraction from what they felt was their core work (keeping their hyperlocal updated with content). In fact, for some it was *any* sense of operating in a commercial space that would be the distraction, by making the endeavour much less pleasurable: "The thought of having the economic pressure of actually having to make a living through it, I think it would just totally take away the enjoyment actually, and it becomes a chore" (Crosspool News). Occasionally the interviewees wanted to discuss what was meant by the term 'hyperlocal', but only one found it a barrier to income generation: "We found that it just took a lot of time to explain what it was we were doing, why we were doing it, how it could benefit the business and why they should do it. So it just wasn't really feasible" (WV11).

Precarity and self-exploitation

Another common thread in the findings was that hyperlocal producers spent more time than perhaps they wanted to on producing content and running their sites. One interviewee said, "It's very rare that I'm not doing something to the paper or the site, finding articles, interacting or whatever" (The Ambler). Even where the hours were modest, the position taken was that it was too much in the light of either slim or no pay: "at least between 14 and 20 hours. It really is an unpaid job" (Broughton Spurtle). The process of doing hyperlocal often feels like it completely takes over the lives of its producers. Although there was a recognition of the extent to which they were exploiting themselves, issues of exploitation extended beyond the individual hyperlocal producer and out to their network of contributors. Many described how their operations relied on sometimes quite large networks of volunteers who gave small amounts of time: "I love that we are able to work with so many community writers and [that] brings a real diversity of content to the site" (Star & Crescent). The value gained by these volunteers was usually expressed in two ways: either they were seen as benefiting by gaining new skills or they were assumed to be benefiting emotionally from the act of contributing: "I think the other volunteers also feel that they're working for the good of the community" (The Ambler).

Clearly, without volunteers, many of the hyperlocals interviewed would not be operating in anywhere near the capacity they were, but even amongst those who talked up the value of volunteerism, there were some concerns about the degree to which volunteers were being exploited. There was much anxiety about the amount paid or not paid to those contributors to hyperlocals and some expressed a limit to volunteerism:

> The number of people who want to blog about the neighbourhood for free, which is basically what I've been doing for quite some time, in a sustained long-term way is very, very small, but what I've found is that crowdsourcing bits of content and stitching it together is a way that can bring people in.
>
> *(Greener Leith)*

Many interviewees had trouble articulating what rewards they felt were due to others:

> I know time is money, whatever the words are. I've made a tiny bit of money out of the site … it might mean that if someone was doing some of the techie

stuff, I could give them a few quid, because I'm a believer you work, you should get paid for it.

(Cwmbran Life)

One hyperlocal seemed to realise that embracing a more enterprise-focused approach would solve their worries about exploiting others:

What I'd like is I'd like to make more money, I'd like everybody who works on it to make more money. I want it to go further afield. I'd love to be able to franchise it out around the country. That would be great. I've no idea how to do that.

(Bedford Clanger)

This tendency to fantasise about possible outcomes where the money issue is solved was a recurring theme. For most, the prospect of being able to pay people on a regular basis felt like a distant prospect and one in which the rewards might take various forms:

I'd like to maybe be able to pay a retainer to some of the people who are regular contributors, on the basis that it might not be much, it might not even be NUJ rates, but it might be if you could post a story a week, you could have £40 a week or something. Just a gesture. I'd like that. It wouldn't even have to be cash. It could be an Amazon voucher … . I'd just like to somehow have something to say thanks to people; that would be nice.

(Abergele Post)

Cross-subsidy, grants and alternative economies

The tendency towards self-exploitation resulted in a degree of informal cross-subsidy whereby time was taken out of personal life to be spent on producing the hyperlocal ("I've got an understanding wife" – Leeds Citizen). But there was more formal cross-subsidising happening as well. Some hyperlocals described doing paid journalism-related freelance work as a form of cross-subsidy, but others discussed how connected business ventures provided the financial underpinning for their hyperlocal. One hyperlocal cross-subsidised through producing magazines for a trade union, and another produced a trade journal. Another ran a business 'expo' that they claimed provided all the resources to employ two people to work on their hyperlocal site.

Despite the lack of desire or confidence to generate income, as detailed above, there was evidence of hyperlocals generating funds in innovative ways that demonstrate an entrepreneurial attitude. In one instance, a hyperlocal site that outwardly seemed to be very successful in drawing in advertising was in fact using a bartering system:

The adverts on there, most of those adverts you see have all been swapped. I wanted some tyres for my car so a guy from [tyre company] swapped me some tyres. I wanted my lawn doing, I've put one on for a lawn care company who's done my lawn for me. So, there's no money there, I've just swapped them all for things.

(Saddleworth News)

In another instance, bartering was a way to get content onto the site and advertising was only used when cash was needed:

If I give you more content, more space with a bit of free advertising, will you write me two or three articles on financial advice and that kind of thing. So there'd be barter, I'd be bartering in – there'd be no cash transaction, it'd be bartering in. And only if I needed to pay for the server that month, I'd go and sell some advertising.

(Knutsford Times)

Another hyperlocal asked for donations rather than seek advertising and used an electronic payment system to allow readers to donate directly. However, he had instances where the donations came in a more direct form:

A guy came up to me – this is amazing – a guy wanted to meet me, this is a few months ago, and he wanted to meet me in the community centre, and he gave me £300 in cash, £150 of which were pound coins. I didn't ask where it came from.

(Salford Star)

But, again, there was tension about how to deal with money. Some hyperlocals had not even the most basic knowledge of what might happen should they attract income: "Being paranoid I rang up the Tax Office to find out what the code was for some unique tax" (Cwmbran Life). Others were keen to dispose of any excess income through philanthropic means:

Any profit we make, we put into local good causes ... it keeps the money circulating locally, but we don't want to bang the drum too much about it because we don't want to be too sanctimonious, be smug about it.

(Broughton Spurtle)

It was no surprise to see take-up of grant initiatives, given the attention this sector receives from public funders. Scott Rodgers (2017) notes that such funding has a broader aim of trying to create the appearance of a viable 'movement' well beyond the small number of experimental hyperlocal projects that are funded. He argues that Destination Local (the 2012 funding programme of UK charity Nesta) in effect brought "the UK hyperlocal space to life ... giving the appearance of

184 Sustaining hyperlocal journalism

motion, by emphasizing experimentation, public engagement and information-sharing" (Rodgers 2017: 13). Further philanthropic investment from Carnegie UK Trust in 2014 saw not only the arrival of more funds for further experimentation by UK hyperlocalists – and thus a continuation of the desire to animate the movement – but also a more direct appeal to government for support and recognition for the sector, with calls for reviews of a skewed media regulatory climate in order "to start levelling the playing field on financial support" (Carnegie UK Trust 2014: 14). The key message though is in line with much of the discourse prevalent in wider creative industries policy literature; that is, a need to support small-scale entrepreneurship in recognition of what is argued to be a shift in the industrial conditions under which news is produced:

> The 20th century model was for news to be gathered and delivered by institutions, very much shaped by the technologies available to them. The 21st century model shaped by new technologies is for news to be gathered and delivered by individuals and small specialist organisations and networks.
>
> *(Carnegie UK Trust 2014: 2)*

For many hyperlocal publishers interviewed, writing funding bids was a key part of their work, although securing funding was not easy: "That's another part of my job to try and find grants, and obviously they're harder and harder to come by" (The Ambler). In this particular instance, the grant income was not directly for doing hyperlocal work but was instead for a related activity that would cross-subsidise the hyperlocal: "I do other work with community groups doing digital media projects" (The Ambler). In a similar example, another interviewee was happy that the funding was for related activities rather than work directly on the hyperlocal, making clear that where cross-subsidy happened, it did not go towards paying individuals. But undoubtedly the income flowing into the sector is seeing an entrepreneurial response, with those securing success noting its competitive nature:

> We were one of ten projects out of 165 to be awarded that funding, and that allowed us to set up the business as a limited company, and really it went from being a side project to being our main project.
>
> *(Kentish Towner)*

Social entrepreneurship as an interpretative repertoire

There are clear tensions in the ways in which finances are discussed by hyperlocals. The language used often draws on an enterprise discourse, and the exploitation of their own labour is certainly explained with language that talks up the benefits of having a diverse skill set, taking risks and being outcome focused. Yet outside of a relatively small group of commercially oriented local news businesses, there is also often a clear rejection of financial motives, with the majority of our interviewees tending to draw on a civic discourse whereby they see their work as creating other forms of value for the communities they write about and engage with. Buckingham and Banaji (2013) offer a useful critique of utopianist positions about the civic potential of the Internet whereby Internet technologies offer unproblematic routes to participation. Such participation is always expressed in positive terms, they argue (Buckingham and Banaji 2013: 9), as is the case in our research. While laudable, this kind of utopianism can also be seen to mask the widespread degree of self-exploitation prevalent in hyperlocal news. Interviewees almost always expressed how their input was above and beyond what was required. They find aspects of it pleasurable and burdensome in turns, and they have a clear sense of the "symbolic nature" (Hesmondhalgh and Baker 2008: 114) of their journalistic outputs. They continue to self-exploit based on the pleasure they get from their work and their belief in the civic value of what they are doing; in turn, though, they also sometimes have a tendency to exploit others.

Even within this dominant civic discourse, there is certainly evidence of a wide range of entrepreneurial attitudes. As tense as many were when it came to talking about money, hyperlocal producers will often try just about anything to draw in funding and, in many cases, they seem to be content with very small amounts. In that broad sense of how we have come to understand entrepreneurship (whereby it might be socially as well as economically focused, as discussed in Jones and Spicer 2009: 10), this is a group who fit the template. They use the interpretative repertoire of enterprise but make it socially focused, always foregrounding the wider community benefit. However, there is a tension in the way they also seek to draw on a repertoire of authenticity with the result that, for many, the notion of making money potentially limits the prospect of further development of their projects. The repeated references to the motivating factor of what we might regard as hyperlocal's 'warm glow' ("the big thing I get out of this is the creative aspect of it and the community aspect of it" – The Kirkbymoorside Town Blog) is, to a degree, a discursive practice that prevents discussion about the complexity of the challenges facing the sustainability of hyperlocal. Many hyperlocal producers are conflicted, self-exploited figures drawing on a contradictory interpretative repertoire that they do not quite believe in.

The need to be seen as acting on behalf of the community is most strongly articulated when the issue of sustainability is discussed. Whilst some have clear financial motives from the outset, for most, undertaking hyperlocal publishing is seen as very much a personal sacrifice, one done for love rather than money and articulated through a social enterprise repertoire. But as Matt Carlson points out, we should not be surprised that this view is articulated: "journalists have long based arguments for their legitimacy on independence from their revenue-generating sides" (2013: 8). In this sense, the desire amongst hyperlocal journalists to sidestep the subject of finances replicates long-standing anxieties in the discourse and practice of mainstream professional journalists. What is different here, of course, is that those being questioned not only play journalistic roles; they are also proprietors (of sorts), small-scale local publishers for whom the sustainability of their operation clearly plays very immediately on their minds.

Conclusion

In purely economic terms, our survey research identified only a small group of financially viable community news services, with advertising as the main source of revenue (although there were also a number of people who were previously hobbyists who were trying but struggling to professionalise and monetise their sites). Nesta's work on the value of the advertising market in the UK for hyperlocal media (Oliver & Ohlbaum Associates Ltd 2013) has sought to outline the market opportunity that exists for those wishing to create commercially sustainable hyperlocal services. The research found that of the £731 million spent on online advertising by "small consumer-facing" businesses, £23 million was spent with hyperlocal websites (Oliver & Ohlbaum Associates Ltd 2013). As the authors themselves describe it: "this may not be heartening reading for hyperlocal providers" (Oliver & Ohlbaum Associates Ltd 2013: 5). From a survey of local businesses undertaken as part of that research, a quarter of respondents were aware of hyperlocal websites but only 6 per cent had advertised on them. The gloominess is compounded by lack of interest by national advertisers in using hyperlocal websites: "growth is therefore likely to be restricted to small businesses advertising expenditure which can be attracted from other platforms" (Oliver & Ohlbaum Associates Ltd 2013: 62). Given the estimated £2.6 billion spent by small businesses in the UK (on- or offline) (Oliver & Ohlbaum Associates Ltd 2013: 8), hyperlocal's slice is marginal at best, but it does at least demonstrate the local advertising sector in the UK is not lacking in revenue-generating opportunities.

By far the largest group identified by our survey research were volunteer-led efforts. Thus, hyperlocal publishing in the UK seems to be a precarious practice, subject to the impact of changes in the professional and personal circumstances of its publishers which often impacts on the time available for community news projects. Hyperlocal news takes time, effort and (to a lesser extent) money to produce and circulate. Although our survey found that the great majority of community news producers in the UK are not in it for the money, the lack of financial security has implications for the medium- to long-term viability of these nascent online publications and perhaps therefore for the security, reach and sustainability of hyperlocal news publishing as a whole.

Hyperlocal publishing therefore seems to be happily resisting marketisation, and given the public service ethos that underpins many hyperlocal operations, it is no surprise that the BBC has taken an interest in them as part of a wider discussion about how to better connect with both commercial and community news operations. Although the BBC hasn't sought to set up its own hyperlocal-style services (having had complaints from local newspaper groups when they trialled a more localised news service in the early 2000s), they have sought to build better relationships with the local press and have recognised hyperlocal websites as part of the local media landscape, inviting them to consult on how they might work together:

The aim of the proposals are to strengthen links between the BBC, hyperlocals and other established forms of local media, as well as directing BBC audiences to the best stories online and ensuring the right credit is given to external news sources.

(BBC 2015)

The resultant dialogue raised hopes that hyperlocal publishers would see a slice of funding come their way as part of the Local Democracy Reporters scheme (Linford 2017). However, when funding was announced, it was the large newspaper groups that saw the bulk of the 143 full-time reporters distributed amongst them. Only two posts went to independent hyperlocal publishers (BBC 2017).

Ultimately, the hyperlocal journalist entrepreneur offers a challenge to those twin notions of the 'hard-nosed' journalist and the 'hard-nosed' entrepreneur. Although the fictive hyperlocal entrepreneur, as projected in the discourse of many commentators and lobbyists, doesn't exist in a widespread way, there is a dominant civic discourse that hyperlocalists draw upon to contextualise their practice. We can see that there is a range of attitudes to the economics of hyperlocal: at one end are those who welcome the market opportunity and are seeking to grow their operations into larger businesses, whilst, at the other, there are those who have a vociferous resistance to any form of income generation. Yet the research findings offer some comfort for academics or organisations who laud the civic activism evident in the output of many sites. They can feel confident that sustaining this activity is not dependent wholly on those hyperlocal sites generating income. Yet, in line with findings by Kurpius *et al.* (2010) and van Kerkhoven and Bakker (2014), there is a sense of precariousness over hyperlocal's viability in the long term as either an alternative media scene or in addressing democratic deficits caused by the withdrawal and decline of mainstream professional local journalism. For those looking to invest funding or to bring the practice to the attention of policymakers, they can take comfort that the sector is home to some small business entrepreneurs seeking to grow media businesses that address concerns over media plurality. Yet such figures are relatively rare, and the risk in looking only for the fictive hyperlocal entrepreneur is that there will be disappointment as the policy gaze moves elsewhere. As Bourdieu and Passeron point out: "if he [the 'fictive' student] does not live up to being which he ought to be – his 'being-for-the-teacher' – the mistakes are wholly attributable to him, whether out of error or out of spite" (1996: 16).

References

Auletta, Ken (2011) You've got news [Online]. *New Yorker*. Available at: www.newyorker.com/magazine/2011/01/24/youve-got-news [Accessed 21 October 2014].

Baines, David (2012) Hyper-local news: A glue to hold rural communities together? *Local Economy*, Vol. 27, No. 2, pp. 152–166.

Baines, David & Kennedy, Ciara (2010) An education for independence. *Journalism Practice*, Vol. 4, No. 1, pp. 97–113.

188 Sustaining hyperlocal journalism

BBC (2015) BBC seeks views of community news websites and bloggers [Online]. Available at: www.bbc.co.uk/mediacentre/latestnews/2015/hyperlocal [Accessed 29 July 2015].

BBC (2017) BBC announces media organisations which will employ Local Democracy Reporters as latest step in the Local News Partnerships [Online]. Available at: www.bbc.co.uk/corporate2/mediacentre/latestnews/2017/local-democracy-reporters [Accessed 11 December 2017].

Bourdieu, Pierre & Passeron, Jean-Claude (1996) Introduction: Language and relationship to language in the teaching situation. In: Bourdieu, P., Passeron, J.-C., De Saint Martin, M. & Teese, R. (eds) *Academic Discourse: Linguistic Misunderstanding and Professorial Power*. Stanford, CA: Stanford University Press, pp. 1–34.

Buckingham, David & Banaji, Shakuntala (2013) *The Civic Web: Young People, the Internet, and Civic Participation*. Cambridge, MA: MIT Press.

Carlson, Matt (2013) Journalistic change in an online age: Disaggregating visibility, legitimacy, and revenue. *JOMEC Journal*, No. 3. doi:10.18573/j.2013.10239

Carnegie UK Trust (2014) *The Future's Bright – the Future's Local*. Dunfermline: Carnegie UK Trust.

Gill, Rosalind & Pratt, Andy (2008) In the social factory? Immaterial labour, precariousness and cultural work. *Theory, Culture & Society*, Vol. 25, No. 7–8, pp. 1–30.

Glaser, Mark (2010) Citizen journalism: Widening world democracy. In: Allan, S. (ed.) *The Routledge Companion to News and Journalism*. London andNew York: Routledge, pp. 578–590.

Gollmitzer, Mirjam (2014) Precariously employed watchdogs? *Journalism Practice*, Vol. 8, No. 6, pp. 826–841.

Hesmondhalgh, David & Baker, Sarah (2008) Creative work and emotional labour in the television industry. *Theory, Culture & Society*, Vol. 25, No. 7–8, pp. 97–118.

Hesmondhalgh, David & Baker, Sarah (2011) *Creative Labour: Media Work in Three Cultural Industries*. London: Routledge.

Jones, Campbell & Spicer, André (2009) *Unmasking the Entrepreneur*. Cheltenham: Edward Elgar.

Jones, Janet & Salter, Lee (2012) *Digital Journalism*. Los Angeles: Sage.

Jones, Sally (2014) Gendered discourses of entrepreneurship in UK higher education: The fictive entrepreneur and the fictive student. *International Small Business Journal*, Vol. 32, No. 3, pp. 237–258.

Kaufman, Leslie (2014, 18 May) Patch sites turn corner after sale and big cuts [Online]. *New York Times*. Available at: www.nytimes.com/2014/05/19/business/media/patch-sites-turn-corner-after-sale-and-big-cuts.html?_r=0 [Accessed 21 October 2014].

Kaye, J. & Quinn, S. (2010) *Funding Journalism in the Digital Age: Business Models, Strategies, Issues and Trends*. New York: Peter Lang.

Kurpius, David D., Metzgar, Emily T. & Rowley, Karen M. (2010) Sustaining hyperlocal media. *Journalism Studies*, Vol. 11, No. 3, pp. 359–376.

Lambourne, Helen (2013, 11 June) Freelance publishers axed from Local World sites [Online]. *holdthefrontpage.co.uk*. Available at: https://www.holdthefrontpage.co.uk/2013/news/freelance-publishers-axed-from-local-world-sites/ [Accessed 12 May 2016].

Linford, Paul (2017, 6 July) Fifteen hyperlocals set to bid for Local Democracy Reporters [Online]. *holdthefrontpage.co.uk*. Available at: https://www.holdthefrontpage.co.uk/2017/news/fifteen-hyperlocals-set-to-bid-for-local-democracy-reporters/ [Accessed 11 December 2017].

Oliver & Ohlbaum Associates Ltd (2013) *Research on Local Advertising Markets*. London: Oliver & Ohlbaum Associates Ltd.

Pavlik, John V. (2013) Trends in new media research: A critical review of recent scholarship. *Sociology Compass*, Vol. 7, No. 1, pp. 1–12.

Pekkala, Pekka & Cook, Clare (2012) Sustaining journalistic entrepreneurship. In: Sirkkunen, E. & Cook, C. (eds) *Chasing Sustainability on the Net*. Tampere, Finland: Tampere Research Centre for Journalism, Media and Communication, pp. 108–115.

Perrin, William (2011, 27 April) Guardian Local closes [Online]. *Talk About Local*. Available at: https://talkaboutlocal.org.uk/guardian-local-closes/ [Accessed 2 December 2017].

Pickard, Meg (2011, 27 April) Guardian Local – an update on the experiment [Online]. *Guardian blog*. Available at: www.theguardian.com/help/insideguardian/2011/apr/27/guardian-local-update [Accessed 27 April 2017].

Potts, Mark (2007, 15 July) Backfence: Lessons learned [Online]. Available at: http://recoveringjournalist.typepad.com/recovering_journalist/2007/07/backfence-lesso.html [Accessed 12 December 2017].

Price, Andy (2010) Local voices: The regional press and user-generated content. In: Monaghan, G. & Tunney, S. (eds) *Web Journalism: A New Form of Citizenship?* Brighton: Sussex Academic Press, pp. 137–149.

Rodgers, Scott (2017) Digitizing localism: Anticipating, assembling and animating a "space" for UK hyperlocal media production. *International Journal of Cultural Studies*. doi:00A0;10.1177/1367877917704495

Ross, Andrew (2008) The new geography of work: Power to the precarious? *Theory, Culture & Society*, Vol. 25, No. 7–8, pp. 31–49.

St John, Burton, Johnson, Kirsten & Nah, Seungahn (2014) Patch.com: The challenge of connective community journalism in the digital sphere. *Journalism Practice*, Vol. 8, No. 2, pp. 197–212.

Thomas, Marc, Waldram, Hannah & Walker, Ed (2013) *Connected: The Power of Modern Community*. London: The Guardian.

Thurman, Neil, Pascal, Jean-Christophe & Bradshaw, Paul (2011) Can big media do "big society"? A critical case study of commercial, convergent hyperlocal news. *International Journal of Media and Cultural Politics*, Vol. 8, No. 2. doi:00A0;10.1386/macp.8.2-3.269_1

van Kerkhoven, Marco & Bakker, Piet (2014) The hyperlocal in practice. *Digital Journalism*, Vol. 2, No. 3, pp. 296–309.

Vehkoo, Johanna & Cook, Clare (2012) UK: Big media friends. In: Sirkkunen, E. & Cook, C. (eds) *Chasing Sustainability on the Net*. Tampere, Finland: Tampere Research Centre for Journalism, Media and Communication, pp. 42–51.

Wilhelm, Alex (2013, 8 August) AOL to "impact" hundreds of Patch employees Friday in a bid for hyper local profits [Online]. *techcrunch.com*. Available at: http://techcrunch.com/2013/08/08/aol-to-impact-hundreds-of-patch-employees-friday-in-a-bid-for-hyper-local-profits [Accessed 21 October 2014].

CONCLUSION

This book has looked at hyperlocal publishers both as contributors to the public sphere, fulfilling to some extent a normative journalistic role, and as chroniclers of the everyday. We have set out research that has offered a context for the necessity of this new form of journalism, provided an overview of the scale of its form and practice in the UK, and given insights into the actions and motivations of its producers. The narrative around the decline of the local press has resulted in much attention being paid to hyperlocal journalism, with such services pitched as filling the democratic deficit left when local newspapers close. There has been a weight of expectation on hyperlocal news services, with those who operate them framed in a way that situates them as heroic figures (Goode 2009: 1290), able to manage both the business and journalistic side of their endeavours while remaining authentic to the communities they serve. Fulfilling all of these roles feels like a rather tall order. Our research has therefore gone about unpicking this idealised image of the hyperlocalist and instead offers a more nuanced sense of the issues they face. Our aim was to raise questions about the value of hyperlocal journalism but to avoid framing those questions wholly around normative assumptions about the role of journalism in a democracy.

In our conclusion we summarise our main arguments and observations of this research before setting out a series of key findings along with the implications they have for scholars of community journalism, policy-lobbyists and policymakers as well as practitioners themselves.

Framing hyperlocal publishing

We began in chapter 1 by highlighting how hyperlocal news was being discussed by commentators and by some academics as potentially playing a role in reinvigorating both communities and the local media sector. The emphasis in definitions has been on the civic value of hyperlocal and the expectation that "the content be original and that engaging with the site results in increased connection to the community" (Metzgar *et al.* 2011: 774). In the UK much discussion has focused on the value of these enterprises sustaining themselves through new business models. Only tentatively has discussion turned to the potential of direct public subsidy (Holdsworth 2015). While much commentary concerns itself with the hope that hyperlocal publishing can help fill the gap left by a declining local press (a decline we outlined in chapter 2) and hold power to account, we have argued that looking at hyperlocals from a cultural practice perspective might be a better way of understanding the broader role they might play. First, drawing on recent work by Kristy Hess and Lisa Waller (2016), this allows us to look beyond the narrow debate about sustainability and newsworthiness and to see value in undertaking hyperlocal journalism as a celebration of place and of the everyday. In chapter 7 we drew attention to the numerous failures of commercial hyperlocal operations, which, Hess and Waller argue, may be down to the impossibility of trying to 'bottle' what is a cultural information-sharing practice rooted in everyday lives, as opposed to than a newsgathering and distribution practice. Highmore (2010), Pink (2012) and Postill (2011) all see value in the conceptual framings of the everyday, and while Highmore attempts to account for the habitual ease with which we incorporate media technologies into our everyday lives, he recognises, as we do, the potential for disruption. Likewise, Pink sees value in the ubiquity of the use of social media and digital technologies and the potential for a kind of slow activism. Postill sees such activism taking place as a result of citizens' interest in the banal matters of everyday living.

Of course, such activism is less direct than the active citizenship that Harcup (2016a) discusses, and we could consider how Nick Couldry's (2006) idea of cultures of citizenship offers a more useful framework for considering the value of what we might call everyday active citizenship. We could argue that the networked search for lost pets is as good an example as any of DIY citizenship with "an activist and communitarian ethic" (Hartley 2010: 240). We also drew on ideas of the public sphere, the private sphere and alternative public spheres. While the debate about hyperlocal may well feel like a discussion about the degraded nature of the public sphere, we should consider hyperlocal not simply as another mechanism through which the public can contribute to civic debate. Much of hyperlocal news doesn't feel particularly newsworthy (the B31 Voices case study shows many examples of banal news), and as Hess and Waller point out: "types of news featured in many hyperlocal publications provide a challenge to the very nature of news itself" (2016: 201). But as Zizi Papacharissi argues, personal blogging is a space of "broadening and overlapping private and public agendas" (2010: 149), and we might consider hyperlocal publishing in the same way. What might concern the individual in the private sphere can also be of wider concern. Sonia Livingstone points out that what is needed here is a reframing of the debate about the value of the private sphere: "the activities these terms characterise can be re-described as independence or even resistance" (2005: 170). It is perhaps more

192 Conclusion

difficult to frame hyperlocal publishing as alternative, but as Chris Atton argues, we should be attentive to process as well as product in looking at alternative media operations, and in its practices and means of production, perhaps there is evidence of alternativeness in hyperlocal's ability to foster "wider social participation in their creation, participation and dissemination" (2002: 25).

The decline of traditional local news and how it affects the citizen

In chapters 2 and 3 we set out the wider media context of the local news landscape and charted the decline of local legacy journalism and the impact of that decline on communities. Circulation and advertising revenue declines matter because of the combined effects of their loss on the ability of news companies to adequately resource their newsgathering and publishing activities, the consequences of which are discussed in depth in the case study of Port Talbot. These revenue declines have been a major factor in cutbacks that have resulted in journalism job losses, especially at a local and regional level in newspapers, which have also affected their associated online publishing platforms (Phillips and Witschge 2012: 13; Williams and Franklin 2007: 2). In spite of their weakened state, newspapers continue to be admired for their reputation for breaking original news and leading the news agenda, and it must be acknowledged that much of this newsgathering muscle has been (and continues to be) enabled by printed news underwritten mainly by advertising. However, the fact that readers are now turning away from newsprint in large numbers has prompted some to forecast newspapers will not survive beyond the middle of this century (Meyer 2009). For other commentators, the ease and convenience of receiving up-to-the-minute news on electronic devices (and the speed of news audiences' uptake of mobile devices) seems to be making newspapers obsolete (Langeveld 2012). Consequently, the need for printed news in today's communities, particularly as digital and mobile devices have grown in popularity – is still very much debated. The tide of general opinion among commentators has become more optimistic since the gloomy predictions of the first decade of the millennium. There are those who now temper the gloom with views that back the ability of newspapers and hybrid print and web "news organisations" to continue fulfilling a valuable role (Satchwell 2012). For some there is an exciting future for collaborative enterprises involving journalists and citizens as well as in new types of digital journalism, data journalism and storytelling that push journalism into new frontiers (Franklin 2014). And of course we should note that there are hyperlocal journalists who are making successes of their independent community news services with print models.

There is some evidence that democratic and civic problems have arisen alongside the withdrawal and weakening of journalism. Port Talbot is a case in point. The market conditions that have prevailed in the UK media led to the closure of several news outlets in Port Talbot, including its dedicated weekly newspaper; its council-published monthly free sheet; its community radio station; a hyperlocal website run by an experienced local news photographer; and a hyperlocal website and newspaper run by professional journalists. It is still served by a regional newspaper and, arguably, by media in regional and national public spheres such as the Welsh and UK press and regional and national television and radio. However, the withdrawal of journalists who lived and worked embedded in the community has been a major factor in impoverishing the local media scene, the decline in local journalists linking to declines in the quantity and quality of news. The quantity of news in Port Talbot dropped sharply, as did staff numbers: in the 1970s, five newspapers had offices in Port Talbot, employing 10 or 11 journalists between them; by 2017 only the *Post* was regularly providing coverage of Port Talbot's news, for which it employed one reporter to cover Port Talbot and Neath from its Swansea headquarters. This constitutes a fall in number of journalists covering the area of more than 90 per cent between 1970 and 2017.

A side effect of this decline has been a reduction in plurality. Reporters working in the area during the 1970s to 1990s spoke of competing against each other to get the scoop, the unique angle or the line that nobody else had. Journalists reported this had ensured lively, healthy local newspapers which were good for "keeping a close eye on [local government]". However, the focus changed and latterly journalists described "filling shapes" or meeting high targets for the smaller stories known as "down-page" (*Post* and *Guardian* journalist interviews), diminishing the time and scope available for carrying out time-consuming journalism practices such as balance and fact-checking. District offices, once a valued resource for both reporters and citizens, also began to close. These limits on resources began to show their effects in the news itself. Indeed, our content analysis shows that over time the news became less local, less likely to use plural sources and more likely to use high-status sources. The effects of this diminished news are in evidence in the experiences of the town's residents: information flows became dominated by word of mouth, rumour, speculation, confusion and lack of foreknowledge, coupled with other effects such as powerlessness and frustration. There were also signs that democratic and civic engagement had been impacted, with election turnouts falling below national averages following newspaper district office closures around the year 2000. These findings suggest that not only were newspapers important to communities, but the presence of locally embedded journalists and their knowledgeable and accountable journalism, situated in accessible district offices, was also key.

The evidence from Port Talbot can perhaps provide hope for local journalists and hyperlocal news providers in demonstrating that their work is essential to communities, civic engagement and democracy and that the absence of local journalism is measurable and missed by those communities. Hyperlocal news can step in to plug news gaps, but it can also supplement existing news publishers and provide plurality and valuable additional voices or alternative perspectives. Much of the evidence points towards high levels of trust between communities and hyperlocals, and their ability to engage local citizens is exciting and offers some hope of repairing the democratic deficit. Indeed, citizens are already beginning to step into the void left by mainstream media, as the case studies in chapter 6 demonstrate.

Arguments have been made in favour of online citizen journalism's ability to provide a substitute for traditional newspapers as "sources of public affairs news and information" (Fico *et al.* 2013: 152) – and there are those who claim a digital age of publishing freedom will allow many voices to join the public debate and open public bodies to scrutiny. One 2012 study in the US found that while websites run by citizen journalists increased the overall number of local government stories in the traditional print press, perhaps through a process of encouraging competition and rivalry for the best stories and scoops, they were not enough to provide a substitute for newspapers; the authors of the study conclude that "citizen journalism sites, particularly citizen blog sites, are more information complements than substitutes, and with respect to news and opinion about some communities they may have been neither complements nor substitutes" (Fico *et al.* 2013: 165). Though we must acknowledge that the capability of many of these news sites to fill the news gap has not yet proved universal nor reliable, there are pockets of innovation, engagement and optimism.

The limits of hyperlocal publishing as components of local news ecologies

In analysing the scale and scope of hyperlocal news, as we did in chapter 3, we noted that the scale of such services has resulted in them being been identified by Ofcom as potentially playing a useful role in ensuring vibrant local news ecologies. Here is an emerging sector, collectively publishing as many as 30 news stories an hour, with some operations seeming to garner large audiences and filling specific geographic news gaps. Ofcom argues that hyperlocal media has "the potential to support and broaden the range of local media content available to citizens and consumers at a time when traditional local media providers continue to find themselves under financial pressure" (2012a: 103). In order to play its public sphere role, hyperlocal publishing needs not just to be visible and to be publishing, but also must be consumed. Our research demonstrates that data on consumption is scarce. Ofcom's own research shows that "only 1 per cent [of people] said that such websites were their most important local media source" (Ofcom 2012a: 106). Thus Ofcom's focus on hyperlocal news may appear contradictory in that it recognises value in a practice that evidence suggests is not paid much attention by audiences. The lack of evidence, however, resulted in Ofcom being unable to judge whether this form of news should be considered as playing a role in ensuring media plurality. Ofcom have noted, in a Public Interest Test for a media takeover, that there is "no evidence to suggest that they [hyperlocals] have the capacity to influence the democratic debate" (2012b: 9).

Through our content analysis we found that hyperlocal news, on the whole, is very oriented toward communities and local areas. By contrast with much professional commercial news, which has become progressively less local in its focus and depth of coverage as resources decline, hyperlocal audiences get lots of locally sourced stories with strong local news angles. Members of the public and local community groups tend to get more of a say as news sources than in mainstream local and regional news. Official sources in local government, business and the emergency services still get a platform, but so do many local citizens. These blogs produce and circulate a significant amount of news about politics, civic life, local economies and the business of local government (which is an area of life in the UK that has been under-reported as the crisis in local commercial news has developed). While some of our findings seem to suggest a rosy picture in terms of the ability of hyperlocal news to foster citizenship, democracy and local community cohesion, others were less positive. One of the ways professional journalists provide us with a plurality of perspectives on local life has traditionally been to speak to numerous news sources to gather the raw materials of news, many of whom they go on to quote in their stories. In our sample, many hyperlocal news producers quote relatively few news sources, and when they are used, rarely are conflicting or oppositional viewpoints provided in the same posts. But our interviews suggest that some hyperlocal producers have developed alternative means to foster and inform plural debate around contentious local issues; for example, opting to enact source balance by spreading interventions from opposing voices out across different stories. In the case of more overtly critical investigative hyperlocal sites, the practice of balancing sources is often rejected on practical and ideological grounds: because council PR departments cannot be relied upon to engage meaningfully with questions, or they use the expectation of being given a right to reply as a tactic to close down debate by stonewalling journalists; because balance is a practice associated with a largely uncritical local mainstream press; and because local elites have enough of a platform for their carefully crafted communications messages in mainstream commercial news media anyway.

Overall, our evidence suggests that hyperlocals provide useful spaces for citizens to participate in the public sphere. They shift the nature of the local news ecology from one dominated by large media corporations to one that has a wide variety of independent operators, although the sustainability of these operations is questionable, relying as they do on volunteerism, shoestring funding or hidden subsidies and cross-subsidies. Collectively, they do represent an alternative to the mainstream, but perhaps not one that is alternative in politics. In that regard, one could not say that they are immediately counter-hegemonic in nature, although of course the celebration of the local, the rejection of the corporate ("if Tesco came along and said they wanted to advertise in your paper ... we wouldn't do it" – *Wayland News*) is itself a form of counter-hegemony. Rather, they often seek to work alongside the mainstream, which in turn plays a role in legitimising them. Of course, as Negt and Kluge (1983) argue, assimilation into dominant practices is an inevitable process in the development of "proletarian" public spheres, which is what we may be seeing in this instance.

Creating authentic reciprocal relationships with audiences

Across our case studies and interviews, a set of key issues emerged, some specific to the cases being presented and some pertinent to the wider hyperlocal practice

196 Conclusion

community. B31 Voices' motivations are similar to other practitioners in wanting to change wider perceptions about their locality. They want to bring back some civic pride to an area that has suffered widespread unemployment as a result of the decline of manufacturing and which has been at the forefront of austerity cuts to public services. While they report on these issues in the same way that mainstream media do, they also utilise reciprocal practices via social media to the point where their audience enthusiastically works together to gather and share positive content. The use of hashtags to highlight stories of good deeds (#B31Positive, #B31Sup-portingLocal) draws citizens into the news-making domain not as witnesses to breaking news, but as observers of the everyday. Our analysis of the social media engagement of B31 Voices certainly suggests that there is an appetite to engage with the more banal aspects of life in South Birmingham. This is not to be dismissed, and it can be seen as a way in which citizens seek to gently push against the dominant myths about the places where they live with stories of their own. The Facebook Page of B31 Voices is a place where "produsers" (Bruns 2008) get a chance to participate in the public sphere through what are now everyday media technologies. Further, citizens' networked actions of sharing, commenting and liking counteract any gatekeeping practices that Sas and Marty Taylor might enact. Reciprocation is key to citizen engagement, a practice we also found amongst the wider group of hyperlocal publishers.

Authenticity is another shared concern for hyperlocal publishers. Our research shows that in general, hyperlocal journalists are at pains to situate themselves as being authentic. One of the interviewees described the need to be authentic to audiences and also to local public bodies from which stories are procured: "[Initially] they [the council] didn't really understand who we were, what we were and why we were doing it, and I think they were quite cautious at getting too involved with us" (WV11). For this interviewee, while the relationship with audience hinged on foregrounding the not-for-profit nature of their operation and the informality of their exchanges on social media, they had to present a more professional face to the council and others in order to convince them "that we are genuine, and in it for the right reasons and worth dealing with" (WV11). As Damian Radcliffe notes in his 2012 report for Nesta, for many hyperlocalists, 'keeping it real' is more important than attracting an audience: "success does not always equate to page views. Engagement, civic impact and plurality of voice can be as important as reach, if not more so" (2012: 11). Yet such a focus on these ideals can unfortunately come at the cost of sustainability (after all, page views can equal income).

How authenticity is operationalised and maintained is demonstrated by On the Wight, who understand that they need to show their audience that they can be the authentic voice for their concerns. While their strategies to do this (e.g. through their method of creating author accounts for republishing press releases) might be different from those of other hyperlocalists, the intended result is the same. However, in the case of *Tyburn Mail*, we see how a more professional approach to hyperlocal journalism seemed to create a disconnect between the hyperlocal operation and its audience. Here, the time-poor journalist operated wholly within a professional journalism discourse and rejected the potential to develop a network of citizen 'produsers' through a more reciprocal use of social media. In turn, there was suspicion among residents about the motives of the community newspaper and the ways in which it sought to represent its community. This hyperlocal did not seem to provide the opportunity for citizens to challenge the residual, stigmatised view of the locality, and by failing to create space for discussion and debate on its social media channels, little will was created amongst residents to offer up content in the hope of a reciprocal response that had not previously been forthcoming. It may be, in this case, that the focus on that traditional stalwart of news, crime (the coverage of which the journalist takes particular pride in), at the expense of the banal was a factor in failing to build sufficient social capital among residents. The research process offered interventions that challenged *Tyburn Mail*'s professional approach through trialling more participatory methods of newsgathering. The use of such practices might have helped break down the consumer/producer barriers and create more authentic relationships, but unfortunately the *Tyburn Mail* did not sustain these participatory approaches, and eventually folded.

Translating personal motivations into civic value

In our analysis of interviews with hyperlocal practitioners in chapter 5 we addressed in detail how emerging practices within hyperlocal journalism act to legitimise it in the eyes of its audience. What norms were developing and how were such norms shaped by the motivations of hyperlocal publishers? A clear motivating factor is a desire to redress reputational issues about the localities in which they live and work, offering up alternative representations of place to those created by mainstream media. It would be simplistic to write this motive off as one that is selfish in nature; that is, the act of someone arriving in a new place (as many hyperlocalists have), realising it is not quite what they expected, and then seeking to resist negative attacks in order to protect their personal financial investment in property or to save face with friends and family. Rather, there seems to be a genuine desire to resist dominant myths about localities and to reshape reputational geographies. This shapes the kind of news that is covered, with the emphasis being on good news and the everyday rather than what might be seen as bad news. What is clear is that many hyperlocal publishers are situating themselves as distinct from mainstream media by choosing not to cover a contentious news genre such as crime. Instead, the focus on the everyday is a characteristic practice of many hyperlocalists. The activities of local shops, clubs and organisations, the banal chat of local citizens, are all material from which content is created. That is not to say that all news covered is soft, with issues of local governance also covered and campaigns carried out around issues of local concern. Indeed, in this respect many hyperlocals play a really valuable role in enriching the public sphere and filling the democratic deficit. However, there was a tendency for interviewees to feel more comfortable in discussing their role in producing soft news.

The notion of "reciprocal journalism" (Lewis *et al.* 2014) is helpful in understanding the hyperlocal journalist as a social actor. Content of all kinds is often found or solicited via social media, with updates used as assets in reciprocal exchanges. Hyperlocals employ reciprocal strategies – both online and offline, on the beat – in order to build relationships with the community to which they are so determined to appear authentic. It would seem that this building of social capital is more important than gaining financial capital. Indeed, there seems to be a clear rejection of an entrepreneurial discourse for most of the hyperlocal journalists we spoke to. Putting effort into making money might spoil the fun of hyperlocal journalism, but more importantly, there is a feeling that this would taint the relationships they have built up with communities; what seems to matter most to the hyperlocal journalist is being seen to be on the community's side.

However, it would be wrong to characterise all hyperlocal journalists in this way. Those with a more focused business sense identified how the news gap in their neighbourhoods created an opportunity to both address the democratic deficit and make some money. Indeed, in the case of the Port Talbot Magnet, the desire to become financially sustainable was equated with their ability to continue public interest news reporting; lack of sustainability eventually caused the company to close. It is also true that for many it is less about wanting to be the authentic voice of a community and more about dealing with personal concerns. Feeling angry about a single issue and wishing to campaign on it is a motivating factor for many, but largely for untrained hyperlocal journalists. In one example, this campaigning, personally situated as it was, resulted in the setting up of a blog that changed into something covering wider local topics once the campaign had run its course. Whatever their initial motivation, many described how their operations had spiralled out of control and, to an extent, were becoming a burden. Yet they continue to operate them, often with the consequence that their own labour is subject to exploitation. Although this was expressed with a degree of grumpiness, it is clear that for many, the buzz of doing journalism is a clear motivating force to continue on.

"New contexts of public communication and trust"

In asking researchers to examine the new "communicative ecology", Nick Couldry (2004: 27) requires us to look closely at the "particular settings where people are generating new contexts of public communication and trust" (26). Hyperlocal journalists have created a public setting that is built on a very different relationship from that of the local press, but it is one that is precarious, built as it is on the contradictions at the heart of the 'fictive' hyperlocalism that Radcliffe (2012) and others have argued for. Set against Couldry's three criteria for emerging models of community media – "1) the actual social inclusiveness of those involved; 2) the dependence of such innovations on hidden subsidies (e.g. a university base); and 3) the stability of the new forms of trust on which they rely" (2004: 27) – we can see that hyperlocal journalism faces issues despite its practitioners attempts to be

Conclusion **199**

authentic brokers of "new networks of trust" (26). While we have not examined the extent of hyperlocal journalism's social inclusiveness, we have argued that 'hidden subsidies' come in the form of the free labour provided by the practitioners themselves. In relation to his third criteria, Couldry imagines this as concerning the degree to which editors make transparent the rules of engagement. It is here perhaps that the authenticity that hyperlocal journalists rely on so much is of most significance, potentially becoming a resource that might suggest a sustainable future for hyperlocal journalism. B31 Voices provides a good example of a hyperlocal publisher that has found a way to deal with the relentlessness of engaging with citizens across social media platforms by developing reciprocal strategies that effectively hand over editorial and news-making control to citizens themselves. Other hyperlocals would do well to take note of their practices and follow suit.

The value of hyperlocal journalism

The development of a network of hyperlocal news operations in the UK has created value for citizens in a number of ways. Here we set out our key findings.

Hyperlocal publishing is a route to participation in the public sphere, supporting everyday active citizenship

The various hyperlocal publishing outlets, although geographically patchy, provide an alternative route to participation in the public sphere at a time when newspaper readership is declining (by an average of 10 per cent year on year according to Turvill 2015). Such participation is often focused on the more banal aspects of living in communities, but this can help foster everyday active citizenship (Postill 2008: 419). Further, hyperlocals invariably celebrate the endeavours of local independent shops, charities and community groups, which can help grow local social capital and enhance community cohesion. In short, they offer a route to civic participation.

The embedded hyperlocal practitioner's lack of objectivity can result in greater civic value

The focus on these everyday concerns should come as no surprise when we are dealing with people who are embedded in their neighbourhoods and whose journey into hyperlocalism started in the private sphere. To a degree, even the professional journalist feels the weight of the civic discourse and can end up in a less critical space than one would expect from local news organisations. Pfau *et al.* (2004) note that journalists embedded within US military units during the Iraq invasion of 2003 lose perspective and inevitably end up displaying bias towards the troops they are embedded with. What is lost is "the idealised standard of reporter objectivity" (Pfau *et al.* 2004: 84). In hyperlocal publishing, similar issues inevitably arise. From a citizen perspective it may well come as something of a relief to find

200 Conclusion

that a news outlet wants to be on your side from the outset, working to counter the media framings that often blight local areas.

Hyperlocal publishers are part of a wider information ecology in localities

There is no doubt that in some localities hyperlocals can contribute to a more plural media ecology. However, their emphasis on good news and tendency to operate in a civic discourse means they are just as likely to be an aspect of local tourist information or an extension of local council information as they are a news source. Paulussen and D'Heer's study of a Belgian newspaper's experiment with hyperlocal news found that citizen journalists were more likely to report on soft news: "coverage about daily community life has become the domain of the citizen reporters" (2013: 599). The practitioners in our research talked at length of the value of good news. One might take this as a reason to dismiss the value of hyperlocal but it does provide a vehicle through which citizens can feel some civic pride in place. In that there is much value.

Reciprocation is a practice through which civic engagement is nurtured

Another form of value comes about as a result of the practices of reciprocation that seem to lie at the heart of many hyperlocal news operations. Through social media there is a constant invitation to participate. This brings citizens' knowledge and opinions into the public domain (as their comments are shared or retweeted) and situates them as co-creators of news content rather than mere observers whose assets are there to be picked off only at the point where their observation is of the extraordinary rather than the ordinary.

Future research directions

This research has taken a perspective that shifts the analytical lens from the public to the private sphere. It argues, as Hess and Waller (2016) also do, that undertaking hyperlocal publishing is akin to a personally motivated cultural endeavour. Practitioners are caught between a civic and a journalistic discourse, but the reality is that much of their motivation is rooted in the personal and therefore scholars should take a research approach with that in mind. Jerome Turner (2015) likewise calls for a recasting of the study of hyperlocal news away from that of the public sphere. He argues that this is not news as we have come to understand it: "editors often need do little more than offer the conduit and curatorial channel by which narratives of everyday, local life are sourced, assessed, and then re-broadcast to the audience" (Turner 2015: 48). His study of hyperlocal audiences shows that hyperlocal media is valuable to residents because it is "key to an everyday understanding of their neighbourhood [and] can encourage unexpected forms of civic engagement" (Turner 2015: 48). Further research with audiences for hyperlocal news is needed (see also Harcup 2016a, 2016b), and Turner's anthropological approach (he observes interactions on social media platforms over an extended period of time) can offer richer detail about the value of producer-audience interactions than a more quantitative approach. Given the role played by social media as platforms for reciprocation, surely this would be a candidate for future fieldwork.

Implications for hyperlocal publishing and its practitioners

From a policymaker's point of view, a conclusion that argues for a celebration of the banality of the local is surely not quite what was hoped for. Clearly there are some examples that show the effectiveness of having a harder investigative edge as the central offer (Bristol Cable, Love Wapping) or the value of employing satire to poke fun at the absurdities of local politics (Paradise Circus in Birmingham; Broughton Spurtle in Edinburgh). The fictive hyperlocalist may well be allowed to celebrate the everyday, but they must also play their public service role in ensuring that local power is held to account. It is for this activity that policy-lobbyists want to help secure funding from a range of parties (Carnegie UK Trust 2014). At first glance, the evidence presented in this book suggests that this call for funding might be at odds with what many hyperlocalists want, given that many express a kind of revulsion at the idea of having to deal with money. Money would "spoil the fun", they argue, and be to the detriment of the authentic relationship they have developed with their audiences. However, although many of our interviewees hold this view, it remains the fact that Nesta received 165 applications for a £500,000 pot of seed funding in 2012, and interest in further funding initiatives was just as keen. A conference in early 2018 aimed at community journalists (Building the Future of Journalism, Cardiff, 11 January, 2018) had a strong focus on funding models, highlighting how even a return to printed newspapers shouldn't be ruled out as a way in which hyperlocal publishers might be able to bring audiences to advertisers and thus allow them to become sustainable. Without a doubt, there are many hyperlocal journalists who would like their bank balance to be full enough to allow them to concentrate on their content.

The Carnegie UK Trust have made useful suggestions for ways in which the market conditions could favour the further development of hyperlocal news operations. They note how local councils are still required to place statutory notices in local newspapers, thus providing a form of hidden subsidy:

> The Department for Communities and Local Government could also intervene to start levelling the playing field on financial support, for instance to permit local authorities to spend some (e.g. 10 per cent) of their statutory advertising budgets through hyperlocal news providers.
>
> *(Carnegie UK Trust 2014: 14)*

Also, whereas newspapers feel the benefit of zero-rated VAT, said to be worth £600 million a year (Carnegie UK Trust 2014: 5), the largely online publications

202 Conclusion

run by hyperlocal operators receive no such benefit. The number operating at the VAT threshold level may be very small, but the issue at stake here is about creating the conditions by which it becomes an option for hyperlocal publishers to attempt to grow if they can or wish to. Market conditions are tricky enough – in terms of dealing with a competitive online advertising market and grappling with the algorithmic nature of social media platforms that often seem to work to keep readers away from income-generating websites – without also having to take on commercial competitors who have an advantage through hidden subsidies.

Should hyperlocal news get the level playing field it deserves, it has a greater chance of forming a more robust part of local media ecologies, becoming part of the news mix as business models settle enough to produce stable income streams. This need not come at the expense of a complete shift to the mainstream in terms of either practice or product. Relatively lightweight organisations such as those in our case studies can survive if they have access to even a small slice of the subsidies of the mainstream press (*Tyburn Mail*, although a print newspaper, had no statutory notices placed in it by the city council). Despite often rejecting a genre of news – that is, crime – that many recognise catches the attention of readers, the focus on the everyday seems to bring the multiple shares, likes and comments that hyperlocals can capitalise on. In fact, it is this genre of content that gives hyperlocal the authentic, warm feel that attracted academics, policymakers and lobbyists to the practice in the first place.

Something will have been lost if hyperlocal news matures into a sector that simply replicates mainstream news media and its practices. We might see a form that once had the potential to create an alternative public sphere "silently reproduce" (Couldry 2004: 27) the hierarchies it had the potential to replace. Yet given the shifts in the UK towards regional devolution, the running down of public services and the reliance on the private or third sector to sustain what's left, it is vital we have more local scrutiny rather than less. The 'more' that hyperlocal offers is independent, participatory and networked. Further, it brings its audience into the domain of journalism to talk about everything, in the everyday. It traverses its digital and real-world news beats in a way that the commercial press no longer has the resource to do. The case of Port Talbot offers a stark reminder of the benefits of plurality, but this plurality has been gradually eroded over decades, with notable effects on citizens including their evident reliance on word of mouth, rumour and speculation since the departure of professional journalists from the town. While our research makes clear that the fictive hyperlocalist remains tantalisingly out of reach, we should look to champion a form that offers a fresh chance for journalism to have a more authentic relationship with its audience and allows us a glimpse of what happens if "everyone is a journalist" (Hartley 2009: 154).

References

Atton, Chris (2002) *Alternative Media*. London: Sage.
Bruns, Axel (2008) *Blogs, Wikipedia, Second Life, and Beyond: From Production to Produsage*. New York: Peter Lang.

Carnegie UK Trust (2014) *The Future's Bright – The Future's Local*. Dunfermline: Carnegie UK Trust.

Couldry, Nick (2004) The productive "consumer" and the dispersed "citizen". *International Journal of Cultural Studies*, Vol. 7, No. 1, pp. 21–32.

Couldry, Nick (2006) Culture and citizenship: The missing link? *European Journal of Cultural Studies*, Vol. 9, No. 3, pp. 321–339.

Fico, Frederick, Lacy, Stephen, Wildman, Steven S., Baldwin, Thomas, Bergan, Daniel & Zube, Paul (2013) Citizen journalism sites as information substitutes and complements for United States newspaper coverage of local governments. *Digital Journalism*, Vol. 1, No. 1, pp. 152–168.

Franklin, Bob (2014) The future of journalism. *Journalism Studies*, Vol. 15, No. 5, pp. 481–499.

Goode, Luke (2009) Social news, citizen journalism and democracy. *New Media & Society*, Vol. 11, No. 8, pp. 1287–1305.

Harcup, Tony (2016a) Alternative journalism as monitorial citizenship? A case study of a local news blog. *Digital Journalism*, Vol. 4, No. 5, pp. 639–657.

Harcup, Tony (2016b) Asking the readers: Audience research into alternative journalism. *Journalism Practice*, Vol. 10, No. 6, pp. 680–696.

Hartley, John (2009) *The Uses of Digital Literacy*. St Lucia, Qld.: University of Queensland Press.

Hartley, John (2010) Silly citizenship. *Critical Discourse Studies*, Vol. 7, No. 4, pp. 233–248.

Hess, Kristy & Waller, Lisa (2016) Hip to be hyper. *Digital Journalism*, Vol. 4, No. 2, pp. 193–210.

Highmore, B. (2010) *Ordinary Lives: Studies in the Everyday*. Abingdon: Routledge.

Holdsworth, David (2015) BBC seeks views of community news websites and bloggers [Online]. *BBC*. Available at: www.bbc.co.uk/blogs/aboutthebbc/entries/d148ee0f-7bc1-4db4-8170-13b13eb2faac [Accessed 8 June 2016].

Langeveld, Martin (2012) The coming death of the seven-day publication [Online]. *Niemen Journalism Lab*. Available at: www.niemanlab.org/2012/12/the-coming-death-of-seven-day-publication/ [Accessed 22 March 2018].

Lewis, Seth C., Holton, Avery E. & Coddington, Mark (2014) Reciprocal journalism: A concept of mutual exchange between journalists and audiences. *Journalism Practice*, Vol. 8, No. 2, pp. 229–241.

Livingstone, Sonia (2005) In defence of privacy: Mediating the public/private boundary at home. In: Livingstone, S. (ed.) *Audiences and Publics: When Cultural Engagement Matters for the Public Sphere*. Changing Media – Changing Europe, Vol. 2. Bristol: Intellect Books, pp. 163–185.

Metzgar, Emily T., Kurpius, David D. & Rowley, Karen M. (2011) Defining hyperlocal media: Proposing a framework for discussion. *New Media & Society*, Vol. 13, No. 5, pp. 772–787.

Meyer, Philip (2009) *The Vanishing Newspaper: Saving Journalism in the Information Age*. Columbia, MO: University of Missouri Press.

Negt, Oskar & Kluge, Alexander (1983) The proletarian public sphere. In Mattelart, A. & Sieglaub, S. (eds) *Communication and Class Struggle*, Vol. 2. New York: International General, pp. 92–94.

Ofcom (2012a) *The Communications Market Report*. London: Ofcom.

Ofcom (2012b) *Report on Public Interest Test on the Acquisition of Guardian Media Group's Radio Stations (Real and Smooth) by Global Radio. Annexes 1–3*. London: Ofcom.

Papacharissi, Zizi (2010) *A Private Sphere: Democracy in a Digital Age*. Cambridge: Polity.

Paulussen, Steve & D'Heer, Evelien (2013) Using citizens for community journalism. *Journalism Practice*, Vol. 7, No. 5, pp. 588–603.

Pfau, Michael, Haigh, Michel, Gettle, Mitchell, Donnelly, Michael, Scott, Gregory, Warr, Dana & Wittenberg, Elaine (2004) Embedding journalists in military combat units: Impact on newspaper story frames and tone. *Journalism & Mass Communication Quarterly*, Vol. 81, No. 1, pp. 74–88.

Phillips, Angela & Witschge, Tamara (2012) The changing business of news: Sustainability of news journalism. In: Lee-Wright, P., Phillips, A. & Witschge, T. (eds) *Changing Journalism*. Abingdon: Routledge, pp. 3–20.

Pink, Sarah (2012) *Situating Everyday Life: Practices and Places.* London: Sage.

Postill, John (2008) Localizing the Internet beyond communities and networks. *New Media & Society*, Vol. 10, No. 3, pp. 413–431.

Postill, John (2011) *Localizing the Internet: An Anthropological Account.* Oxford: Berghahn Books.

Radcliffe, Damian (2012) *Here and Now: UK Hyperlocal Media Today.* London: Nesta.

Satchwell, Bob (2012) Local news crisis: Publishers and editors must get back to basics [Online]. *The Guardian*. Available at: www.guardian. co.uk/media/greenslade/2012/jun/26/local-newspapers-digital-media [Accessed 20 June 2016].

Turner, Jerome (2015) Good dog, bad dog: Exploring audience uses and attitudes to hyperlocal community news media through the prism of banal pet stories. *Anthropological Notebooks*, Vol. 21, No. 3, pp. 39–50.

Turvill, William (2015) UK regional dailies see sales decline by average of 10 per cent year on year [Online]. *Press Gazette*. Available at: www.pressgazette.co.uk/regional-daily-newspaper-abcs-second-half-2014-paid-titles-lose-average-10-cent-circulations-year/ [Accessed 20 June 2016].

Williams, Andrew & Franklin, Bob (2007) *Turning Around the Tanker: Implementing Trinity Mirror's Online Strategy.* Cardiff: Cardiff University. Available at: http://image.guardian.co.uk/sys-files/Media/documents/2007/03/13/Cardiff.Trinity.pdf [Accessed 2 December 2015].

INDEX

A Little Bit of Stone 123, 168
Abergele Post 182
activism: banal activism 27–30, 146;
    civic activism 33–34, 187 everyday
    activism 31, 146; online activism
    29–30, 120; slow activism 30, 191
active citizenship 9, 32–33, 36, 191, 199
advertising see business models; local
    newspapers: advertising; social media:
    advertising
alternative economies 182–3
alternative media 9, 21–4, 31, 33, 36,
    187, 192
alternative press 9, 21, 92
alternative public sphere 20–24, 191, 202
amateur journalism 155
Archant 51
armchair auditors 74
Atton, Chris 23–24, 27, 30, 36, 152, 192
audience fragmentation 44–45, 53, 95
audiences 90–91, 96, 100, 102–104, 107,
    119, 130, 133–134, 136–137, 142, 145,
    172, 187, 192, 194–196, 200–201
Audit Bureau of Circulation 49, 54, 91
austerity 146, 155, 196

B31 Voices 136–146, 151, 157–158, 160,
    162, 166–168, 191, 196, 199
Balsall Common 118
banal chat
banal news 3, 15, 27, 37, 142, 191, 197
BBC (British Broadcasting Corporation) 2,
    33, 36, 47, 58, 89, 93, 156, 159, 186–187

BBC Wales 45–47
beat reporting 131–133, 167, 198
Beckett, Charles 5
Bedford Clanger 118, 182
Bexley Is Bonkers 120
Birmingham 99, 136–137, 140, 146–147
Birmingham Mail 167
Bitterne Park 117, 119–120, 132, 179
Bourdieu, Pierre 9, 29–30, 187
Bristol Cable 201
Brixton Bugle 90
Broughton Spurtle 127, 129, 131–132, 181,
    183, 201
Bruns, Axel 5, 7, 33–34, 129, 133, 152, 196
business models: hyperlocal 84, 105–107,
    119–121, 166, 191, 202; newspapers
    7, 8, 17, 43, 51, 55, 57

Caerphilly Observer 59, 85, 179
capitalism 6, 19, 173
Cardiff 46, 52, 59
Carmarthen Journal 46
Carnegie UK Trust 6, 84, 93, 109,
    159–160, 184, 201
Castle Vale 136, 146–149, 151–152, 155,
    167, 169–170
Castle Vale Community Radio (CVCR) 148
Celtic Weeklies 53
Centre for Community Journalism 6, 8,
    90, 93
churnalism 58
Cincinnati Post 81
circulation see local newspapers: circulation

206 Index

citizen journalism 2–3, 5, 7, 9–10, 19, 31–3, 48, 132, 194, 200
citizenship 15, 19, 31–36, 115, 119, 140, 191, 195; *see also* active citizenship
clickbait 56–58
co–operatives 59
Comedia 21
Communications Market Report 5, 93
communities: advertising to 97; and campaigns 107; communication within 126; creating value for 185; deprived 85; everyday life in 11, 104, 199; fractured 24; hyperlocals engaging with 2; informing 96, 159; of interest 35; journalists' relationship with 8, ,131, 132, 167, 198; journalists representing 6, 16, 68; 102, 125, 134, 137, 167, 176, 190; online 25, 126–127, 131; social capital and bonding within 10, 94, 116, 125, 133, 144; in Wales 43, 48, 79; withdrawal of news from 51, 52, 56, 86, 89, 121, 192–194
community journalism 111, 126, 127, 136, 145, 155, 167, 190
community media 93, 115, 137, 146–149, 159, 168, 198
community newspaper 48, 148, 167, 197; *see also* papurau bro
Couldry, Nick 29, 34–36, 115–116, 136, 167–168, 191, 198–199, 202
counter–hegemony 37, 167, 195
counter–public sphere *see* alternative public sphere
crime reporting 3, 33, 77, 101, 109, 118–119, 121–122, **140**, 141, 146, 148, 150, 152, 157, 197, 202
Crosspool News 121, 125, 132, 181
crowdfunding 59, 84
crowdsourcing 31, **141**, 143, 145, 181
Cymru Fyw 47

democracy 11, 15–16, 19–20, 25, 29, 34, 56, 69, 72, 75, 79, 85, 190, 193, 195; see also democratic deficit
democratic deficit 3, 10, 36–37, 57–58, 83, 86, 94, 187, 190, 193, 198
digital literacy 78, 134
Digbeth is Good 117, 131, 180

education 46, 107, 108, 141, 148, 174
elections: coverage 18, 56; turnouts 81, 82, 83, 85
Enders, Clare 65
England 17, 47, 72, 99, 109, 155,

entrepreneurship 9, 173–174, 178–180; *see also* social entrepreneurship
everyday life 28, 34, 69, 93, 104, 155, 196, 199, 201
exclusive news 70, 160

Facebook 53, 57, 77–78, 81, 90, 123, 127, 129–131, 133, 137, 140–142, 144–145, 150–151, 153, 157, 162, 196
Fenton, Natalie 5, 21, 53
Filton Voice 85, 121, 178
fourth estate 9–10, 16, 71–72, 80–81, 159; *see also* watchdog role of press
Fox, Simon 57
Franklin, Bob 16–18, 56
free newspapers 46, 48, 49, 59, 67, 69, 84, 90, 149, 192
Freedom of Information 84, 110

Glamorgan Gazette 68
Goode, Luke 9, 19, 31–32, 35, 152, 190
Google 53, 57, 79
Google Analytics 161
graffiti 77, 167
grant funding 10, 145, 148–149, 154, 159, 166–168, 172, 177, 182–184
Greener Leith 181
Greenslade, Roy 24
Grenfell Tower Fire 1
The Guardian 2, 128, 159, 174
Guardian Local 174–175
Gurn Nurn 118–119, 129–130, 180

Habermas, Jurgen 4, 16, 18–22, 24–25, 35
Harcup, Tony 9–10, 21–22, 33, 36, 44, 97, 115, 143, 191, 201
Hartley, John 24, 26–27, 34–36, 159, 191, 202
Hedon Blog 107, 119, 123–124, 131, 133
Here and Now report 159
Highmore, Ben 27–28 191
Higgerson, David 57
hyperlocal journalism: accountability reporting 108–110, audiences 33, 90–91, 97, 194; civic value of 83, 101, 114, 134, 139, 145, 166, 178, 185, 191, 197, 199; commercial operations 174–176; as cultural practice 26–27, 191; definition 4–6, 9–10, 36; economics of 176–178; in Europe 5; and the everyday 30–31, 37, 191 geographical spread in UK 92–93, 97, 99, *100*, 110; localness 101–102; motivations of practitioners 70, 86, 116–125; newsgathering practices 125–134; newsrooms 138–140, 146,

155, 160, 162–163, 165–166, 168; and
place 6–8, 116–119; and precarious
labour 173, 181–182; and print 65, 84;
role in public sphere 16, 18–20, 191,
195, 199; publishing frequency 97–99;
use of social media 125, 127–131,
196; use of sources 102–105; stories
covered 99–101; subsidies 59, 83, 177,
182–184, 191, 195, 198–199, 201–202;
sustainability of 8–9, 84–85, 86, 172,
177–181, 185, 186–187, 191, 195–196,
198–199, 201; in the US 4–5; in Wales
59, 83

Independent Community News Network
8, 90
Independently Funded News Consortia 90
information subsidies 17, 58
informed citizenry 19, 55, 75, 101, 119
inner-city 147
Inside Croydon 105, 109, 122, 128
Internet 3–4, 7, 19, 25–7, 29–30, 34–5,
43–5, 52, 59, 90, 94, 96, 99, 115, 120,
126–27, 129, 134, 140, 153, 185
investigative reporting 79, 105, 108–110
Ireland 92
ITV 89
ITV Cymru Wales 47

Johnston Press 51
Joint Industry Committee for Regional
Media Research (JICREG) 91
Journalism: role of informing 16, 20, 73–74,
80; role of representing 68, 72, 79, 80;
role of scrutiny 68, 72, 80; use of sources
18, 56, 72–73; and trust 77, 78, 84;
see also amateur journalism; citizen
journalism; hyperlocal journalism,
networked journalism; participatory
journalism; public interest journalism;
reciprocal journalism

Kentish Towner 184
Knutsford Times 117, 122, 129, 183

The Labour party 76
LeaderLive.co.uk 59; see also Wrexham
Leader
Leeds 2, 10, 33, 175
Leeds Citizen 109, 122, 182
Lefebvre, Henri 31
Leicester Mercury 50, 52
Lewis, Justin 32, 119, 134–135, 143,
145, 170, 198
listicles 56–7

literacy 45 see also digital literacy
Livingstone, Sonia 24–25, 191
Llanelli Star 46
local authority districts 55, 99
Local Democracy Reporter Scheme 58
Local Digital Programme Services Scheme
see local television
local government reporting 2, 69–72, 74–5,
76–8, 82, 84, 85, 92, 96, 100–101,
104–05, 106, 107–10, 120–22, 142–44,
147–49, 152–54, 156, 160, 163, 165,
192, 193–96, 200–02
local newspapers: advertising 44, 49–51, 53,
58, 70, 156; advertising monopolies 46;
campaigns 80; changing workloads 55,
67,71; circulation 43–44, 46, 47, 48–50,
53, 66; civic value of content 2, 55–56;
closures 46, 48, 65, 71, 85–86;
competition, rivalry and plurality 46,
70–71, 86, 193; and cuts 46, 51, 71,
101; district offices 53, 67–68, 71, 72;
economics of 16–17, 43–45, 49–51, 54,
66, 71; localness 16; online content
56–57; ownership of 44, 46, 55, 67;
reduction in workforce 1–2, 50–54,
66, 71
Local People network 98–99, 175
local radio 45, 47
local television 47, 156
Local World 46, 55, 95, 98
Localism Act 15, 107
London 2, 6, 66, 81, 90, 99, 105, 109, 128,
156–57
London SE1 90
lost pets 162, 167, 191
Love Wapping 105, 131–132, 201

mass media 18, 20–1, 22, 26, 44, 45, 116,
media ecologies 93–96, 194, 200
media plurality 4, 11, 19, 36, 45–6, 55,
95–7, 103–04, 110, 137, 174, 187,
193–96, 200, 202
Media Wales 43, 46, 50–53, 57–58

National Assembly of Wales 46, 76, 82,
84, 85
National Theatre Wales 83
National Union of Journalists 15, 51, 52,
83, 182
Neath Guardian 53
Neath Port Talbot Courier 70
Neighbourhood News 84; see also Carnegie
UK Trust
neighbourhood forums 107
Neighbourhood Networks study 6, 124

208 Index

networked public sphere 144
Nesta 5–7, 91, 93, 159, 183, 186, 196, 201
news black holes 65, 76, 79–80, 85–86
news café 152, 154
News Media Association 51
news values 130, 143, 152
newspapers *see* local newspapers
newsrooms *see* hyperlocal journalism:
   newsrooms
North Wales Daily Post 46
Northern Ireland 99
NUJ see National Union of Journalists

Ofcom 5–6, 44–45, 55, 89–91, 93–97, 99,
   159, 194
online forums 93, 97, 158
online news 16–17, 43, 45, 47, 53–54, 56,
   59, 76–77, 94
Openly Local 91–93, 97–98, 113

Papacharissi, Zizi 25–26, 36, 45, 191
papurau bro 48, 59
Paradise Circus 201
participatory journalism 133, 146, 155
patch reporters 66
Perrin, William 1
Pink, Sarah 28–30, 37, 191
police 17, 67, 73, 102, 103, **108**, **109**,
   143–144; *see also* crime reporting
policy–makers 6
politics 17–18, 22, 30, 47, 56, 76–77, 99,
   101, 103, 115, 120, 140–141, 145, 167,
   195, 201
Port Talbot 48–49, 59, 65, 66, 68–69,
   71–80, 82–83, 85–86, 125, 192–193, 202
Port *Talbot Guardian* 48–49, 53
Port Talbot Magnet 59, 65, 66, 68–69, 70,
   74, 77, 83, 86, 198
public interest journalism 43, 56–58, 71,
   72, 84
public relations 18, 56, 58, 72–73, 115, 117,
   148
public service broadcasting 90
public sphere 3–5, 10, 15–20, 22, 24–25,
   27, 33, 35–37, 56, 69–70, 73, 81, 86, 89,
   107, 110, 115, 190–191, 193, 194–197,
   199–200; *see also* networked public sphere
press releases 74, 84, 105, 110, 122, 163,
   166, 168n3, 168n4, 169n5, 196; *see also*
   churnalism
Preston, Peter 2

Radcliffe, Damian 6, 9, 93, 99, 159,
   196, 198
Reach plc *see* Trinity Mirror

readers' buying habits 44, 36, 132
recession 44, 51, 66, 89
reciprocal journalism 125–134,
   198, 200
rural 46, 99, 109, 155
Rowland, Paul 57

S4C 47
Saddleworth News 8, 130, 180, 183
Salford Online 127, 179
Salford Star 121, 183
Scotland 96, 99
search engines 5, 17
Sheen, Michael 79
Shove, Elizabeth 28
Snapchat 27
social capital 6, 10, 34, 125–126, 133,
   147, 197–199; *see also* communities:
   social capital and bonding within
social entrepreneurship 184–185
Social Media Surgeries 140
social media: advertising 57; and
   audience growth 90–91, 97; for
   breaking news 3; everyday use
   by citizens 29, 31, 45, 130, 153,
   191; and gatekeeping 142; 191,
   196–202; use of hashtags 27, 129,
   142–143, 145, 156, 196; use by
   hyperlocal journalists 8, 37, 125–131,
   133–134, 136–138, 140, 143–145,
   151, 157, 159–160, 166, 169,
   196–202; use by newspaper journalists
   68, 72; as news platform 53, 77;
   use by public officials 143; *see*
   also Facebook; Snapchat; Twitter;
   YouTube
South Leeds Life 90
South Wales Echo 46, 48, 71
South *Wales Evening Post* 46, 48, 65–66,
   68–69, 71
Southwark Living 120, 180
sports reporting 44, 72, 77, 120, 140–41,
   149, 156
Star and Crescent 120
statutory notices 201–202
steel industry 66, 84–85, 86
Swansea 46–47, 66–67, 83, 193

Talk About Local 1, 3, 6, 36, 90, 93,
   159, 175
television 5, 18, 26, 28, 44–5, 47, 76, 78,
   89, 95–6, 105, 156, 173, 193 *see also*
   local television
The Ambler 110, 118–119, 131,
   181, 184

Index 209

The Kirkbymoorside Town Blog 127, 180, 185
The Lincolnite 130, 179
top–slicing 47
training 3, 9, 75, 104, 115, 124, 137, 148, 157, 165, 174
Trinity Mirror 43, 46, 51, 53, 54, 55, 58, 60n3, 175
Trunk Road Agency 75
Twitter 8, 90, 127–129, 133, 137–138, 139–140, 143–145, 150, 157, 162
Tyburn Mail 146, 149–155, 166–168, 196–197, 202

unreported news, see news black holes
user data 29, 57; see also Google Analytics
user–generated content 32, 33, 133

volunteer journalists 9, 59, 83–84, 91, 93, 98, 128, 181

Wahl–Jorgensen, Karin 20, 30, 33
Wales 11, 43, 46–59, 65, 79, 82–3, 85, 93, 96, 99, 109
Wales on Sunday 46
Wales Online 46, 53, 57
watchdog role of press 16, 74, 108
Wayland News 117, 121, 123, 132–133, 180, 195
Welsh Government 75, 85
Welsh language 47
West Hampstead Life 128–130, 179–180
West Leeds Dispatch 122
Western Mail 46, 48–52, 71, 79, 80
whistle–blowers 84, 85, 120
Wrexham 48, 59
Wrexham.com 59, 64, 116, 120
WV11 179, 181, 196

YouTube 25, 35

zombie newspapers 86

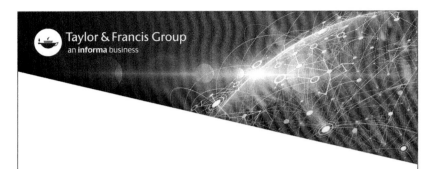